Captains Of The Civil War
A Chronicle Of The Blue And The Gray

by

William Wood

Double 9
BOOKS

Captains Of The Civil War
A Chronicle Of The Blue And The Gray
by William Wood

ISBN: 978-93-59322-75-9

Published by

DOUBLE 9 BOOKS

2/13-B, Ansari Road
Daryaganj, New Delhi – 110002
info@double9books.com
www.double9books.com
Tel. 011-40042856

ABOUT THE AUTHOR

William Wood, William Charles Henry Wood was a Canadian historian, Scout leader, and naturalist who lived from 7 June 1864 to 2 September 1947. He was born in the city of Quebec and served as a Lieutenant-Colonel in the Royal Rifles of Canada from 1887 to the end of World War I. He was involved in literary and historical circles, and he was the President of the Quebec Literary and Historical Society. He was engaged in wildlife conservation and lobbied for Labrador bird sanctuaries. In 1909, he was also the president of the Quebec Scouts. He was a prolific chronicler of Canadian history and produced several works on the subject, most notably The Storied Province of Quebec, a five-volume series on the history of Quebec. He died at the age of 83 in Quebec City in 1947. Wood was laid to rest in Sillery's Mount Hermon Cemetery.

CONTENTS

PREFACE

Sixty years ago today the guns that thundered round Fort Sumter began the third and greatest modern civil war fought by English-speaking people. This war was quite as full of politics as were the other two—the War of the American Revolution and that of Puritan and Cavalier. But, though the present Chronicle never ignores the vital correlations between statesmen and commanders, it is a book of warriors, through and through.

I gratefully acknowledge the indispensable assistance of Colonel G. J. Fiebeger, a West Point expert, and of Dr. Allen Johnson, chief editor of the series and Professor of American History at Yale.

WILLIAM WOOD,

Late Colonel commanding 8th Royal Rifles, and Officer-in-charge, Canadian Special Mission Overseas.

QUEBEC,
April 18, 1921.

CHAPTER I
THE CLASH: 1861

States which claimed a sovereign right to secede from the Union naturally claimed the corresponding right to resume possession of all the land they had ceded to that Union's Government for the use of its naval and military posts. So South Carolina, after leading the way to secession on December 20, 1860, at once began to work for the retrocession of the forts defending her famous cotton port of Charleston. These defenses, being of vital consequence to both sides, were soon to attract the strained attention of the whole country.

There were three minor forts: Castle Pinckney, dozing away, in charge of a solitary sergeant, on an island less than a mile from the city; Fort Moultrie, feebly garrisoned and completely at the mercy of attackers on its landward side; and Fort Johnson over on James Island. Lastly, there was the world-renowned Fort Sumter, which then stood, unfinished and ungarrisoned, on a little islet beside the main ship channel, at the entrance to the harbor, and facing Fort Moultrie just a mile away. The proper war garrison of all the forts should have been over a thousand men. The actual garrison—including officers, band, and the Castle Pinckney sergeant—was less than a hundred. It was, however, loyal to the Union; and its commandant, Major Robert Anderson, though born in the slave-owning State of Kentucky, was determined to fight.

The situation, here as elsewhere, was complicated by Floyd, President Buchanan's Secretary of War, soon to be forced out of office on a charge of misapplying public funds. Floyd, as an ardent Southerner, was using the last lax days of the Buchanan Government to get the army posts ready for capitulation whenever secession should have become an accomplished fact. He urged on construction, repairs, and armament at Charleston, while refusing to strengthen the garrison, in order, as he said, not to provoke Carolina. Moreover, in November he had replaced old Colonel Gardner, a Northern veteran of "1812," by Anderson the Southerner, in whom he hoped to find a good capitulator. But this time Floyd was wrong.

The day after Christmas Anderson's little garrison at Fort Moultrie slipped over to Fort Sumter under cover of the dark, quietly removed Floyd's workmen, who were mostly Baltimore Secessionists, and began to prepare for defense. Next morning Charleston was furious and began to prepare for attack. The South Carolina authorities at once took formal possession of Pinckney and Moultrie; and three days later seized the United States Arsenal in Charleston itself. Ten days later again, on January 9, 1861, the *Star of the West*, a merchant vessel coming in with reinforcements and supplies for Anderson, was fired on and forced to turn back. Anderson, who had expected a man-of-war, would not fire in her defense, partly because he still hoped there might yet be peace.

While Charleston stood at gaze and Anderson at bay the ferment of secession was working fast in Florida, where another tiny garrison was all the Union had to hold its own. This garrison, under two loyal young lieutenants, Slemmer and Gilman, occupied Barrancas Barracks in Pensacola Bay. Late at night on the eighth of January (the day before the *Star of the West* was fired on at Charleston) some twenty Secessionists came to seize the old Spanish Fort San Carlos, where, up to that time, the powder had been kept. This fort, though lying close beside the barracks, had always been unoccupied; so the Secessionists looked forward to an easy capture. But, to their dismay, an unexpected guard challenged them, and, not getting the proper password in reply, dispersed them with the first shots of the Civil War.

Commodore Armstrong sat idle at the Pensacola Navy Yard, distracted between the Union and secession. On the ninth Slemmer received orders from Winfield Scott, General-in-Chief at Washington, to use all means in defense of Union property. Next morning Slemmer and his fifty faithful men were landed on Santa Rosa Island, just one mile across the bay, where the dilapidated old Fort Pickens stood forlorn. Two days later the Commodore surrendered the Navy Yard, the Stars and Stripes were lowered, and everything ashore fell into the enemy's hands. There was no flagstaff at Fort Pickens; but the Union colors were at once hung out over the northwest bastion, in full view of the shore, while the *Supply* and *Wyandotte*, the only naval vessels in the bay, and both commanded by loyal men, mastheaded extra colors and stood clear. Five days afterwards they had to sail for New York; and Slemmer, whose total garrison had been raised to eighty by the addition of thirty sailors, was left to hold Fort Pickens if he could.

He had already been summoned to surrender by Colonel Chase and Captain Farrand, who had left the United States Army and Navy for the service of the South. Chase, like many another Southern officer, was stirred to his inmost depths by his own change of allegiance. "I have come," he said, "to ask of you young officers, officers of the same army in which I have spent the best and happiest years of my life, the surrender of this fort; and fearing that I might not be able to say it as I ought, and also to have it in proper form, I have put it in writing and will read it." He then began to read. But his eyes filled with tears, and, stamping his foot, he said: "I can't read it. Here, Farrand, you read it." Farrand, however, pleading that his eyes were weak, handed the paper to the younger Union officer, saying, "Here, Gilman, you have good eyes, please read it." Slemmer refused to surrender and held out till reinforced in April, by which time the war had begun in earnest. Fort Pickens was never taken. On the contrary, it supported the bombardment of the Confederate 'longshore positions the next New Year (1862) and witnessed the burning and evacuation of Pensacola the following ninth of May.

While Charleston and Pensacola were fanning the flames of secession the wildfire was running round the Gulf, catching well throughout Louisiana, where the Governor ordered the state militia to seize every place belonging to the Union, and striking inland till it reached the farthest army posts in Texas. In all Louisiana the Union Government had only forty men. These occupied the Arsenal at Baton Rouge under Major Haskins. Haskins was loyal. But when five hundred state militiamen surrounded him, and his old brother-officer, the future Confederate General Bragg, persuaded him that the Union was really at an end, to all intents and purposes, and when he found no orders, no support, and not even any guidance from the Government at Washington, he surrendered with the honors of war and left by boat for St. Louis in Missouri.

There was then in Louisiana another Union officer; but made of sterner stuff. This was Colonel W. T. Sherman, Superintendent of the State Seminary of Learning and Military Academy at Alexandria, up the Red River. He was much respected by all the state authorities, and was carefully watching over the two young sons of another future Confederate leader, General Beauregard. William Tecumseh Sherman had retired from the Army without seeing any war service, unlike Haskins, who was a one-armed veteran of the Mexican campaign. But Sherman was determined to stand by the Union, come what might. Yet he was equally determined to wind up the affairs of the State Academy so as to hand them over in perfect order. A few days after the seizure of the Arsenal, and before the formal secession of the State, he wrote to the Governor:

"Sir: As I occupy a *quasi*-military position under the laws of the State, I deem it proper to acquaint you that I accepted such position when Louisiana was a State of the Union, and when the motto of this seminary was inserted in marble over the main door: "By the liberality of the General Government of the United States. The Union—*esto perpetua*." Recent events foreshadow a great change, and it becomes all men to choose.... I beg you to take immediate steps to relieve me as superintendent, the moment the State determines to secede, for on no earthly account will I do any act or think any thought hostile to, or in defiance of, the old Government of the United States."

Then, to the lasting credit of all concerned, the future political enemies parted as the best of personal friends. Sherman left everything in perfect order, accounted for every cent of the funds, and received the heartiest thanks and best wishes of all the governing officials, who embodied the following sentence in their final resolution of April 1, 1861: "They cannot fail to appreciate the manliness of character which has always marked the actions of Colonel Sherman." Long before this Louisiana had seceded, and Sherman had gone north to Lancaster, Ohio, where he arrived about the time of Lincoln's inauguration.

Meanwhile, on the eighteenth of February, the greatest of all surrenders had taken place in Texas, where nineteen army posts were handed over to the State by General Twiggs. San Antonio was swarming with Secessionist rangers. Unionist companies were marching up and down. The Federal garrison was leaving the town on parole, with the band playing Union airs and Union colors flying. The whole place was at sixes and sevens, and anything might have happened.

In the midst of this confusion the colonel commanding the Second Regiment of United States Cavalry arrived from Fort Mason. He was on his way to Washington, where Winfield Scott, the veteran General-in-Chief, was anxiously waiting to see him; for this colonel was no ordinary man. He had been Scott's Chief of Staff in Mexico, where he had twice won promotion for service in the field. He had been a model Superintendent at West Point and an exceedingly good officer of engineers before he left them, on promotion, for the cavalry. Very tall and handsome, magnificently fit in body and in mind, genial but of commanding presence, this flower of Southern chivalry was not only every inch a soldier but a leader born and bred. Though still unknown to public fame he was the one man to whom the most insightful leaders of both sides turned, and rightly turned; for this was Robert Lee, Lee of Virginia, soon to become one of the very few really great commanders of the world.

As Lee came up to the hotel at San Antonio he was warmly greeted by Mrs. Darrow, the anxious wife of the confidential clerk to Major Vinton, the staunch Union officer in charge of the pay and quartermaster services. "Who are those men?" he asked, pointing to the rangers, who wore red flannel shoulder straps. "They are McCulloch's," she answered; "General

Twiggs surrendered everything to the State this morning." Years after, when she and her husband and Vinton had suffered for one side and Lee had suffered for the other, she wrote her recollection of that memorable day in these few, telling words: "I shall never forget his look of astonishment, as, with his lips trembling and his eyes full of tears, he exclaimed, 'Has it come so soon as this?' In a short time I saw him crossing the plaza on his way to headquarters and noticed particularly that he was in citizen's dress. He returned at night and shut himself into his room, which was over mine; and I heard his footsteps through the night, and sometimes the murmur of his voice, as if he was praying. He remained at the hotel a week and in conversations declared that the position he held was a neutral one."

Three other Union witnesses show how Lee agonized over the fateful decision he was being forced to make. Captain R. M. Potter says: "I have seldom seen a more distressed man. He said, 'When I get to Virginia I think the world will have one soldier less. I shall resign and go to planting corn.'" Colonel Albert G. Brackett says: "Lee was filled with sorrow at the condition of affairs, and, in a letter to me, deploring the war in which we were about to engage, made use of these words: 'I fear the liberties of our country will be buried in the tomb of a great nation.'" Colonel Charles Anderson, quoting Lee's final words in Texas, carries us to the point of parting: "I still think my loyalty to Virginia ought to take precedence over that which is due to the Federal Government; and I shall so report myself in Washington. If Virginia stands by the old Union, so will I. But if she secedes (though I do not believe in secession as a constitutional right, nor that there is sufficient cause for revolution) then I will still follow my native State with my sword, and, if need be, with my life. I know you think and feel very differently. But I can't help it. These are my principles; and I must follow them."

Lee reached Washington on the first of March. Lincoln, delivering his Inaugural on the fourth, brought the country one step nearer war by showing the neutrals how impossible it was to reconcile his principles as President of the whole United States with those of Jefferson Davis as President of the seceding parts. "The power confided to me will be used to hold, occupy, and possess the property and places belonging to the government." Three days later the provisional Confederate Congress at Montgomery in Alabama passed an Army Act authorizing the enlistment of one hundred thousand men for one year's service. Nine days later again, having adopted a Constitution in the meantime, this Congress passed a Navy Act, authorizing the purchase or construction of ten little gunboats.

In April the main storm center went whirling back to Charleston, where Sherman's old friend Beauregard commanded the forces that encircled Sumter. Sumter, still unfinished, had been designed for a garrison of six hundred and fifty combatant men. It now contained exactly sixty-five. It was to have been provisioned for six months. The actual supplies could not be made to last beyond two weeks. Both sides knew that Anderson's gallant little garrison must be starved out by the fifteenth. But the excited Carolinians would not wait, because they feared that the arrival of reinforcements might balk them of their easy prey. On the eleventh Beauregard, acting under orders from the Confederate Government, sent in a summons to surrender. Anderson refused. At a quarter to one the next morning the summons was repeated, as pilots had meanwhile reported a Federal vessel approaching the harbor. Anderson again refused and again admitted that he would be starved out on the fifteenth. Thereupon Beauregard's aides declared immediate surrender the only possible alternative to a bombardment and signed a note at 3:20 A.M. giving Anderson formal warning that fire would be opened in an hour.

Fort Sumter stood about half a mile inside the harbor mouth, fully exposed to the converging fire of four relatively powerful batteries, three about a mile away, the fourth nearly twice as far. At the northern side of the harbor mouth stood Fort Moultrie; at the southern stood the batteries on Cummings Point; and almost due west of Sumter stood Fort Johnson. Near Moultrie was a four-gun floating battery with an iron shield. A mile northwest of Moultrie, farther up the harbor, stood the Mount Pleasant battery, nearly two miles off from Sumter. At half-past four, in the first faint light of a gray morning, a sudden spurt of flame shot out from Fort Johnson, the dull roar of a mortar floated through the misty air, and the big shell—the first shot of the real war—soared up at a steep angle, its course distinctly marked by its burning fuse, and then plunged down on Sumter. It was a capital shot, right on the center of the target, and was followed by an admirable burst. Then all the converging batteries opened full; while the whole population of perfervid Charleston rushed out of doors to throng their beautiful East Battery, a flagstone marine parade three miles in from Sumter, of which and of the attacking batteries it had a perfect view.

But Sumter remained as silent as the grave. Anderson decided not to return the fire till it was broad daylight. In the meantime all ranks went to breakfast, which consisted entirely of water and salt pork. Then the gun crews went to action stations and fired back steadily with solid shot. The ironclad battery was an exasperating target; for the shot bounced off it like dried peas. Moultrie seemed more vulnerable. But appearances were deceptive; for it was thoroughly quilted with bales of cotton, which the solid shot simply rammed into an impenetrable mass. Wishing to save his men, in which he was quite successful, Anderson had forbidden the use of the shell-guns, which were mounted on the upper works and therefore more exposed.

Shell fire would have burst the bales and set the cotton flaming. This was so evident that Sergeant Carmody, unable to stand such futile practice any longer, quietly stole up to the loaded guns and fired them in succession. The aim lacked final correction; and the result was small, except that Moultrie, thinking itself in danger, concentrated all its efforts on silencing these guns. The silencing seemed most effective; for Carmody could not reload alone, and so his first shots were his last.

At nightfall Sumter ceased fire while the Confederates kept on slowly till daylight. Next morning the officers' quarters were set on fire by red-hot shot. Immediately the Confederates redoubled their efforts. Inside Sumter the fire was creeping towards the magazine, the door of which was shut only just in time. Then the flagstaff was shot down. Anderson ran his colors up again, but the situation was rapidly becoming impossible. Most of the worn-out men were fighting the flames while a few were firing at long intervals to show they would not yet give in. This excited the generous admiration of the enemy, who cheered the gallantry of Sumter while sneering at the caution of the Union fleet outside. The fact was, however, that this so-called fleet was a mere assemblage of vessels quite unable to fight the Charleston batteries and without the slightest chance of saving Sumter.

Having done his best for the honor of the flag, though not a man was killed within the walls, Anderson surrendered in the afternoon. Charleston went wild with joy; but applauded the generosity of Beauregard's chivalrous terms. Next day, Sunday the fourteenth, Anderson's little garrison saluted the Stars and Stripes with fifty guns, and then, with colors flying, marched down on board a transport to the strains of *Yankee Doodle*.

Strange to say, after being four years in Confederate hands, Sumter was recaptured by the Union forces on the anniversary of its surrender. It was often bombarded, though never taken, in the meantime.

The fall of Sumter not only fired all Union loyalty but made Confederates eager for the fray. The very next day Lincoln called for 75,000 three-month volunteers. Two days later Confederate letters of marque were issued to any privateers that would prey on Union shipping. Two days later again Lincoln declared a blockade of every port from South Carolina round to Texas. Eight days afterwards he extended it to North Carolina and Virginia.

But in the meantime Lincoln had been himself marooned in Washington. On the nineteenth of April, the day he declared his first blockade, the Sixth Massachusetts were attacked by a mob in Baltimore, through which the direct rails ran from North to South. Baltimore was full of secession, and the bloodshed roused its fury. Maryland was a border slave State out of which the District of Columbia was carved. Virginia had just seceded. So when the would-be Confederates of Maryland, led by the Mayor of Baltimore, began tearing up rails, burning bridges, and cutting the wires, the Union Government found itself enisled in a hostile sea. Its own forces abandoned the Arsenal at Harper's Ferry and the Navy Yard at Norfolk. The work of demolition at Harper's Ferry had to be bungled off in haste, owing to shortness of time and lack of means. The demolition of Norfolk was better done, and the ships were sunk at anchor. But many valuable stores fell into enemy hands at both these Virginian outposts of the Federal forces. Through six long days of dire suspense not a ship, not a train, came into Washington. At last, on the twenty-fifth, the Seventh New York got through, having come south by boat with the Eighth Massachusetts, landed at Annapolis, and commandeered a train to run over relaid rails. With them came the news that all the loyal North was up, that the Seventh had marched through miles of cheering patriots in New York, and that these two fine regiments were only the vanguard of a host.

But just a week before Lincoln experienced this inexpressible relief he lost, and his enemy won, a single officer, who, according to Winfield Scott, was alone worth more than fifty thousand veteran men. On the seventeenth of April Virginia voted for secession. On the eighteenth Lee had a long confidential interview with his old chief, Winfield Scott. On the twentieth he resigned, writing privately to Scott at the same time: "My resignation would have been presented at once but for the struggle it has cost me to separate myself from a service to which I have devoted the best years of my life. During the whole of that time I have experienced nothing but kindness from my superiors and a most cordial friendship from my comrades. I shall carry to the grave the most grateful recollections of your kind consideration, and your name and fame shall always be dear to me. Save in the defense of my native State I never desire again to draw my sword."

The three great motives which finally determined his momentous course of action were: first, his aversion from taking any part in coercing the home folks of Virginia; secondly, his belief in State rights, tempered though it was by admiration for the Union; and thirdly, his clear perception that war was now inevitable, and that defeat for the South would inevitably mean a violent change of all the ways of Southern life, above all, a change imposed by force from outside, instead of the gradual change he wished to see effected from within. He was opposed to slavery; and both his own and his wife's slaves had long been free. Like his famous lieutenant, Stonewall Jackson, he was particularly kind to the blacks; none of whom ever wanted to leave, once they had been domiciled at Arlington, the estate that came to him through his wife, Mary Custis, great-granddaughter of Martha Washington. But, like Lincoln before the war, he wished emancipation to come from the slave States themselves, as in time it must have come, with due regard for compensation.

On the twenty-third of this eventful April Lee was given the chief command of all Virginia's forces. Three days later "Joe" Johnston took command of the Virginians at Richmond. One day later again "Stonewall" Jackson took command at Harper's Ferry. Johnston played a great and noble part throughout the war; and we shall meet him again and again, down to the very end. But Jackson claims our first attention here.

Like all the great leaders on both sides Jackson had been an officer of regulars. He was, however, in many ways unlike the army type. He disliked society amusements, was awkward, shy, reserved, and apparently recluse. Moderately tall, with large hands and feet, stiff in his movements, ungainly in the saddle, he was a mere nobody in public estimation when the war broke out. A few brother-officers had seen his consummate skill and bravery as a subaltern in Mexico; and still fewer close acquaintances had seen his sterling qualities at Lexington, where, for ten years, he had been a professor at the Virginia Military Institute. But these few were the only ones who were not surprised when this recluse of peace suddenly became a very thunderbolt of war—Puritan in soul, Cavalier in daring: a Cromwell come to life again.

Harper's Ferry was a strategic point in northern Virginia. It was the gate to the Shenandoah Valley as well as the point where the Baltimore and Ohio Railroad crossed the Potomac some sixty miles northwest of Washington. Harper's Ferry was known by name to North and South through John Brown's raid two years before. It was now coveted by Virginia for its Arsenal as well as for its command of road, rail, and water routes. The plan to raid it was arranged at Richmond on the sixteenth of April. But when the raiders reached it on the eighteenth they found it abandoned and its Arsenal in flames. The machine shops, however, were saved, as well as the metal parts of twenty thousand stand of arms. Then the Virginia militiamen and volunteers streamed in, to the number of over four thousand. They were a mere conglomeration of semi-independent units, mostly composed of raw recruits under officers who themselves knew next to nothing. As usual with such fledgling troops there was no end to the fuss and feathers among the members of the busybody staffs, who were numerous enough to manage an army but clumsy enough to spoil a platoon. It was said, and not without good reason, that there was as much gold lace at Harper's Ferry, when the sun was shining, as at a grand review in Paris.

Into this gaudy assemblage rode Thomas Jonathan Jackson, mounted on Little Sorrel, a horse as unpretentious as himself, and dressed in his faded old blue professor's uniform without one gleam of gold. He had only two staff officers, both dressed as plainly as himself. He was not a major-general, nor even a brigadier; just a colonel. He held no trumpeting reviews. He made no flowery speeches. He didn't even swear. The armed mob at Harper's Ferry felt that they would lose caste on Sunday afternoons under a commandant like this. Their feelings were still more outraged when they heard that every officer above the rank of captain was to lose his higher rank, and that all new reappointments were to be made on military merit and direct from Richmond. Companies accustomed to elect their officers according to the whim of the moment eagerly joined the higher officers in passing adverse resolutions. But authorities who were unanimous for Lee were not to be shaken by such absurdities in face of a serious war. And when the froth had been blown off the top, and the dregs drained out of the bottom, the solid mass between, who really were sound patriots, settled down to work.

There was seven hours' drill every day except Sunday; no light task for a mere armed mob groping its ignorant way, however zealously, towards the organized efficiency of a real army. The companies had to be formed into workable battalions, the battalions into brigades. There was a deplorable lack of cavalry, artillery, engineers, commissariat, transport, medical services, and, above all, staff. Armament was bad; other munitions were worse. There would have been no chance whatever of holding Harper's Ferry unless the Northern conglomeration had been even less like a fighting army than the Southern was.

Harper's Ferry was not only important in itself but still more important for what it covered: the wonderfully fruitful Shenandoah Valley, running southwest a hundred and forty miles to the neighborhood of Lexington, with an average width of only twenty-four. Bounded on the west by the Alleghanies and on the east by the long Blue Ridge this valley was a regular covered way by which the Northern invaders might approach, cut Virginia in two (for West Virginia was then a part of the State) and, after devastating the valley itself (thus destroying half the food-base of Virginia) attack eastern Virginia through whichever gaps might serve the purpose best. More than this, the only direct line from Richmond to the Mississippi ran just below the southwest end of the valley, while a network of roads radiated from Winchester near the northeast end, thirty miles southwest of Harper's Ferry.

Throughout the month of May Jackson went on working his men into shape and watching the enemy, three thousand strong, at Chambersburg, forty-five miles north of Harper's Ferry, and twelve thousand strong farther north still. One day he made a magnificent capture of rolling stock on the twenty-seven miles of double track that centered in Harper's Ferry. This greatly hampered the accumulation of coal at Washington besides helping the railroads of the South. Destroying the line was out of the question, because it ran through West Virginia and Maryland, both of which he hoped to see on the Confederate side. He was himself a West Virginian, born at Clarksburg; and it grieved him greatly when West Virginia stood by the Union.

Apart from this he did nothing spectacular. The rest was all just sheer hard work. He kept his own counsel so carefully that no one knew anything about what he would do if the enemy advanced. Even the officers of outposts were forbidden to notice or mention his arrival or departure on his constant tours of inspection, lest a longer look than usual at any point might let an awkward inference be drawn. He was the sternest of disciplinarians when the good of the service required it. But no one knew better that the finest discipline springs from self-sacrifice willingly made for a worthy cause; and no one was readier to help all ranks along toward real efficiency in the kindest possible way when he saw they were doing their best.

At the end of May Johnston took over the command of the increasing force at Harper's Ferry, while Jackson was given the First Shenandoah Brigade, a unit soon, like himself, to be raised by service into fame.

On the first and third of May Virginia issued calls for more men; and on the third Lincoln, who quite understood the signs of the times, called for men whose term of service would be three years and not three months.

Just a week later Missouri was saved for the Union by the daring skill of two determined leaders, Francis P. Blair, a Member of Congress who became a good major-general, and Captain Nathaniel Lyon, an excellent soldier, who commanded the little garrison of regulars at St. Louis. When Lincoln called upon Governor Claiborne Jackson to supply Missouri's quota of three-month volunteers the Governor denounced the proposed coercion as "illegal, unconstitutional, revolutionary, inhuman, and diabolical"; and thereafter did his best to make Missouri join the South. But Blair and Lyon were too quick for him. Blair organized the Home Guards, whom Lyon armed from the arsenal. Lyon then sent all the surplus arms and stores across the river into Illinois, while he occupied the most commanding position near the arsenal with his own troops, thus forestalling the Confederates, under Brigadier-General D. M. Frost, who was now forced to establish Camp Jackson in a far less favorable place. So vigorously had Blair and Lyon worked that they had armed thousands while Frost had only armed hundreds. But when Frost received siege guns and mortars from farther south Lyon felt the time had come for action.

Lyon was a born leader, though Grant and Sherman (then in St. Louis as junior ex-officers, quite unknown to fame) were almost the only men, apart from Blair, to see any signs of preëminence in this fiery little redheaded, weather-beaten captain, who kept dashing about the arsenal, with his pockets full of papers, making sure of every detail connected with the handful of regulars and the thousands of Home Guards.

On the ninth of May Lyon borrowed an old dress from Blair's mother-in-law, completing the disguise with a thickly veiled sunbonnet, and drove through Camp Jackson. That night he and Blair attended a council of war, at which, overcoming all opposition, answering all objections, and making all arrangements, they laid their plans for the morrow. When Lyon's seven thousand surrounded Frost's seven hundred the Confederates surrendered at discretion and were marched as prisoners through St. Louis. There were many Southern sympathizers among the crowds in the streets; one of them fired a pistol; and the Home Guards fired back, killing several women and children by mistake. This unfortunate incident hardened many neutrals and even Unionists against the Union forces; so much so that Sterling Price, a Unionist and former governor, became a Confederate general, whose field for recruiting round Jefferson City on the Missouri promised a good crop of enemies to the Union cause.

Lyon and Blair wished to march against Price immediately and smash every hostile force while still in the act of forming. But General Harney, who commanded the Department of the West, returned to St. Louis the day after the shooting and made peace instead of war with Price. By the end of the month, however, Lincoln removed Harney and promoted Lyon in his place; whereupon Price and Governor Jackson at once prepared to fight. Then sundry neutrals, of the gabbling kind who think talk enough will settle anything, induced the implacables to meet in St. Louis. The conference was ended by Lyon's declaration that he would see every Missourian under the sod before he would take any orders from the State about any Federal matter, however small. "This," he said in conclusion, "means war." And it did.

Again a single week sufficed for the striking of the blow. The conference was held on the eleventh of June. On the fourteenth Lyon reached Jefferson City only to find that the Governor had decamped for Boonville, still higher up the Missouri. Here, on the seventeenth, Lyon attacked him with greatly superior numbers and skill, defeated him utterly, and sent him flying south with only a few hundred followers left. Boonville was, in itself, a very small affair indeed. But it had immense results. Lyon had seized the best strategic point of rail and river junction on the Mississippi by holding St. Louis. He had also secured supremacy in arms, munitions, and morale. By turning the Governor out of Jefferson City, the State capital, he had deprived the Confederates of the prestige and convenience of an acknowledged headquarters. Now, by defeating him at Boonville and driving his forces south in headlong flight he had practically made the whole Missouri River a Federal line of communication as well as a barrier between would-be Confederates to the north and south of it. More than this, the possession of Boonville struck a fatal blow at Confederate recruiting and organization throughout the whole of that strategic area; for Boonville was the center to which pro-Southern Missourians were flocking. The tide of battle was to go against the Federals at Wilson's Creek in the southwest of the State, and even at Lexington on the Missouri, as we shall presently see; but this was only the breaking of the last Confederate waves. As a State, Missouri was lost to the South already.

In Kentucky, the next border State, opinions were likewise divided; and Kentuckians fought each other with help from both sides. Anderson, of Fort Sumter fame, was appointed to the Kentucky command in May. But here the crisis did not occur for months, while a border campaign was already being fought in West Virginia.

West Virginia, which became a separate State during the war, was strongly Federal, like eastern Tennessee. These Federal parts of two Confederate States formed a wedge dangerous to the whole South, especially to Virginia and the Carolinas. Each side therefore tried to control this area itself. The Federals, under McClellan, of whom we shall soon hear more, had two lines of invasion into West Virginia, both based on the Ohio. The northern converged by rail, from Wheeling and Parkersburg, on Grafton, the only junction in West Virginia. The southern ran up the Great Kanawha, with good navigation to Charleston and water enough for small craft on to Gauley Bridge, which was the strategic point.

In May the Confederates cut the line near Grafton. As this broke direct communication between the West and Washington, McClellan sent forces from which two flying columns, three thousand strong, converged on Philippi, fifteen miles south of Grafton, and surprised a thousand Confederates. These thereupon retired, with little loss, to Beverly, thirty miles farther south still. Here there was a combat at Rich Mountain on the eleventh of July. The Confederates again retreated, losing General Garnett in a skirmish the following day. This ended McClellan's own campaign in West Virginia.

But the Kanawha campaign, which lasted till November, had only just begun, with Rosecrans as successor to McClellan (who had been recalled to Washington for very high command) and with General Jacob D. Cox leading the force against Gauley. The Confederates did all they could to keep their precarious foothold. They sent political chiefs, like Henry A. Wise, ex-Governor of Virginia, and John B. Floyd, the late Federal Secretary of War, both of whom were now Confederate brigadiers. They even sent Lee himself in general commend. But, confronted by superior forces in a difficult and thoroughly hostile country, they at last retired east of the Alleghanies, which thenceforth became the frontier of two warring States.

The campaign in West Virginia was a foregone conclusion. It was not marked by any real battles; and there was no scope for exceptional skill of the higher kind on either side. But it made McClellan's bubble reputation.

McClellan was an ex-captain of United States Engineers who had done very well at West Point, had distinguished himself in Mexico, had represented the American army with the Allies in the Crimea, had written a good official report on his observations there, had become manager of a big railroad after leaving the service, and had so impressed people with his ability and modesty on the outbreak of war that his appointment to the chief command in West Virginia was hailed with the utmost satisfaction. Then came the two affairs at Philippi and Rich Mountain, the first of which was planned and carried out by other men, while the second was, if anything, spoiled by himself; for here, as afterwards on a vastly greater scene of action, he failed to strike home at the critical moment.

Yet though he failed in arms he won by proclamations; so much so, in fact, that *Words not Deeds* might well have been his motto. He began with a bombastic address to the inhabitants and ended with another to his troops, whom he congratulated on having "annihilated two armies, commanded by educated and experienced soldiers, intrenched in mountain fastnesses fortified at their leisure."

It disastrously happened that the Union public were hungering for heroes at this particular time and that Union journalists were itching to write one up to the top of their bent. So all McClellan's tinsel was counted out for gold before an avaricious mob of undiscriminating readers; and when, at the height of the publicity campaign, the Government wanted to retrieve Bull Run they turned to the "Man of Destiny" who had been given the noisiest advertisement as the "Young Napoleon of the West." McClellan had many good qualities for organization, and even some for strategy. An excited press and public, however, would not acclaim him for what he was but for what he most decidedly was not.

Meanwhile, before McClellan went to Washington and Lee to West Virginia, the main Union army had been disastrously defeated by the main

Confederate army at Bull Run, on that vital ground which lay between the rival capitals.

In April Lincoln had called for three-month volunteers. In May the term of service for new enlistments was three years. In June the military chiefs at Washington were vainly doing all that military men could do to make something like the beginnings of an army out of the conglomerating mass. Winfield Scott, the veteran General-in-Chief, rightly revered by the whole service as a most experienced, farsighted, and practical man, was ably assisted by W. T. Sherman and Irvin McDowell. But civilian interference ruined all. Even Lincoln had not yet learned the quintessential difference between that civil control by which the fighting services are so rightly made the real servants of the whole people and that civilian interference which is very much the same as if a landlubber owning a ship should grab the wheel repeatedly in the middle of a storm. Simon Cameron, then Secretary of War, was good enough as a party politician, but all thumbs when fumbling with the armies in the field. The other members of the Cabinet had war nostrums of their own; and every politician with a pull did what he could to use it. Behind all these surged a clamorous press and an excited people, both patriotic and well meaning; but both wholly ignorant of war, and therefore generating a public opinion that forced the not unwilling Government to order an armed mob "on to Richmond" before it had the slightest chance of learning how to be an army.

The Congress that met on the Fourth of July voted five hundred thousand men and two hundred and fifty million dollars. This showed that the greatness of the war was beginning to be seen. But the men, the money, and the Glorious Fourth were so blurred together in the public mind that the distinction between a vote in Congress and its effect upon some future battlefield was never realized. The result was a new access of zeal for driving McDowell "on to Richmond." Making the best of a bad business, Scott had already begun his preparations for the premature advance.

By the end of May Confederate pickets had been in sight of Washington, while McDowell, crossing the Potomac, was faced by his friend of old West Point and Mexican days, General Beauregard, fresh from the capture of Fort Sumter. By the beginning of July General Patterson, a veteran of "1812" and Mexico, was in command up the Potomac near Harper's Ferry. He was opposed by "Joe" Johnston, who had taken over that Confederate command from "Stonewall" Jackson. Down the Potomac and Chesapeake Bay there was nothing to oppose the Union navy. General Benjamin Butler, threatening Richmond in flank, along the lower Chesapeake, was watched by the Confederates Huger and Magruder. Meanwhile, as we have seen already, the West Virginian campaign was in full swing, with superior Federal forces under McClellan.

Thus the general situation in July was that the whole of northeastern Virginia was faced by a semicircle of superior forces which began at the Kanawha River, ran northeast to Grafton, then northeast to Cumberland, then along the Potomac to Chesapeake Bay and on to Fortress Monroe. From the Kanawha to Grafton there were only roads. From Grafton to Cumberland there was rail as well. From Cumberland to Washington there were road, rail, river, and canal. From Washington to Fortress Monroe there was water fit for any fleet. The Union armies along this semicircle were not only twice as numerous as the Confederates facing them but they were backed by a sea-power, both naval and mercantile, which the Confederates could not begin to challenge, much less overcome. Lee was the military adviser to the Confederate Government at Richmond as Scott then was to the Union Government at Washington.

Such was the central scene of action, where the first great battle of the war was fought. The Union forces were based on the Potomac from Washington to Harper's Ferry. The Confederates faced them from Bull Run to Winchester, which points were nearly sixty miles apart by road and rail. The Union forces were fifty thousand strong, the Confederate thirty-three thousand. The Union problem was how to keep "Joe" Johnston in the Winchester position by threatening or actually making an invasion of the Shenandoah Valley with Patterson's superior force, while McDowell's superior force attacked or turned Beauregard's position at Bull Run. The Confederate problem was how to give Patterson the slip and reach Bull Run in time to meet McDowell with an equal force. The Confederates had the advantage of interior lines both here and in the semicircle as a whole, though the Union forces enjoyed in general much better means of transportation. The Confederates enjoyed better control from government headquarters, where the Cabinet mostly had the sense to trust in Lee. Scott, on the other hand, was tied down by orders to defend Washington by purely defensive means as well as by the "on to Richmond" march. Patterson was therefore obliged to watch the Federal back door at Harper's Ferry as well as the Confederate side doors up the Shenandoah: an impossible task, on exterior lines, with the kind of force he had. The civilian chiefs at Washington did not see that the best of all defense was to destroy the enemy's means of destroying *them*, and that his greatest force of fighting *men*, not any particular *place*, should always be their main objective.

On the fourteenth of June Johnston had destroyed everything useful to the enemy at Harper's Ferry and retired to Winchester. On the twentieth Jackson's brigade marched on Martinsburg to destroy the workshops of the

Baltimore and Ohio Railway and to support the three hundred troopers under J. E. B. Stuart, who was so soon to be the greatest of cavalry commanders on the Confederate side. Unknown at twenty-nine, killed at thirty-one, "Jeb" Stuart was a Virginian ex-officer of United States Dragoons, trained in frontier fighting, and the perfect type of what a cavalry commander should be: tall, handsome, splendidly supple and strong, hawk-eyed and lion-hearted, quick, bold, determined, and inspiring, yet always full of knowledge and precaution too; indefatigable at all times, and so persistent in carrying out a plan that the enemy could no more shake him off than they could escape their shadows.

On the second of July the first brush took place at Falling Waters, five miles south of the Potomac, where Jackson came into touch with Patterson's advanced guard. As Jackson withdrew his handful of Virginian infantry the Federal cavalry came clattering down the turnpike and were met by a single shot from a Confederate gun that smashed the head of their column and sent the others flying. Meanwhile Stuart, who had been reconnoitering, came upon a company of Federal infantry resting in a field. Galloping among them suddenly he shouted, "Throw down your arms or you are all dead men!" Whereupon they all threw down their arms; and his troopers led them off. Patterson, badly served by his very raw staff, reported Jackson's little vanguard as being precisely ten times stronger than it was. He pushed out cautiously to right and left; and when he tried to engage again he found that Jackson had withdrawn. Falling Waters was microscopically small as a fight. But it served to raise Confederate morale and depress the Federals correspondingly.

Patterson occupied Martinsburg, while Johnston, drawn up in line of battle, awaited his further advance four days before retiring. Then, with his fourteen thousand, Patterson advanced again, stood irresolute under distracting orders from the Government in Washington, and finally went to Charlestown on the seventeenth of July—almost back to Harper's Ferry. Johnston, with his eleven thousand, now stood fast at Winchester, fifteen miles southwest, while Stuart, like a living screen, moved to and fro between them.

Meanwhile McDowell's thirty-six thousand had marched past the President with bands playing and colors flying amid a scene of great enthusiasm. The press campaign was at its height; so was the speechifying; and ninety-nine people out of every hundred thought Beauregard's twenty-two thousand at Bull Run would be defeated in a way that would be sure to make the South give in. McDowell had between two and three thousand regulars: viz., seven troops of cavalry, nine batteries of artillery, eight companies of infantry, and a little battalion of marines. Then there was the immense paper army voted on the Glorious Fourth. And here, for the general public to admire, was a collection of armed and uniformed men that members of Congress and writers in the press united in calling one of the best armies the world had ever seen. Moreover, the publicity campaign was kept up unflaggingly till the very clash of arms began. Reporters marched along and sent off reams of copy. Congressmen, and even ladies, graced the occasion in every way they could. "The various regiments were brilliantly uniformed according to the æsthetic taste of peace," wrote General Fry, then an officer on McDowell's staff, and "during the nineteenth and twentieth the bivouacs at Centreville, almost within cannon range of the enemy, were thronged with visitors, official and unofficial, who came in carriages from Washington, were under no military restraint, and passed to and fro among the troops as they pleased, giving the scene the appearance of a monster military picnic."

Had McDowell been able to attack on either of these two days he must have won. But previous Governments had never given the army the means of making proper surveys; so here, within a day's march of the Federal capital, the maps were worthless for military use. Information had to be gleaned by reconnaissance; and reconnaissance takes time, especially without trustworthy guides, sufficient cavalry, and a proper staff. Moreover, the army was all parts and no whole, through no fault of McDowell's or of his military chiefs. The three-month volunteers, whose term of service was nearly over, had not learned their drill as individuals before being herded into companies, battalions, and brigades, of course becoming more and more inefficient as the units grew more and more complex. Of the still more essential discipline they naturally knew still less. There was no lack of courage; for these were the same breed of men as those with whom Washington had won immortal fame, the same as those with whom both Grant and Lee were yet to win it. But, as Napoleon used to say, mere men are not the same as soldiers. Nor are armed mobs the same as armies.

The short march to the front was both confused and demoralizing. No American officer had ever had the chance even of seeing, much less handling, thirty-six thousand men under arms. This force was followed by an immense and unwieldy train of supplies, manned by wholly undisciplined civilian drivers; while other, and quite superfluous, civilians clogged every movement and made confusion worse confounded. "The march," says Sherman, who commanded a brigade, "demonstrated little save the general laxity of discipline; for, with all my personal efforts, I could not prevent the men from straggling for water, blackberries, or anything on the way they fancied." In the whole of the first long summer's day, the sixteenth of July, the army only marched six miles; and it took the better part of the seventeenth to herd its stragglers back again. "I wished them," says McDowell, "to go to Centreville the second day [only another six miles out] but the men were foot-weary, not so much by the distance marched as by the time they had been on foot." That observant private, Warren Lee Goss, has told us how hard it is to soldier suddenly. "My canteen banged against my bayonet; both tin cup and bayonet badly interfered with the butt of my musket, while my cartridge-box and haversack were constantly flopping up and down—the whole jangling like loose harness and chains on a runaway horse." The weather was hot. The roads were dusty. And many a man threw away parts of his kit for which he suffered later on. There was food in superabundance. But, with that unwieldy and grossly undisciplined supply-and-transport service, the men and their food never came together at the proper time.

Early on the eighteenth McDowell, whose own work was excellent all through, pushed forward a brigade against Blackburn's Ford, toward the Confederate right, in order to distract attention from the real objective, which was to be the turning of the left. The Confederate outposts fell back beyond the ford. The Federal brigade followed on; when suddenly sharp volleys took it in front and flank. The opposing brigade, under Longstreet (of whom we shall often hear again), had lain concealed and sprung its trap quite neatly. Most of the Federals behaved extremely well under these untoward circumstances. But one whole battery and another whole battalion, whose term of service expired that afternoon, were officially reported as having "moved to the rear to the sound of the enemy's cannon." Thereafter, as military units, they simply ceased to exist.

At one o'clock in the morning of this same day Johnston received a telegram at Winchester, from Richmond, warning him that McDowell was advancing on Bull Run, with the evident intention of seizing Manassas Junction, which would cut the Confederate rail communication with the Shenandoah Valley and so prevent all chance of immediate concentration at Bull Run. Johnston saw that the hour had come. It could not have come before, as Lee and the rest had foreseen; because an earlier concentration at Bull Run would have drawn the two superior Federal forces together on the selfsame spot. There was still some risk about giving Patterson the slip. True, his three-month special-constable array was semi-mutinous already; and its term of service had only a few more days to run. True, also, that the men had cause for grievance. They were all without pay, and some of them were reported as being still "without pants." But, despite such drawbacks, a resolute attack by Patterson's fourteen thousand could have at least held fast Johnston's eleven thousand, who were mostly little better off in military ways. Patterson, however, suffered from distracting orders, and that was his undoing. Johnston, admirably screened by Stuart, drew quietly away, leaving his sick at Winchester and raising the spirits of his whole command by telling them that Beauregard was in danger and that they were to "make a forced march to save the country."

Straining every nerve they stepped out gallantly and covered mile after mile till they reached the Shenandoah, forded it, and crossed the Blue Ridge at Ashby's Gap. But lack of training and march discipline told increasingly against them. "The discouragement of that day's march," said Johnston, "is indescribable. Frequent and unreasonable delays caused so slow a rate of marching as to make me despair of joining General Beauregard in time to aid him." Even the First Brigade, with all the advantages of leading the march and of having learnt the rudiments of drill and discipline, was exhausted by a day's work that it could have romped through later on. Jackson himself stood guard alone till dawn while all his soldiers slept.

As Jackson's men marched down to take the train at Piedmont, Stuart gayly trotted past, having left Patterson still in ignorance that Johnston's force had gone. By four in the afternoon of the nineteenth Jackson was detraining at Manassas. But, as we shall presently see, it was nearly two whole days before the last of Johnston's brigades arrived, just in time for the crisis of the battle. When Johnston had joined Beauregard their united effective total was thirty thousand men. There had been a wastage of three thousand. McDowell also had no more than thirty thousand effectives present on the twenty-first; for he left one division at Centreville and lost the rest by straggling and by the way in which the battery and battalion already mentioned had "claimed their discharge" at Blackburn's Ford. Throughout the nineteenth and twentieth, while, sorely against his will, the Federals were having their "monster military picnic" at Centreville, he was reconnoitering his constantly increasing enemy under the greatest difficulties, with his ill-trained staff, bad maps, and lack of proper guides.

Lee had chosen six miles of Bull Run as a good defensive position. But Beauregard intended to attack, hoping to profit by the Federal disjointedness. Consequently none of the eight fords were strongly defended except at Union Mills on the extreme right and the Stone Bridge on the extreme left, where the turnpike from Centreville to Warrenton crossed the Run. Bull Run itself was a considerable obstacle, having fairly high banks and running along the Confederate front like the ditch of a fortress. Three miles in rear stood Manassas Junction on a moderate plateau intersected by several creeks. The most important of these creeks, Young's Branch, joined Bull Run on the extreme left, near the Stone Bridge and Warrenton turnpike, after flowing through the little valley between the Henry Hill and Matthews Hill.

Three miles in front, across Bull Run, stood Centreville, the Federal camp and field base during the battle.

Sunday, July 21, 1861, was a beautiful midsummer day. Both armies were stirring soon after dawn. But a miscarriage of orders delayed the Confederate offensive so much that the initiative of attack passed to the Federals, who advanced against the Stone Bridge shortly after six. This attack, however, though made by a whole division against a single small brigade, was immediately recognized as a mere feint when, two hours later, Evans, commanding the Confederate brigade, saw dense clouds of dust rising above the woods on his left front, where the road crossed Sudley Springs, nearly two miles beyond his own left. Perceiving that this new development must be a regular attempt to turn the whole Confederate left by crossing Bull Run, he sent back word to Beauregard, posted some men to hold the Stone Bridge, and marched the rest to crown the Matthews Hill, facing Sudley Springs a mile away. Meanwhile four of "Joe" Johnston's five Shenandoah brigades—Bee's, Bartow's, Bonham's, and Jackson's—had been coming over from the right reserve to strengthen Evans at the Bridge. As the great Federal turning movement developed against the Confederate left these brigades followed Evans and were themselves followed by other troops, till the real battle raged not along Bull Run but across the Matthews Hill and Henry Hill.

Forming the new front at right angles to the old, so as to attack and defend the Confederate left on the Matthews and Henry Hills, caused much confusion on both sides; but more on the Federal, as the Confederates knew the ground better. By eleven Bee had reached Evans and sent word back to hurry Bartow on. But the Federals, having double numbers and a great preponderance in guns, soon drove the Confederates off the Matthews Hill. As the Confederates recrossed Young's Branch and climbed the Henry Hill the regular artillery of the Federals limbered up smartly, galloped across the Matthews Hill, and from its nearer slope plied the retreating Confederates on the opposite slope with admirably served shell. Under this fire the raw Confederates ran in confusion, while their uncovered guns galloped back to find a new position.

"Curse them for deserting the guns," snapped Imboden, whose battery came face to face with Jackson's brigade. "I'll support you," said Jackson, "unlimber right here." At the same time, half-past eleven, Bee galloped up on his foaming charger, saying, "General, they're beating us back." "Then, Sir," said Jackson, "we'll give them the bayonet"; and his lips shut tight as a vice.

Bee then went back behind the Henry Hill, where his broken brigade was trying to rally, and, pointing toward the crest with his sword, shouted in a voice of thunder: "Rally behind the Virginians! Look! There's Jackson standing like a stone wall!" From that one cry of battle Stonewall Jackson got his name.

While the rest of the Shenandoahs were rallying, in rear of Jackson, Beauregard and Johnston came up, followed by two batteries. Miles behind them, all the men that could be spared from the fords were coming too. But the Federals on the Matthews Hill were still in more than double numbers; and they enjoyed the priceless advantage of having some regulars among them. If the Federal division at the Stone Bridge had only pushed home its attack at this favorable moment the Confederates must have been defeated. But the division again fumbled about to little purpose; and for the second time McDowell's admirable plan was spoilt.

It was now past noon on that sweltering midsummer day; and there was a welcome lull for the rallying Confederates while the Federals were coming down the Matthews Hill, struggling across the swamps and thickets of Young's Branch, and climbing the Henry Hill. Within another hour the opposing forces were at close grips again, and the Federals, flushed with success and steadied by the regulars, seemed certain to succeed.

Imboden has vividly described his meeting Jackson at this time. "The fight was just then hot enough to make him feel well. His eyes fairly blazed. He had a way of throwing up his left hand with the open palm towards the person he was addressing; and, as he told me to go, he made this gesture. The air was full of flying missiles, and as he spoke he jerked down his hand, and I saw that blood was streaming from it. I exclaimed, 'General, you are wounded.' 'Only a scratch—a mere scratch,' he replied; and, binding it hastily with a handkerchief, he galloped away along his line."

Five hundred yards apart the opposing cannon thundered, while the musketry of the long lines of infantry swelled the deafening roar. Suddenly two Federal batteries of regulars dashed forward to even shorter range, covered by two battalions on their flank. But the gaudy Zouaves of the outer battalion lost formation in their advance; whereupon "Jeb" Stuart, with only a hundred and fifty horsemen, swooped down and smashed them to pieces by a daring charge. Then, just as the scattered white turbans went wildly bobbing about, into the midst of the inner battalion, out rushed the Thirty-third Virginians, straight at the guns. The battery officers held their fire, uncertain in the smoke whether the newcomers were friend or foe, till a deadly volley struck home at less than eighty yards. Down went the gunners to a man; down went the teams to a horse; and off ran the Zouaves and the other supporting battalion, helter-skelter for the rear.

But other Federals were still full of fight and in superior numbers. They came on with great gallantry, considering they were raw troops who were now without the comfort of the guns. Once more a Federal victory seemed secure; and if the infantry had only pressed on (not piecemeal, by disjoined battalions, but by brigades) without letting the Confederates recover from one blow before another struck them, the day would have certainly been theirs. Moreover, they would have inflicted not simply a defeat but a severe disaster on their enemy, who would have been caught in flank by the troops at the Stone Bridge; for these troops, however dilatory, must have known what to do with a broken and flying Confederate flank right under their very eyes. Premonitory symptoms of such a flight were not wanting. Confederate wounded, stragglers, and skulkers were making for the rear; and the rallied brigades were again in disorder, with Bee and Bartow, two first-rate brigadiers, just killed, and other seniors wounded. Another ominous sign was the limbering up of Confederate guns to cover the expected retreat from the Henry Hill.

But on its reverse slope lay Jackson's Shenandoahs, three thousand strong, and by far the best drilled and disciplined brigade that either side had yet produced — apart, of course, from regulars. Jackson had ridden up and down before them, calm as they had ever seen him on parade, quietly saying, "Steady, men, steady! All's well." In this way he had held them straining at the leash for hours. Now, at last, their time had come. Riding out to the center of his line he gave his final orders: "Reserve your fire till they come within fifty yards. Then fire and give them the bayonet; and yell like furies when you charge!" Five minutes later, as the triumphant Federals topped the crest, the long gray line rose up, stood fast, fired one crashing point-blank volley, and immediately charged home with the first of those wild, high rebel yells that rang throughout the war. The stricken and astounded Federal front caved in, turned round, and fled. At the same instant the last of the Shenandoahs — Kirby Smith's brigade, detrained just in the nick of time — charged the wavering flank. Then, like the first quiver of an avalanche, a tremor shook the whole massed Federals one moment on that fatal hill: the next, like a loosened cliff, they began the landslide down.

There, in the valley, along Young's Branch, McDowell established his last line of battle, based on the firm rock of the regulars. But by this time the Confederates had brought up troops from the whole length of their line; the balance of numbers was at last in their favor; and nothing could stay the Federal recoil. Lack of drill and discipline soon changed this recoil into a disorderly retreat. There was no panic; but most of the military units dissolved into a mere mob whose heart was set on getting back to Washington in any way left open. The regulars and a few formed bodies in reserve did their best to stem the stream. But all in vain.

One mile short of Centreville there was a sudden upset and consequent block on the bridge across Cub Run. Then the stream of men retreating, mixed with clogging masses of panic-struck civilians, became a torrent.

Bull Run was only a special-constable affair on a gigantic scale. The losses were comparatively small—3553 killed and wounded on both sides put together: not ten per cent of the less than forty thousand who actually fought. Moreover, the side that won the battle lost the war. And yet Bull Run had many points of very great importance. In spite of all shortcomings it showed the good quality of the troops engaged: if not as soldiers, at all events as men. It proved that the war, unlike the battle, would not be fought by special constables, some of whom first fired their rifles when their target was firing back at them. It brought one great leader—Stonewall Jackson— into fame. Above all, it profoundly affected the popular points of view, both North and South. In the South there was undue elation, followed by the absurd belief that one Southerner could beat two Northerners any day and that the North would now back down *en masse*, as its army had from the Henry Hill. A dangerous slackening of military preparation was the unavoidable result. In the North, on the other hand, a good many people began to see the difference between armed mobs and armies; and the thorough Unionists, led by the wise and steadfast Lincoln, braced themselves for real war.

CHAPTER II
THE COMBATANTS

No map can show the exact dividing line between the actual combatants of North and South. Eleven States seceded: Virginia, the Carolinas, Georgia, Florida, Alabama, Mississippi, Tennessee, Louisiana, Texas, and Arkansas. But the mountain folk of western Virginia and eastern Tennessee were strong Unionists; and West Virginia became a State while the war was being fought. On the other hand, the four border States, though officially Federal under stress of circumstances, were divided against themselves. In Maryland, Kentucky, Missouri, and Kansas, many citizens took the Southern side. Maryland would have gone with the South if it had not been for the presence of overwhelming Northern sea-power and the absence of any good land frontier of her own. Kentucky remained neutral for several months. Missouri was saved for the Union by those two resourceful and determined men, Lyon and Blair. Kansas, though preponderantly Unionist, had many Confederates along its southern boundary. On the whole the Union gained greatly throughout the borderlands as the war went on; and the remaining Confederate hold on the border people was more than counterbalanced by the Federal hold on those in the western parts of old Virginia and the eastern parts of Tennessee. Among the small seafaring population along the Southern coast there were also some strongly Union men.

Counting out Northern Confederates and Southern Federals as canceling each other, so far as effective fighting was concerned a comparison made between the North and South along the line of actual secession reveals the one real advantage the South enjoyed all through—an overwhelming party in favor of the war. When once the die was cast there was certainly not a tenth of the Southern whites who did not belong to the war party; and the peace party always had to hold its tongue. The Southerners formed simpler and far more homogeneous communities of the old long-settled stock, and were more inclined to act together when once their feelings were profoundly stirred.

The Northern communities, on the other hand, being far more complex and far less homogeneous, were plagued with peace parties that grew like human weeds, clogging the springs of action everywhere. There were immigrants new to the country and therefore not inclined to take risks for a cause they had not learned to make their own. There were also naturalized, and even American-born, aliens, aliens in speech, race, thought, and every way of life. Then there were the oppositionists of different kinds, who would not support any war government, however like a perfect coalition it might be. Among these were some Northerners who did business with the South, especially the men who financed the cotton and tobacco crops. Others, again, were those loose-tongued folk who think any vexed question can be settled by unlimited talk. Next came those "defeatist" cranks who always think their own side must be wrong, and who are of no more practical use than the out-and-out "pacifists" who think everybody wrong except themselves. Finally, there were those slippery folk who try to evade all public duty, especially when it smacks of danger. These skulkers flourish best in large and complex populations, where they may even masquerade as patriots of the kind so well described by Lincoln when he said how often he had noticed that the men who were loudest in proclaiming their readiness to shed their last drop of blood were generally the most careful not to shed the first.

Many of these fustian heroes formed the mushroom secret societies that played their vile extravaganza right under the shadow of the real tragedy of war. Worse still, not content with the abracadabra of their silly oaths, the busybody members made all the mischief they could during Lincoln's last election. Worst of all, they not only tried their hands at political assassination in the North but they lured many a gallant Confederate to his death by promising to rise in their might for a "Free Northwest" the moment the Southern troopers should appear. Needless to say, not a single one of the whole bombastic band of cowards stirred a finger to help the Confederate troopers who rode to their doom on Morgan's Raid through Indiana and Ohio. The peace party wore a copper as a badge, and so came to be known as "Copperheads," much to the disgust of its more inflated members, who called themselves the Sons of Liberty. The war party, with a better appreciation of how names and things should be connected, used their own descriptive "Copperhead" in its appropriate meaning of a poisonous snake in the grass behind.

The Indians would have preferred neutrality between the two kinds of inevitably dispossessing whites. But neutrality was impossible in what was then the Far West. Not ten thousand Indians fought for both sides put together. On the whole they fought well as skirmishers, though they rarely withstood shell fire, even when their cover was good and their casualties small.

The ten times more numerous negroes were naturally a much more serious factor. The North encouraged the employment of colored labor corps and even colored soldiers, especially after Emancipation. But the vast majority of negroes, whether slave or free, either preferred or put up with their Southern masters, whom they generally served faithfully enough either in military labor corps or on the old plantations. As the colored population of the South was three and a half millions this general fidelity was of great importance to the forces in the field.

The total population of the United States in 1861 was about thirty-one and a half millions. Of this total twenty-two and a half belonged to the North and nine to the South. The grand total odds were therefore five against two. The odds against the South rise to four against one if the blacks are left out. There were twenty-two million whites in the North against five and a half in the South. But to reach the real fighting odds of three to one we must also eliminate the peace parties, large in the North, small in the South. If we take a tenth off the Southern whites and a third off the Northern grand total we shall get the approximate war-party odds of three to one; for these subtractions leave fifteen millions in the North against only five in the South.

This gives the statistical key to the startling contrasts which were so often noted by foreign correspondents at the time, and which are still so puzzling in the absence of the key. The whole normal life of the South was visibly changed by the war. But in the North the inquiring foreigner could find, on one hand, the most steadfast loyalty and heroic sacrifice, both in the Northern armies and among their folks at home, while on the other he could find a wholly different kind of life flaunting its most shameless features in his face. The theaters were crowded. Profiteers abounded, taking their pleasures with ravenous greed; for the best of their blood-money would end with the war. Everywhere there was the same fundamental difference between the patriots who carried on the war and the parasites who hindered them. Of course the two-thirds who made up the war party were not all saints or even perfect patriots. Nor was the other third composed exclusively of wanton sinners. There were, for instance, the genuine settlers whom the Union Government encouraged to occupy the West, beyond the actual reach of war. But the distinction still remains.

Though sorely hampered, the Union Government did, on the whole, succeed in turning the vast and varied resources of the North against the much smaller and less varied resources of the South. The North held the machinery of national government, though with the loss of a good quarter of the engineers. In agriculture of, all kinds both North and South were very strong for purposes of peace. Each had food in superabundance. But the trading strength of the South lay in cotton and tobacco, neither of which could be turned into money without going north or to sea. In finance the North was overwhelmingly strong by comparison, more especially because Northern sea-power shut off the South from all its foreign markets. In manufactures the South could not compare at all. Northern factories alone could not supply the armies. But finance and factories together could. The Southern soldier looked to the battlefield and the raiding of a base for supplying many of his most pressing needs in arms, equipment, clothing, and even food—for Southern transport suffered from many disabilities. Fierce wolfish cries would mingle with the rebel yell in battle when the two sides closed. "You've got to leave your rations!"—"Come out of them clothes!"—"Take off them boots, Yank!"—"Come on, blue bellies, we want them blankets!"

It was the same in almost every kind of goods. The South made next to none for herself and had to import from the North or overseas. The North could buy silk for balloons. The South could not. The Southern women gave in their whole supply of silk for the big balloon that was lost during the Seven Days' Battle in the second year of the war. The Southern soldiers never forgave what they considered the ungallant trick of the Northerners who took this many-hued balloon from a steamer stranded on a bar at low tide down near the mouth of the James. Thus fell the last silk dress, a queer tribute to Northern sea-power! Northern sea-power also cut off nearly everything the sick and wounded needed; which raised the death rate of the Southern forces far beyond the corresponding death rate in the North. Again, preserved rations were almost unknown in the South. But they were plentiful throughout the Northern armies: far too plentiful, indeed, for the taste of the men, who got "fed up" on the dessicated vegetables and concentrated milk which they rechristened "desecrated vegetables" and "consecrated milk."

There is the same tale to tell about transport and munitions. Outside the Tredegar Iron Works at Richmond the only places where Southern cannon could be made were Charlotte in North Carolina, Atlanta and Macon in Georgia, and Selma in Alabama. The North had many places, each with superior plant, besides which the oversea munition world was far more at the service of the open-ported North than of the close-blockaded South. What sea-power meant in this respect may be estimated from the fact that out of the more than three-quarters of a million rifles bought by the North in the first fourteen months of the war all but a beggarly thirty thousand came from overseas.

Transport was done by road, rail, sea, and inland waters. Other things being equal, a hundred tons could be moved by water as easily as ten by rail or one by road. Now, the North not only enjoyed enormous advantages in sea-power, both mercantile and naval, but in road, rail, canal, and river transport too. The road transport that affected both sides most was chiefly in the South, because most maneuvering took place there. "Have you been through Virginia?—Yes, in several places" is a witticism that might be applied to many another State where muddy sloughs abounded. In horses, mules, and vehicles the richer North wore out the poorer and blockaded South. Both sides sent troops, munitions, and supplies by rail whenever they could; and here, as a glance at the map will show, the North greatly surpassed the South in mileage, strategic disposition, and every other way.

The South had only one through line from the Atlantic to the Mississippi; and this ran across that Northern salient which threatened the South from the southwestern Alleghanies. The other rails all had the strategic defect of not being convenient for rapid concentration by land; for most of the Southern rails were laid with a view to getting surplus cotton and tobacco overseas. The strategic gap at Petersburg was due to a very different cause; for there, in order to keep its local transfers, the town refused to let the most important Virginian lines connect.

Taking sea-power in its fullest sense, to include all naval and mercantile parts on both salt and fresh water, we can quite understand how it helped the nautical North to get the strangle-hold on the landsman's South. The great bulk of the whole external trade of the South was done by shipping. But, though the South was strong in exportable goods, it was very weak in ships. It owned comparatively few of the vessels that carried its rice, cotton, and tobacco crops to market and brought back made goods in return. Yankees, Britishers, and Bluenoses (as Nova Scotian craft were called) did most of the oversea transportation.

Moreover, the North was vastly stronger than the South on all the inland waters that were not "Secesh" from end to end. The map shows how Northern sea-power could not only divide the South in two but almost enisle the eastern part as well. Holding the Mississippi would effect the division, while holding the Ohio would make the eastern part a peninsula, with the upper end of the isthmus safe in Northern hands between Pittsburgh, the great coal and iron inland port, and Philadelphia, the great seaport, less than three hundred miles away. The same isthmus narrows to less than two hundred miles between Pittsburgh and Harrisburg (on the Susquehanna River); and its whole line is almost equally safe in Northern hands. A little farther south, along the disputed borderlands, it narrows to less than one hundred miles, from Pittsburgh to Cumberland (on the Potomac canal). Even this is not the narrowest part of the isthmus, which is less than seventy miles across from Cumberland to Brownsville (on the Monongahela) and less than fifty from Cumberland to the Ohiopyle Falls (on the Youghiogheny). These last distances are measured between places that are only fit for minor navigation. But even small craft had an enormous advantage over road and rail together when bulky stores were moved. So Northern sea-power could make its controlling influence felt in one continuous line all round the eastern South, except for fifty miles where small craft were concerned and for two hundred miles in the case of larger vessels. These two hundred miles of land were those between the Ohio River port of Wheeling and the Navy Yard at Washington.

Nor was this virtual enislement the only advantage to be won. For while the strong right arm of Union sea-power, facing northward from the Gulf, could hold the coast, and its sinewy left could hold the Mississippi, the supple left fingers could feel their way along the tributary streams until the clutching hand had got its grip on the whole of the Ohio, Cumberland, Tennessee, Missouri, Arkansas, and Red rivers. This meant that the North would not only enjoy the vast advantages of transport by water over transport by land but that it would cause the best lines of invasion to be opened up as well.

Of course the South had some sea-power of her own. Nine-tenths of the United States Navy stood by the Union. But, with the remaining tenth and some foreign help, the South managed to contrive the makeshift parts of what might have become a navy if the North had only let it grow. The North, however, did not let it grow.

The regular navy of the United States, though very small to start with, was always strong enough to keep the command of the sea and to prevent the makeshift Southern parts of a navy from ever becoming a whole. Privateers took out letters of marque to prey on Northern shipping. But privateering soon withered off, because prizes could not be run through the blockade in sufficient numbers to make it pay; and no prize would be recognized except in a Southern port. Raiders did better and for a much longer time. The *Shenandoah* was burning Northern whalers in Bering Sea at the end of the war. The *Sumter* and the *Florida* cut a wide swath under instructions which "left much to discretion and more to the torch." The famous *Alabama* only succumbed to the U.S.S. *Kearsarge* after sinking the *Hatteras* man-of-war and raiding seventy other vessels. Yet still the South, in spite of her ironclads, raiders, and rams, in spite of her river craft, of the home ships or foreigners that ran the blockade, and of all her other efforts, was a landsman's country that could make no real headway against the native sea-power of the North.

Perhaps the worst of all the disabilities under which the abortive Southern navy suffered was lubberly administration and gross civilian interference. The Administration actually refused to buy the beginnings of a ready-made sea-going fleet when it had the offer of ten British East Indiamen specially built for rapid conversion into men-of-war. Forty thousand bales of cotton would have bought the lot. The Mississippi record was even worse. Five conflicting authorities divided the undefined and overlapping responsibilities between them: the Confederate Government, the State governments, the army, the navy, and the Mississippi skippers. A typical result may be seen in the fate of the fourteen "rams" which were absurdly mishandled by fourteen independent civilian skippers with two civilian commodores. This "River Defense Fleet" was "backed by the whole Missouri delegation" at Richmond, and blessed by the Confederate Secretary of War, Judah P. Benjamin, that very clever lawyer-politician and ever-smiling Jew. Six of the fourteen "rams" were lost, with sheer futility, at New Orleans in April, '62; the rest at Memphis the following June.

As a matter of fact the Confederate navy never had but one real man-of-war, the famous *Merrimac*; and she was a mere razee, cut down for a special purpose, and too feebly engined to keep the sea. Even the equally famous *Alabama* was only a raider, never meant for action with a fleet. Over three hundred officers left the United States Navy for the South; but, as in the case of the Army, they were followed by very few men. The total personnel of the regular Confederate navy never exceeded four thousand at any one time. The irregular forces afloat often did gallant, and sometimes even skillful, service in little isolated ways. But when massed together they were always at sixes and sevens; and they could never do more than make the best of a very bad business indeed. The Secretary of the Confederate navy, Stephen R. Mallory, was not to blame. He was one of the very few civilians who understood and tried to follow any naval principles at all. He had done good work as chairman of the Naval Committee in the Senate before the war, and had learnt a good deal more than his Northern rival, Gideon Welles. He often saw what should have been done. But men and means were lacking.

Men and means were also lacking in the naval North at the time the war began. But the small regular navy was invincible against next to none; and it enjoyed many means of expansion denied to the South.

On the outbreak of hostilities the United States Navy had ninety ships and about nine thousand men—all ranks and ratings (with marines) included. The age of steam had come. But fifty vessels had no steam at all. Of the rest one was on the Lakes, five were quite unserviceable, and thirty-four were scattered about the world without the slightest thought of how to mobilize a fleet at home. The age of ironclads had begun already overseas. But in his report to Congress on July 4, 1861, Gideon Welles, Secretary of the

Navy, only made some wholly non-committal observations in ponderous "officialese." In August he appointed a committee which began its report in September with the sage remark that "Opinions differ amongst naval and scientific men as to the policy of adopting the iron armament for ships-of-war." In December Welles transmitted this report to Congress with the still sager remark that "The subject of iron armature for ships is one of great general interest, not only to the navy and country, but is engaging the attention of the civilized world." Such was the higher administrative preparation for the ironclad battle of the following year.

It was the same in everything. The people had taken no interest in the navy and Congress had faithfully represented them by denying the service all chance of preparing for war till after war had broken out. Then there was the usual hurry and horrible waste. Fortunately for all concerned, Gideon Welles, after vainly groping about the administrative maze for the first five months, called Gustavus V. Fox to his assistance. Fox had been a naval officer of exceptional promise, who had left the service to go into business, who had a natural turn for administration, and who now made an almost ideal Assistant Secretary of the Navy. He was, indeed, far more than this; for, in most essentials, he acted throughout the war as a regular Chief of Staff.

One of the greatest troubles was the glut of senior officers who were too old and the alarming dearth of juniors fit for immediate work afloat. It was only after the disaster at Bull Run that Congress authorized the formation of a Promotion Board to see what could be done to clear the active list and make it really a list of officers fit for active service. Up to this time there had been no system of retiring men for inefficiency or age. An officer who did not retire of his own accord simply went on rising automatically till he died. The president of this board had himself turned sixty. But he was the thoroughly efficient David Glasgow Farragut, a man who was to do greater things afloat than even Fox could do ashore. How badly active officers were wanted may be inferred from the fact that before the appointment of Farragut's promotion board the total number of regular officers remaining in the navy was only 1457. Intensive training was tried at the Naval Academy. Yet 7500 volunteer officers had to be used before the war was over. These came mostly from the merchant service and were generally brave, capable, first-rate men. But a nautical is not the same as a naval training; and the dearth of good professional naval officers was felt to the end. The number of enlisted seamen authorized by Congress rose from 7600 to 51,500. But the very greatest difficulty was found in "keeping up to strength," even with the most lavish use of bounties.

The number of vessels in the navy kept on growing all through. Of course not nearly all of them were regular men-of-war or even fighting craft "fit to go foreign." At the end of the first year there were 264 in commission; at the end of the second, 427; at the end of the third, 588; and at the end of the fourth, 671.

Bearing this in mind, and remembering the many other Northern odds, one might easily imagine that the Southern armies fought only with the courage of despair. Yet such was not the case. This was no ordinary war, to be ended by a treaty in which compromise would play its part. There could be only two alternatives: either the South would win her independence or the North would have to beat her into complete submission. Under the circumstances the united South would win whenever the divided North thought that complete subjugation would cost more than it was worth. The great aim of the South was, therefore, not to conquer the North but simply to sicken the North of trying to conquer her. "Let us alone and we'll let you alone" was her insinuating argument; and this, as she knew very well, was echoed by many people in the North. Thus, as regards her own objective, she began with hopes that the Northern peace party never quite let die.

Then, so far as her patriotic feelings were concerned, the South was not fighting for any one point at issue—not even for slavery, because only a small minority held slaves—but for her whole way of life, which, rightly or wrongly, she wanted to live in her own Southern way; and she passionately resented the invasion of her soil. This gave her army a very high morale, which, in its turn, inclined her soldiers the better to appreciate their real or imagined advantages over the Northern hosts. First, they and their enemies both knew that they enjoyed the three real advantages of fighting at home under magnificent leaders and with interior lines. Robert Lee and Stonewall Jackson stood head and shoulders above any Northern leaders till Grant and Sherman rose to greatness during the latter half of the war. Lee himself was never surpassed; and he, like Jackson and several more, made the best use of home surroundings and of interior lines. Anybody can appreciate the prime advantage of interior lines by imagining two armies of equal strength operating against each other under perfectly equal conditions except that one has to move round the circumference of a circle while the other moves to meet it along the shorter lines inside. The army moving round the circumference is said to be operating on exterior lines, while the army moving from point to point of the circumference by the straighter, and therefore shorter, lines inside is said to be operating on interior lines. In more homely language the straight road beats the crooked one. In plain slang, it's best to have the inside track.

Of course there is a reverse to all this. If the roads, rails, and waterways are better around the circle than inside it, then the odds may be turned the other way; and this happens most often when the forces on the exterior lines are the better provided with sea-power. Again, if the exterior forces are so much stronger than the interior forces that these latter dare not leave any strategic point open in case the enemy breaks through, then it is evident that the interior forces will suffer all the disadvantages of being surrounded, divided, worn out, and defeated.

This happened at last to the South, and was one of the four advantages she lost. Another was the hope of foreign intervention, which died hard in Southern hearts, but which was already moribund halfway through the war. A third was the hope of dissension in the North, a hope which often ran high till Lincoln's reëlection in November, '64, and one which only died out completely with the surrender of Lee. The fourth was the unfounded belief that Southerners were the better fighting men. They certainly had an advantage at first in having a larger proportion of men accustomed to horses and arms and inured to life in the open. But, other things being equal, there was nothing to choose between the two sides, so far as natural fighting values were concerned.

Practically all the Southern "military males" passed into the ranks; and a military male eventually meant any one who could march to the front or do non-combatant service with an army, from boys in their teens to men in their sixties. Conscription came after one year; and with very few exemptions, such as the clergy, Quakers, many doctors, newspaper editors, and "indispensable" civil servants. Lee used to express his regret that all the greatest strategists were tied to their editorial chairs. But sterner feelings were aroused against that recalcitrant State Governor, Joseph Brown of Georgia, who declared eight thousand of his civil servants to be totally exempt. From first to last, conscripts and volunteers, nearly a million men were enrolled: equaling one-fifth of the entire war-party white population of the seceding States.

All branches of the service suffered from a constant lack of arms and munitions. As with the ships for the navy so with munitions for the army, the South did not exploit the European markets while her ports were still half open and her credit good, Jefferson Davis was spotlessly honest, an able bureaucrat, and full of undying zeal. But, though an old West Pointer, he was neither a foresightful organizer nor fit to exercise any of the executive power which he held as the constitutional commander-in-chief by land and sea. He ordered rifles by the thousand instead of by the hundred thousand; and he actually told his Cabinet that if he could only take one wing while Lee took the other they would surely beat the North. Worse still, he and his politicians kept the commissariat under civilian orders and full of civilian interference, even at the front, which, in this respect, was always a house divided against itself.

The little regular army of '61, only sixteen thousand strong, stood by the Union almost to a man; though a quarter of the officers went over to the South. Yet the enlisted man was despised even by the common loafers who would not fight if they could help it. "Why don't you come in?" asked a zealous lady at a distribution of patriotic gifts, "aren't you one of our heroes?" "No, ma'am," answered the soldier, "I'm only a regular."

The question of command was often a very vexed one; and many mistakes were made before the final answers came. The most significant of all emergent facts was this: that though the officers who had been regulars before the war did not form a hundredth part of all who held commissions during it, yet these old regulars alone supplied every successful high commander, Federal and Confederate alike, both afloat and ashore.

The North had four times as many whites as the South; it used more blacks as soldiers; and the complete grand total of all the men who joined its forces during the war reached two millions and three-quarters. But this gives a quite misleading idea of the real odds in favor of the North, especially the odds available in battle. A third of the Northern people belonged to the peace party and furnished no recruits at all till after conscription came in. The late introduction of conscription, the abominable substitution clause, and the prevalence of bounty-jumping combined to reduce both the quantity and quality of the recruits obtained by money or compulsion. The Northerners that did fight were generally fighting in the South, among a very hostile population, which, while it made the Southern lines of communication perfectly safe, threatened those of the North at every point and thus obliged the Northern armies to leave more and more men behind to guard the communications that each advance made longer still. Finally, the South generally published the numbers of only its actual combatants, while the Northern returns always included every man drawing pay, whether a combatant or not. On the whole, the North had more than double numbers, even if compared with a Southern total that includes noncombatants. But it should be remembered that a Northern army fighting in the heart of the South, and therefore having to guard every mile of the way back home, could not meet a Southern one with equal strength in battle unless it had left the North with fully twice as many.

Conscription came a year later (1863) in the North than in the South and was vitiated by a substitution clause. The fact that a man could buy himself out of danger made some patriots call it "a rich man's war and a poor man's fight." And the further fact that substitutes generally became regular bounty-jumpers, who joined and deserted at will, over and over again, went far to increase the disgust of those who really served. Frank Wilkeson's *Recollections of a Private Soldier in the Army of the Potomac* is a true voice from the ranks when he explains "how the resort to volunteering, the unprincipled dodge of cowardly politicians, ground up the choicest seed-corn of the nation; how it consumed the young, the patriotic, the intelligent, the generous, and the brave; and how it wasted the best moral, social, and political elements of the Republic, leaving the cowards, shirkers, egotists, and moneymakers to stay at home and procreate their kind."

That is to say, it was so arranged that the foxy-witted lived, while the lion-hearted died.

The organization of the vast numbers enrolled was excellent whenever experts were given a free hand. But this free hand was rare. One vital point only needs special notice here: the wastefulness of raising new regiments when the old ones were withering away for want of reinforcements. A new local regiment made a better "story" in the press; and new and superfluous regiments meant new and superfluous colonels, mostly of the speechifying kind. So it often happened that the State authorities felt obliged to humor zealots set on raising those brand-new regiments which doubled their own difficulties by having to learn their lesson alone, halved the efficiency of the old regiments they should have reinforced, and harassed the commanders and staff by increasing the number of units that were of different and ever-changing efficiency and strength. It was a system of making and breaking all through.

The end came when Northern sea-power had strangled the Southern resources and the unified Northern armies had worn out the fighting force. Of the single million soldiers raised by the South only two hundred thousand remained in arms, half starved, half clad, with the scantiest of munitions, and without reserves of any kind. Meanwhile the Northern hosts had risen to a million in the field, well fed, well clothed, well armed, abundantly provided with munitions, and at last well disciplined under the unified command of that great leader, Grant. Moreover, behind this million stood another million fit to bear arms and obtainable at will from the two millions of enrolled reserves.

The cost of the war was stupendous. But the losses of war are not to be measured in money. The real loss was the loss of a million men, on both sides put together, for these men who died were of the nation's best.

CHAPTER III
THE NAVAL WAR: 1862

Bull Run had riveted attention on the land between the opposing capitals and on the armies fighting there. Very few people were thinking of the navies and the sea. And yet it was at sea, and not on land, that the Union had a force against which the Confederates could never prevail, a force which gradually cut them off from the whole world's base of war supplies, a force which enabled the Union armies to get and keep the strangle-hold which did the South to death.

The blockade declared in April was no empty threat. The sails of Federal frigates, still more the sinister black hulls of the new steam men-of-war, meant that the South was fast becoming a land besieged, with every outwork accessible by water exposed to sudden attack and almost certain capture by any good amphibious force of soldiers and sailors combined.

Sea-power kept the North in affluence while it starved the South. Sea-power held Maryland in its relentless grip and did more than land-power to keep her in the Union. Sea-power was the chief factor in saving Washington. Seapower enabled the North to hold such points of vantage as Fortress Monroe right on the flank of the South. And sea-power likewise enabled the North to take or retake other points of similar importance: for instance, Hatteras Island.

In a couple of days at the end of August, 1861, the Confederate forts at Hatteras Inlet, North Carolina, were compelled to surrender to a joint naval and military expedition under Flag-Officer Stringham and Major-General B. F. Butler. The immediate result, besides the capture of seven hundred men, was the control of the best entrance to North Carolina waters, which entailed the stoppage of many oversea supplies for the Confederate army. The ulterior result was the securing of a base from which a further invasion could be made with great advantage.

The naval campaign of the following year was truly epoch-making; for the duel between the *Monitor* and *Merrimac* in Hampton Roads on March 9, 1862, was the first action ever fought between ironclad steam men-of-war.

Eleven months earlier the Federal Government had suddenly abandoned the Norfolk Navy Yard; though their strongest garrison was at Fortress Monroe, only twelve miles north along a waterway which was under the absolute control of their navy, and though the Confederates' had nothing but an inadequate little untrained force on the spot. Among the spoils of war falling into Confederate hands were twelve hundred guns and the *Merrimac*, a forty-gun steam frigate. The *Merrimac*, though fired and scuttled by the Federals, was hove up, cut down, plated over, and renamed the *Virginia*. (History, however, knows her only as the *Merrimac*.) John L. Porter, Naval Constructor to the Confederate States, had made a model of an ironclad at Pittsburgh fifteen years before; and he now applied this model to the rebuilding of the *Merrimac*. He first cut down everything above the water line, except the gun deck, which he converted into a regular citadel with flat top, sides sloping at thirty-five degrees, and ends stopping short of the ship's own ends by seventy feet fore and aft. The effect, therefore, was that of an ironclad citadel built on the midships of a submerged frigate's hull. The four-inch iron plating of the citadel knuckled over the wooden sides two feet under water. The engines, which the South had no means of replacing, were the old ones which had been condemned before being sunk. A four-foot castiron ram was clamped on to the bow. Ten guns were mounted: six nine-inch smooth-bores, with two six-inch and two seven-inch rifles. Commodore Franklin Buchanan took command and had magnificent professional officers under him. But the crew, three hundred strong, were mostly landsmen; for, as in the case of the Army, the men of the Navy nearly all took sides with the North, and the South had very few seamen of any other kind.

To oppose the *Merrimac* the dilatory North contracted with John Ericsson the Swede, who had to build the *Monitor* much smaller than the Merrimac owing to pressure of time. He enjoyed, however, enormous advantages in every other respect, owing to the vastly superior resources of the North in marine engineering, armor-plating, and all other points of naval construction. The *Monitor* was launched at New York on January 30, 1862, the hundredth day after the laying of her keel-plate. Her length over all was 172 feet, her beam was 41, and her draught only 10—less than half the draught of the *Merrimac*. Her whole crew numbered only 58; but every single one was a trained professional naval seaman who had volunteered for dangerous service under Captain John L. Worden. She was not a good sea boat; and she nearly foundered on her way down from New York to Fortress Monroe. Her underwater hull was shipshape enough; but her superstructure—a round iron tower resting on a very low deck—was not. Contemptuous eyewitnesses described her very well as looking like a tin can on a shingle or a cheesebox on a raft. She carried only two guns, eleven-inchers, both mounted inside her turret, which revolved by machinery; but their 180-pound shot were far more powerful than any aboard the *Merrimac*. In maneuvering the *Monitor* enjoyed an immense advantage, with her light draft, strong engines, and well-protected screws and rudder.

On the eighth of March, a lovely spring day, the *Merrimac* made her trial trip by going into action with her wheezy old engines, lubberly crew, and the guns she had never yet fired. She shoveled along at only five knots; but the Confederate garrisons cheered her to the echo. Seven miles north she came upon the astonished fifty-gun *Congress* and thirty-gun *Cumberland* swinging drowsily at anchor off Newport News, with their boats alongside and the men's wash drying in the rigging. Yet the surprised frigates opened fire at twelve hundred yards and were joined by the shore batteries, all converging on the *Merrimac*, from whose iron sides the shot glanced up without doing more than hammer her hard and start a few rivets. Closing in at top speed—barely six knots—the *Merrimac* gave the *Congress* a broadside before ramming the *Cumberland* and opening a hole "wide enough to drive in a horse and cart." Backing clear and turning the after-pivot gun, the *Merrimac* then got in three raking shells against the *Congress*, which grounded when trying to escape. Meanwhile the *Cumberland* was listing over and rapidly filling, though she kept up the fight to the very last gasp. When she sank with a roar her topmasts still showed above water and her colors waved defiance. An hour later the terribly mauled *Congress* surrendered; whereupon her crew was rescued and she was set on fire. By this time various smaller craft on both sides had joined the fray. But the big *Minnesota* still remained, though aground and apparently at the mercy of the *Merrimac*. The great draught of the *Merrimac* and the setting in of the ebb tide, however, made the Confederates draw off for the night.

Next morning they saw the "tin can on the shingle" between them and their prey. The *Monitor* and *Merrimac* then began their epoch-making fight. The patchwork engines of the deep-draught *Merrimac* made her as unhandy as if she had been water-logged, while the light-draught *Monitor* could not only play round her when close-to but maneuver all over the surrounding shallows as well. The *Merrimac* put her last ounce of steam into an attempt to ram her agile opponent. But a touch of the *Monitor's* helm swung her round just in time to make the blow perfectly harmless. The *Merrimac* simply barged into her, grated harshly against her iron side, and sheered off beaten. The firing was furious and mostly at pointblank range. Once the *Monitor* fired while the sides were actually touching. The concussion was so tremendous that all the *Merrimac's* gun-crews aft were struck down flat, with bleeding ears and noses. But in spite of this her boarders were called away; whereupon every man who could handle cutlass and revolver made ready and stood by. The *Monitor*, however, dropped astern too quickly; and the wallowing *Merrimac* had no chance of catching her. The fight had lasted all through that calm spring morning when the *Monitor* steamed off, across the shallows, still keeping carefully between the *Merrimac* and *Minnesota*. It was a drawn battle. But the effect was that of a Northern victory; for the *Merrimac* was balked of her easy prey, and the North gained time to outbuild the South completely.

Outbuilding the South of course meant tightening the "anaconda" system of blockade, in the entangling coils of which the South was caught already. Three thousand miles of Southern coastline was, however, more than the North could blockade or even watch to its own satisfaction all at once. Fogs, storms, and clever ruses played their part on behalf of those who ran the blockade, especially during the first two years; and it was almost more than human nature could stand to keep forever on the extreme alert, day after dreary day, through the deadly boredom of a long blockade. Like caged eagles the crews passed many a weary week of dull monotony without the chance of swooping on a chase. "Smoke ho!" would be called from the main-topgallant cross-tree. "Where away?" would be called back from the deck. "Up the river, Sir!"—and there it would stay, the very mark of hope deferred. Occasionally a cotton ship would make a dash, with lights out on a dark night, or through a dense fog, when her smoke might sometimes be conned from the tops. Occasionally, too, a foreigner would try to run in, and not seldom succeed, because only the fastest vessels tried to run the blockade after the first few months. But the general experience was one of utter boredom rarely relieved by a stroke of good luck.

The South could not break the blockade. But the North could tighten it, and did so repeatedly, not only at sea but by establishing strong strategic centers of its own along the Southern coast. We have seen already how Hatteras Island was taken in '61, five weeks after Bull Run. Within another three weeks Ship Island was also taken, to the great disadvantage of the Gulf ports and the corresponding advantage of the Federal fleet blockading them; for Ship Island commanded the coastwise channels between Mobile and New Orleans, the two great scenes of Farragut's success. Then, on the seventh of November, the day that Grant began his triumphant career by dealing the Confederates a shrewd strategic blow at Belmont in Missouri, South Carolina suffered a worse defeat at Port Royal (where she lost Forts Beauregard and Walker) than North Carolina had suffered at Hatteras Island. Admiral S. F. Du Pont managed the naval part of the Port Royal expedition with consummate skill, especially the fine fleet action off Hilton

Head against the Southern ships and forts. He was ably seconded by General Thomas West Sherman, commanding the troops.

North Carolina's turn soon came again, when she lost Roanoke Island (and with it the command of Albemarle Sound) on February 8, 1862; and when she also had Pamlico Sound shut against her by a joint expedition that struck down her defenses as far inland as Newbern on the fourteenth of March. Then came the turn of Georgia, where Fort Pulaski, the outpost of Savannah, fell to the Federals on the eleventh of April. Within another month Florida was even more hardly hit when the pressure of the Union fleet and army on Virginia compelled the South to use as reinforcements the garrison that had held Pensacola since the beginning of the war.

These were all severe blows to the Southern cause. But they were nothing to the one which immediately followed.

The idea of an attack on New Orleans had been conceived in June, '61, by Commander (afterwards Admiral) D. D. Porter, of the U.S.S. *Powhatan*, when he was helping to blockade the Mississippi. The Navy Department had begun thinking over the same idea in September and had worked out a definite scheme. New Orleans was of immense strategic importance, as being the link between the sea and river systems of the war. The mass of people and their politicians, on both sides, absurdly thought of New Orleans as the objective of a land invasion from the north. Happily for the Union cause, Gustavus Fox, Assistant Secretary of the Navy, knew better and persuaded his civilian chief, Gideon Welles, that this was work for a joint expedition, with the navy first, the army second. The navy could take New Orleans. The army would have to hold it.

The squadron destined for this enterprise was commanded by David Glasgow Farragut, who arrived at Ship Island on February 20, 1862, in the *Hartford*, the famous man-of-war that carried his flag in triumph to the end. Unlike Lee and Jackson, Grant and Sherman, the other four great leaders in the Civil War, Farragut was not an American whose ancestors on both sides had come from the British Isles. Like Lee, however, he was of very ancient lineage, one of his ancestors, Don Pedro Farragut, having held a high command under the King of Aragon in the Moorish wars of the thirteenth century. Farragut's father was a pure-blooded Spaniard, born under the British flag in Minorca in 1755. Half Spanish, half Southern by descent, Farragut was wholly Southern by family environment. His mother, Elizabeth Shine, was a native of North Carolina. He spent his early boyhood in New Orleans. Both his first and second wives came from Virginia; and he made his home at Norfolk. On the outbreak of the war, however, he immediately went North and applied for employment with the Union fleet.

Farragut was the oldest of the five great leaders, being now sixty years of age, while Lee was fifty-five, Sherman forty-two, Grant forty, and Jackson thirty-eight. He was, however, fit as an athlete in training, able to turn a handspring on his birthday and to hold his own in swordsmanship against any of his officers. Of middle height, strong build, and rather plain features, he did not attract attention in a crowd. But his alert and upright carriage, keenly interested look, and genial smile impressed all who ever knew him with a sense of native kindliness and power. Though far too great a master of the art of war to interfere with his subordinates he always took care to understand their duties from their own points of view so that he could control every part of the complex naval instruments of war—human and material alike—with a sure and inspiring touch. His one weakness as a leader was his generous inclination to give subordinates the chance of distinguishing themselves when they could have done more useful service in a less conspicuous position.

Farragut's base at Ship Island was about a hundred miles east from the Confederate Forts Jackson and St. Philip. These forts guarded the entrance to the Mississippi. Ninety miles above them stood New Orleans, to which they gave protection and from which they drew all their supplies. The result of a conference at Washington was an order from Welles to "reduce the defenses which guard the approaches to New Orleans." But Farragut's own infinitely better plan was to run past the forts and take New Orleans first. By doing this he would save the extra loss required for reducing the forts and would take the weak defenses of New Orleans entirely by surprise. Then, when New Orleans fell, the forts, cut off from all supplies, would have to surrender without the firing of another shot. Everything depended on whether Farragut could run past without too much loss. Profoundly versed in all the factors of the problem, he foresaw that his solution would prove right, while Washington's would as certainly be wrong. So, taking the utmost advantage of all the freedom that his general instructions allowed, he followed a course in which anything short of complete success would mean the ruin of his whole career.

The forts were strong, had ninety guns that would bear on the fleet, and were well placed, one on each side of the river. But they suffered from all the disadvantages of fixed defenses opposed by a mobile enemy, and their own mobile auxiliaries were far from being satisfactory. The best of the "River Defense Fleet," including several rams, had been ordered up to Memphis, so sure was the Confederate Government that the attack would come from the north. Two home-made ironclads were failures. The *Louisiana's* engines were not ready in time; and her captain refused to be towed into the position near the boom where he could do the enemy most harm. The *Mississippi*, a mere floating house, built by ordinary carpenters, never reached the forts at all and was burnt by her own men at New Orleans.

Farragut felt sure of his fleet. He had four splendid new men-of-war that formed a homogeneous squadron, four other sizable warships, and nine new gunboats. All spars and rigging that could be dispensed with were taken down; all hulls camouflaged with Mississippi mud; and all decks whitened for handiness at night. A weak point, however, was the presence of mortar-boats that would have been better out of the way altogether. These boats had been sent to bombard the forts, which, according to the plan preferred by the Government, were to be taken before New Orleans was attacked. In other words, the Government wished to cut off the branches first; while Farragut wished to cut down the tree itself, knowing the branches must fall with the trunk.

On the eighteenth of April the mortar-boats began heaving shells at the forts. But, after six days of bombardment, the forts were nowhere near the point of surrendering, and the supply of shells had begun to run low.

Meanwhile the squadron had been busy preparing for the great ordeal. The first task was to break the boom across the river. This boom was placed so as to hold the ships under the fire of the forts; and the four-knot spring current was so strong that the eight-knot ships could not make way enough against it to cut clear through with certainty. Moreover, the middle of the boom was filled in by eight big schooners, chained together, with their masts and rigging dragging astern so as to form a most awkward entanglement. Farragut's fleet captain, Henry H. Bell, taking two gunboats, *Itasca* and *Pinola*, under Lieutenants Caldwell and Crosby, slipped the chains of one schooner; whereupon this schooner and the *Itasca* swung back and grounded under fire of the forts. The *Pinola* gallantly stood by, helping *Itasca* clear. Then Caldwell, with splendid audacity and skill, steamed up through the narrow gap, turned round, put on the *Itasca's* utmost speed, and, with the current in his favor, charged full tilt against the chains that still held fast. For one breathless moment the little *Itasca* seemed lost. Her bows rose clear out, as, quivering from stem to stern, she was suddenly brought up short from top speed to nothing. But, in another fateful minute, with a rending crash, the two nearest schooners gave way and swept back like a gate, while the *Itasca* herself shot clear and came down in triumph to the fleet.

The passage was made on the twenty-fourth, in line-ahead (that is, one after another) because Farragut found the opening narrower than he thought it should be for two columns abreast, at night, under fire, and against the spring current. Owing to the configuration of the channel the starboard column had to weigh first, which gave the lead to the 500-ton gunboat *Cayuga*. This was the one weak point, because the leading vessel, drawing most fire, should have been the strongest. The fault was Farragut's; for his heart got the better of his head when it came to placing Captain Theodorus Bailey, his dauntless second-in-command, on board a vessel fit to lead the starboard column. He could not bear to obscure any captain's chances of distinction by putting another captain over him. So Bailey was sent to the best vessel commanded by a lieutenant.

The *Cayuga's* navigating officer, finding that the guns of the forts were all trained on midstream, edged in towards Fort St. Philip. His masts were shot to pieces, but his hull drew clear without great damage. "Then," he says, "I looked back for some of our vessels; and my heart jumped up into my mouth when I found I could not see a single one. I thought they must all have been sunk by the forts." But not a ship had gone down. The three big ones of the starboard column—*Pensacola, Mississippi,* and *Oneida*—closed with the fort (so that the gunners on both sides exchanged jeers of defiance) and kept up a furious fire till the lighter craft astern slipped past safely and joined the *Cayuga* above.

Meanwhile the *Cayuga* had been attacked by a mob of Mississippi steamers, six of which belonged to the original fourteen blessed with their precious independence by Secretary Benjamin, "backed by the whole Missouri Delegation." So when the rest of the Federal light craft came up, "all sorts of things happened" in a general free fight. There was no lack of Confederate courage; but an utter absence of concerted action and of the simplest kind of naval skill, except on the part of the two vessels commanded by ex-officers of the United States Navy. The Federal light craft cut their way through their unorganized opponents as easily as a battalion of regulars could cut through a mob throwing stones. But the only two Confederate naval officers got clear of the scrimmage and did all that skill could do with their makeshift little craft against the Federal fleet. Kennon singled out the *Varuna* (the only one of Farragut's vessels that was not a real man-of-war), raked her stern with the two guns of his own much inferior vessel, the *Governor Moore*, and rammed her into a sinking condition. Warley flew at bigger game with his little ram, the *Manassas*, trying three of the large men-of-war, one after another, as they came upstream. The *Pensacola* eluded him by a knowing turn of her helm that roused his warmest admiration. The *Mississippi* caught the blow glancingly on her quarter and got off with little damage. The *Brooklyn* was taken fair and square amidships; but, though her planking was crushed in, she sprang no serious leak and went on with the fight. The wretched little Confederate engines had not been able to drive the ram home.

The *Brooklyn* was the flagship *Hartford's* next-astern and the *Richmond's* next-ahead, these three forming the main body of Farragut's own port column, which followed hard on the heels of the starboard one, so hard, indeed, that there were only twenty minutes between the first shot fired by the forts at the *Cayuga* and the first shot fired by the *Hartford* at the forts. Besides the forts there was the *Louisiana* floating battery that helped to swell the storm of shot and shell; and down the river came a fire-raft gallantly towed by a tug. The *Hartford* sheered off, over towards Fort St. Philip, under whose guns she took ground by the head while the raft closed in and set her ablaze. Instantly the hands on fire duty sprang to their work. But the flames rushed in through the ports; and the men were forced a step back. Farragut at once called out: "Don't flinch from the fire, boys. There's a hotter fire than that for those who don't do their duty!" Whereupon they plied their hoses to such good effect that the fire was soon got under control. Farragut calmly resumed his walk up and down the poop, while the gunners blew the gallant little tug to bits and smashed the raft in pieces. Then he stood keenly watching the *Hartford* back clear, gather way, and take the lead upstream again. Every now and then he looked at the pocket compass that hung from his watch chain; though, for the most part, he tried to scan a scene of action lit only by the flashes of the guns. The air was dense and very still; so the smoke of guns and funnels hung like a pall over both the combatants while the desperate fight went on.

At last the fleet fought through and reached the clearer atmosphere above the forts; all but the last three gunboats, which were driven back by the fire. Then Farragut immediately sent word to General Benjamin F. Butler that the troops could be brought up by the bayous that ran parallel to the river out of range of the forts. But the General, having taken in the situation at a glance from a transport just below the scene of action, had begun to collect his men at Sable Island, twelve miles behind Fort St. Philip, long before Farragut's messenger could reach him by way of the Quarantine Bayou. From Sable Island the troops were taken by the transports to a point on the Mississippi five miles above Fort St. Philip.

After a well-earned rest the whole fleet moved up to New Orleans on the twenty-fifth, turning the city's lines five miles downstream without the loss of a man, for the simple reason that these had been built only to resist an army, and so lay with flanks entirely open to a fleet. General Lovell (the able commander who had so often warned the Confederate Government of the danger from the sea) at once evacuated the defenseless city. The best of the younger men were away with the armies. The best of the older men were too few for the storm. And so pandemonium broke loose. Burning boats, blazing cotton, and a howling mob greeted Farragut's arrival. But after the forts (now completely cut off from their base) had surrendered on the twenty-eighth a landing party from the fleet soon brought the mob to its senses by planting howitzers in the streets and lowering the Confederate colors over the city hall. On the first of May a garrison of Federal troops took charge of New Orleans and kept it till the war was over.

New Orleans was a most pregnant Federal victory; for it established a Union base at the great strategic point where sea-power and land-power could meet most effectively in Mississippi waters.

But it was followed by a perfect anti-climax; for the Federal Government, having planned a naval concentration at Vicksburg, determined to put the plan in operation; though all the naval and military means concerned made such a plan impossible of execution in 1862. Amphibious forces—fleets and armies combined—were essential. There was no use in parading up and down the river, however triumphantly, so long as the force employed could only hold the part of the channel within actual range of its guns. The Confederates could be driven off the Mississippi at any given point. But there was nothing to prevent them from coming back again when once the ships had passed. An army to seize and hold strategic points ashore was absolutely indispensable. Then, and only then, Farragut's long line of communication with his base at New Orleans would be safe, and the land in which the Mississippi was the principal highway could itself be conquered.

"If the Mississippi expedition from Cairo shall not have descended the river, you will take advantage of the panic to push a strong force up the river to take all their defenses in rear." These were the orders Farragut had to obey if he succeeded in taking New Orleans. They were soon reinforced by this reminder: "The only anxiety we feel is to know if you have followed up your instructions and pushed a strong force up the river to meet the Western flotilla." Farragut therefore felt bound to obey and do all that could be done to carry on a quite impossible campaign. So, with a useless landing party of only fifteen hundred troops, he pushed up to Vicksburg, four hundred miles above New Orleans. The nearest Federal army had been halted by the Confederate defenses above Memphis, another four hundred higher still.

There were several reasons why Farragut should not have gone up. His big ships would certainly be stranded if he went up and waited for the army to come down; moreover, when stranded, these ships would be captured while waiting, because both banks were swarming with vastly outnumbering Confederate troops. Then, such a disaster would more than offset the triumph of New Orleans by still further depressing Federal morale at a time when the Federal arms were doing none too well near Washington.

Finally, all the force that was being worse than wasted up the Mississippi might have been turned against Mobile, which, at that time, was much weaker than the defenses Farragut had already overcome. But the people of the North were clamorous for more victories along the line to which the press had drawn their gaze. So the Government ordered the fleet to carry on this impossible campaign.

Farragut did his best. Within a month of passing the forts he had not only captured New Orleans and repaired the many serious damages suffered by his fleet but had captured Baton Rouge, and taken even his biggest ships to Vicksburg, five hundred miles from the Gulf, against a continuous current, and right through the heart of a hostile land. Finding that there were thirty thousand Confederates in, near, or within a day of Vicksburg he and General Thomas Williams agreed that nothing could be done with the fifteen hundred troops which formed the only landing party. Sickness and casualties had reduced the ships' companies; so there were not even a few seamen to spare as reinforcements for these fifteen hundred soldiers, whom Butler had sent, under Williams, with the fleet. Then Farragut turned back, his stores running dangerously short owing to the enormous difficulties of keeping open his long, precarious line of communications. "I arrived in New Orleans with five or six days' provisions and one anchor, and am now trying to procure others.... Fighting is nothing to the evils of the river—getting on shore, running foul of one another, losing anchors, etc." In a confidential letter home he is still more outspoken. "They will keep us in this river till the vessels break down and all the little reputation we have made has evaporated. The Government appears to think that we can do anything. They expect me to navigate the Mississippi nine hundred miles in the face of batteries, ironclad rams, etc.; and yet with all the ironclad vessels they have North they could not get to Norfolk or Richmond."

Back from Washington came still more urgent orders to join the Mississippi flotilla which was coming down to Vicksburg from the north under Flag Officer Charles H. Davis. So once more the fleet worked its laboriously wasteful way up to Vicksburg, where it passed the forts with the help of Porter's flotilla of mortar-boats on the twenty-eighth of June and joined Davis on the first of July. There, in useless danger, the joint forces lay till the fifteenth, the day on which Grant's own "most anxious period of the war" began on the Memphis-Corinth line, four hundred miles above.

Farragut, getting very anxious about the shoaling of the water, was then preparing to run down when he heard firing in the Yazoo, a tributary that joined the Mississippi four miles higher up. This came from a fight between one of his reconnoitering gunboats, the *Carondelet*, and the *Arkansas*, an ironclad Confederate ram that would have been very dangerous indeed if her miserable engines had been able to give her any speed. She was beating the *Carondelet*, but getting her smoke-stack so badly holed that her speed dropped down to one knot, which scarcely gave her steerage way and made her unable to ram. Firing hard she ran the gauntlet of both fleets and took refuge under the Vicksburg bluffs, whence she might run out and ram the Union vessels below. Farragut therefore ran down himself, hoping to smash her by successive broadsides in passing. But the difficulties of the passage wasted the daylight, so that he had to run by at night. She therefore survived his attack, and went downstream to join the Confederates against Baton Rouge. But her engines gave way before she got there; and she had to be blown up.

Farragut was back at New Orleans before the end of July. On the fifth of August the Confederates made their attack on Baton Rouge; but were beaten back by the Union garrison aided by three of Farragut's gunboats and two larger vessels from Davis's command. The losses were not very severe on either side; but the Union lost a leader of really magnificent promise in its commanding general, Thomas Williams, a great-hearted, cool-headed man and most accomplished officer. The garrison of Baton Rouge, being too small and sickly and exposed, was withdrawn to New Orleans a few days later.

Then Farragut at last returned to the Gulf blockade. Davis went back up the river, where he was succeeded by D. D. Porter in October. And the Confederates, warned of what was coming, made Port Hudson and Vicksburg as strong as they could. Vicksburg was now the only point they held on the Mississippi where there were rails on both sides; and the Red River, flowing in from the West between Vicksburg and Port Hudson, was the only good line of communication connecting them with Texas, whence so much of their meat was obtained.

For three months Farragut directed the Gulf blockade from Pensacola, where, on the day of his arrival, the twentieth of August, he was the first American to hoist an admiral's flag. The rank of rear-admiral in the United States Navy had been created on the previous sixteenth of July; and Farragut was the senior of the first three officers upon whom it was conferred.

Farragut became the ranking admiral just when the United States Navy was having its hardest struggle to do its fivefold duty well. There was commerce protection on the high seas, blockade along the coast, coöperation with the army on salt water and on fresh, and of course the destruction of the nascent Confederate forces afloat. But perhaps a knottier problem than any part of its combatant duty was how to manage, in the very midst of war, that rapid expansion of its own strength for which no government had let it prepare in time of peace. During this year the number of vessels in commission grew from 264 to 427. Yet such a form of expansion was much simpler than that of the enlisted men; and the expansion of even the most highly trained enlisted personnel was very much simpler than the corresponding expansion of the officers. Happily for the United States Navy it started with a long lead over its enemy. More happily still it could expand with the help of greatly superior resources. Most happily of all, the sevenfold expansion that was effected before the war was over could be made under leaders like Farragut: leaders, that is, who, though in mere numbers they were no more, in proportion to their whole service, than the flag as mere material is to a man-of-war, were yet, as is the flag, the living symbol of a people's soul.

Commerce protection on the high seas was an exceedingly harassing affair. A few swift raiders, having the initiative, enjoyed great advantages over a far larger number of defending vessels. Every daring raid was trumpeted round the world, bringing down unmeasured, and often unmerited, blame on the defense. The most successful vigilance would, on the other hand, pass by unheeded. The Union navy lacked the means of patrolling the sea lanes of commerce over millions and millions of desolate square miles. Consequently the war-risk insurance rose to a prohibitive height on vessels flying the Stars and Stripes; and, as a further result, enormous transfers were made to other flags. The incessant calls for recruits, afloat and ashore, and to some extent the lure of the western lands, also robbed the merchant service of its men. Thus, one way and another, the glory of the old merchant marine departed with the Civil War.

Blockade was more to the point than any attempt to patrol the sea lanes. Yet it was even more harassing; for it involved three distinct though closely correlated kinds of operation: not only the seizure, in conjunction with the army, of enemy ports, and the patrolling of an enemy coastline three thousand miles long, but also the patrolling of those oversea ports from which most contraband came. This oversea patrol was the most effective, because it went straight to the source of trouble. But it required extraordinary vigilance, because it had to be conducted from beyond the three-mile limit, and with the greatest care for all the rights of neutrals.

By mid-November Farragut was back at New Orleans. A month later General Banks arrived with reinforcements. He superseded General Butler and was under orders to coöperate with McClernand, Grant's second-in-command, who was to come down the Mississippi from Cairo. But the proposed meeting of the two armies never took place. Banks remained south of Port Hudson, McClernand far north of Vicksburg; for, as we shall see in the next chapter, Sherman's attempt to take Vicksburg from the North failed on the twenty-ninth of December.

The naval and river campaigns of '62 thus ended in disappointment for the Union. And, on New Year's Day, Galveston, which Farragut had occupied in October without a fight and which was lightly garrisoned by three hundred soldiers, fell into Confederate hands under most exasperating circumstances. After the captain and first lieutenant of the U.S.S. *Harriet Lane* had been shot by the riflemen aboard two cotton-clad steamers the next officer tamely surrendered. Commander Renshaw, who was in charge of the blockade, amply redeemed the honor of the Navy by refusing to surrender the *Westfield*, in spite of the odds against him, and by blowing her up instead. But when he died at the post of duty the remaining Union vessels escaped; and the blockade was raised for a week.

After that Commodore H. H. Bell, one of Farragut's best men, closed in with a grip which never let go. Yet even Bell suffered a reverse when he sent the U.S.S. *Hatteras* to overhaul a strange vessel that lured her off some fifteen miles and sank her in a thirteen-minute fight. This stranger was the *Alabama*, then just beginning her famous or notorious career. Nor were these the only Union troubles in the Gulf during the first three weeks of the new year. Commander J. N. Matt ran the *Florida* out of Mobile, right through the squadron that had been specially strengthened to deal with her; and the shore defenses of the Sabine Pass, like those of Galveston, fell into Confederate hands again, to remain there till the war was over.

In spite of all failures, however, Farragut still had the upper hand along the Gulf, and up the Mississippi as far as New Orleans, without which admirable base the River War of '62 could never have prepared the way for Grant's magnificent victory in the River War of '63.

CHAPTER IV
THE RIVER WAR: 1862

The military front stretched east and west across the border States from the Mississippi Valley to the sea. This immense and fluctuating front, under its various and often changed commanders, was never a well coördinated whole. The Alleghany Mountains divided the eastern or Virginian wing from the western or "River" wing. Yet there was always more or less connection between these two main parts, and the fortunes of one naturally affected those of the other. Most eyes, both at home and abroad, were fixed on the Virginian wing, where the Confederate capital stood little more than a hundred miles from Washington, where the greatest rival armies fought, and where decisive victory was bound to have the most momentous consequences. But the River wing was hardly less important; for there the Union Government actually hoped to reach these three supreme objectives in this one campaign: the absolute possession of the border States, the undisputed right of way along the Mississippi from Cairo to the Gulf, and the triumphant invasion of the lower South in conjunction with the final conquest of Virginia.

We have seen already how the Union navy, aided by the army, won its way up the Mississippi from the Gulf to Baton Rouge, but failed to secure a single point beyond. We shall now see how the Union army, aided by the navy, won its way down the Mississippi from Cairo to Memphis, and fairly attained the first objective—the possession of the border States; but how it also failed from the north, as the others had failed from the south, to gain a footing on the crucial stretch between Vicksburg and Port Hudson. One more year was required to win the Mississippi; two more to invade the lower South; three to conquer Virginia.

Just after the fall of Fort Sumter the Union Government had the foresight to warn James B. Eads, the well-known builder of Mississippi jetties, that they would probably draw upon his "thorough knowledge of our Western rivers and the use of steam on them." But it was not till August that they gave him the contract for the regular gunboat flotilla; and it was not till the following year that his vessels began their work. In the meantime the armies were asking for all sorts of transport and protective craft. So the first flotilla on Mississippi waters started under the War (not the Navy) Department, though manned under the executive orders of Commander John Rodgers, U. S. N., who bought three river steamers at Cincinnati, lowered their engines, strengthened their frames, protected their decks, and changed them into gunboats.

The first phase of the clash in this land of navigable rivers had ended, as we have seen already, with the taking of Boonville on the Missouri by that staunch and daring Union regular, General Nathaniel Lyon, on June 17, 1861. Boonville was a stunning blow to secession in those parts. Confederate hopes, however, again rose high when the news of Bull Run came through. At this time General John C. Frémont was taking command of all the Union forces in the "Western Department," which included Illinois and everything between the Mississippi and the Rockies. Frémont's command, however, was short and full of trouble. Round his headquarters at St. Louis the Confederate colors were flaunted in his face. His requisitions for arms and money were not met at Washington. Union regiments marched in without proper equipment and with next to no supplies. There were boards of inquiry on his contracts. There were endless cross-purposes between him and Washington. And early in November he was transferred to West Virginia just as he was about to attack with what seemed to him every prospect of success. He had not succeeded. But he had done good work in fortifying St. Louis; in ordering gunboats, tugs, and mortar-boats; in producing some kind of system out of utter confusion; in trusting good men like Lyon; and in sending the then unknown Ulysses Grant to take command at Cairo, the excellent strategic base where the Ohio joins the Mississippi.

The most determined fighting that took place during Frémont's command was brought on by Lyon, who attacked Ben McCulloch at Wilson's Creek, in southwest Missouri, on the tenth of August. Though McCulloch had ten thousand, against not much over five, Lyon was so set on driving the Confederates away from such an important lead-bearing region that he risked an attack, hoping by surprise, skillful maneuvers, and the help of his regulars to shake the enemy's hold, even if he could not thoroughly defeat him. Disheartened by his repeated failure to get reinforcements, and very anxious about the fate of his flanking column under Sigel, whose attack from the rear was defeated, he expressed his forebodings to his staff. But the light of battle shone bright as ever in his eyes; he was killed leading a magnificent charge; and when, after his death, his little army drew off in good order, the Confederates, by their own account, "were glad to see him go."

On the twentieth of September the Confederates under Sterling Price won a barren victory by taking Lexington, Missouri, where Colonel James

Mulligan made a gallant defense. That was the last Confederate foothold on the Missouri; and it could not be maintained.

In October, Anderson, who had never recovered from the strain of defending Fort Sumter, turned over to Sherman the very troublesome Kentucky command. Sherman pointed out to the visiting Secretary of War, Simon Cameron, that while McClellan had a hundred thousand men for a front of a hundred miles in Virginia, and Frémont had sixty thousand for about the same distance, he (Sherman) had been given only eighteen thousand to guard the link between them, although this link stretched out three hundred miles. Sherman then asked for sixty thousand men at once; and said two hundred thousand would be needed later on. "Good God!" said Cameron, "where are they to come from?" Come they had to, as Sherman foresaw. Cameron made trouble at Washington by calling Sherman's words "insane"; and Sherman's "insanity" became a stumbling-block that took a long time to remove.

Grant, in command at Cairo, began his career as a general by cleverly forestalling the enemy at Paducah, where the Tennessee flows into the Ohio. Then, on the seventh of November, he closed the first confused campaign on the Mississippi by attacking Belmont, Missouri, twenty miles downstream from Cairo, in order to prevent the Confederates at Columbus, Kentucky, right opposite, from sending reinforcements to Sterling Price in Arkansas. There was a stiff fight, in which the Union gunboats did good work. Grant handled his soldiers equally well; and the Union objective was fully attained.

Halleck, the Federal Commander-in-Chief for the river campaign of '62, fixed his headquarters at St. Louis. From this main base his right wing had rails as far as Rolla, whence the mail road went on southwest, straight across Missouri. At Lebanon, near the middle of the State, General Samuel R. Curtis was concentrating, before advancing still farther southwest against the Confederates whom he eventually fought at Pea Ridge. From St. Louis there was good river, rail, and road connection south to Halleck's center in the neighborhood of Cairo, where General Ulysses S. Grant had his chief field base, at the junction of the Mississippi and Ohio. A little farther east Grant had another excellent position at Paducah, beside the junction of the Ohio and the Tennessee. Naval forces were of course indispensable for this amphibious campaign; and in Flag-Officer Andrew Hull Foote the Western Flotilla had a commander able to coöperate with the best of his military colleagues. Halleck's left—a semi-independent command—was based on the Ohio, stretched clear across Kentucky, and was commanded by a good organizer and disciplinarian, General Don Carlos Buell, whose own position at Munfordville was not only near the middle of the State but about midway between the important railway junctions of Louisville and Nashville.

Henry W. Halleck was a middle-aged, commonplace, and very cautious general, who faithfully plodded through the war without defeat or victory. He looked so long before he leaped that he never leaped at all—not even on retreating enemies. Good for the regular office-work routine, he was like a hen with ducklings for this river war, in which Curtis, Grant, Buell, and his naval colleague Foote, were all his betters on the fighting line.

His opponent, Albert Sidney Johnston, was also middle-aged, being fifty-nine; but quite fit for active service. Johnston had had a picturesque career, both in and out of the army; and many on both sides thought him likely to prove the greatest leader of the war. He was, however, a less formidable opponent than Northerners were apt to think. He was not a consummate genius like Lee. He had inferior numbers and resources; and the Confederate Government interfered with him. Yet they did have the good sense to put both sides of the Mississippi under his unified command, including not only Kentucky and Tennessee, Missouri and Arkansas, but the whole of the crucial stretch from Vicksburg to Port Hudson. In this they were wiser than the Federal Government with Halleck's command, which was neither so extensive nor so completely unified.

Johnston took post in his own front line at Bowling Green, Kentucky, not far south of Buell's position at Munfordville. He was very anxious to keep a hold on Kentucky and Missouri, along the southern frontiers of which his forces were arrayed. His extreme right was thrown northward under General Marshall to Prestonburg, near the border of West Virginia, in the dangerous neighborhood of many Union mountain folk. His southern outpost on the right was also in the same kind of danger at Cumberland Gap, a strategic pass into the Alleghanies at a point where Kentucky, Tennessee, and Virginia meet. Halfway west from there, to Bowling Green the Confederates hoped to hold the Cumberland near Logan's Cross Roads and Mill Springs. Westwards from Bowling Green Johnston's line held positions at Fort Donelson on the Cumberland, Fort Henry on the Tennessee, and Columbus on the Mississippi. All his Trans-Mississippi troops were under the command of the enthusiastic Earl Van Dorn, who hoped to end his spring campaign in triumph at St. Louis.

The fighting began in January at the northeastern end of the line, where the Union Government, chiefly for political reasons, was particularly anxious to strengthen the Unionists that lived all down the western Alleghanies and so were a thorn in the side of the solid South beyond. On the tenth Colonel James A. Garfield, a future President, attacked and defeated Marshall near Prestonburg and occupied the line of Middle Creek. The Confederates, half starved, half clad, ill armed, slightly outnumbered, and with no advantage except their position, fought well, but unavailingly. Only some three thousand men were engaged on both sides put together. Yet the result was important because it meant that the Confederates had lost their hold on the eastern end of Kentucky, which was now in unrestricted touch with West Virginia.

Within eight days a greater Union commander, General G. H. Thomas, emerged as the victor of a much bigger battle at Mill Springs and Logan's Cross Roads on the upper Cumberland, ninety miles due east of Bowling Green. The victory was complete, and Thomas's name was made. Thomas, indeed, was known already as a man whose stentorian orders had to be obeyed; and a clever young Confederate prisoner used this reputation as his excuse for getting beaten: "We were doing pretty good fighting till old man Thomas rose up in his stirrups, and we heard him holler out: 'Attention, Creation! By kingdoms, right wheel!' Then we knew you had us."

There were only about four thousand men a side. But in itself, and in conjunction with Garfield's little victory at Prestonburg, the battle of Logan's Cross Roads was important as raising the Federal morale, as breaking through Johnston's right, and as opening the road into eastern Tennessee. Short supplies and almost impassable roads, however, prevented a further advance. One brigade was therefore detached against Cumberland Gap, while the rest joined Buell's command, which was engaged in organizing, drilling hard, and keeping an eye on Johnston.

In February the scene of action changed to Johnston's left center, where Forts Donelson and Henry were blocking the Federal advance up the Cumberland and the Tennessee.

On the fourth, Flag-Officer Foote, with seven gunboats, of which four were ironclads, led the way up the Tennessee, against Fort Henry. That day the furious current was dashing driftwood in whirling masses against the flotilla, which had all it could do to keep station, even with double anchors down and full steam up. Next morning a new danger appeared in the shape of what looked like a school of dead porpoises. These were Confederate torpedoes, washed from their moorings. As it was now broad daylight they were all successfully avoided; and the crews felt as if they had won the first round.

The sixth of February dawned clear, with just sufficient breeze to blow the smoke away. The flotilla steamed up the swollen Tennessee between the silent, densely wooded banks. Not a sound was heard ashore until, just after noon, Fort Henry came into view and answered the flagship's signal shot with a crashing discharge of all its big guns. Then the fire waxed hot and heavy on both sides, the gunboats knocking geyser-spouts of earth about the fort, and the fort knocking gigantic splinters out of the gunboats. The *Essex* ironclad was doing very well when a big shot crashed into her middle boiler, which immediately burst like a shell, scalding the nearest men to death, burning others, and sending the rest flying overboard or aft. With both pilots dead and Commander W. D. Porter badly scalded, the *Essex* was drifting out of action when the word went round that Fort Henry had surrendered: and there, sure enough, were the Confederate colors coming down. Instantly Porter rallied for the moment, called for three cheers, and fell back exhausted at the third.

The Confederate General Tilghman surrendered to Foote with less than a hundred men, all the rest, over twenty-five hundred, having started towards Fort Donelson before the flag came down. The Western Flotilla had won the day alone. But it was the fear of Grant's approaching army that hurried the escaping garrison. An hour after the surrender Grant rode in and took command. That night victors and vanquished were dining together when a fussy staff officer came in to tell Grant that he could not find the Confederate reports. On this Captain Jesse Taylor, the chief Confederate staff officer, replied that he had destroyed them. The angry Federal then turned on him with the question, "Don't you know you've laid yourself open to punishment?" and was storming along, when Grant quietly broke in: "I should be very much surprised and mortified if one of my subordinate officers should allow information which he could destroy to fall into the hands of the enemy."

The surrender of Fort Henry, coming so soon after Prestonburg and Logan's Cross Roads, caused great rejoicing in the loyal North. The victory, effective in itself, was completed by sending the ironclad *Carondelet* several miles upstream to destroy the Memphis-Ohio railway bridge, thus cutting the shortest line from Bowling Green to the Mississippi. But the action, in which the army took no part, was only a preliminary skirmish compared with the joint attack of the fleet and army on Fort Donelson. Fort Donelson was of great strategic importance. If it held fast, and the Federals were defeated, then Johnston's line would probably hold from Bowling Green to Columbus, and the rails, roads, and rivers would remain Confederate in western Tennessee. If, on the other hand, Fort Donelson fell, and more especially if its garrison surrendered, then Johnston's line would have to be withdrawn at once, lest the same fate should overtake the outflanked remains of it. Both sides understood this perfectly well; and all concerned looked anxiously to see how the new Federal commander, General Grant, would face the crisis.

Ulysses Simpson Grant came of sturdy New England stock, being eighth in descent from Matthew Grant, who landed in 1630 and was

Surveyor of Connecticut for over forty years. Grant's mother was one of the Simpsons who had been Pennsylvanians for several generations. His family was therefore as racy of the North as Lee's was of the South. His great-grandfather and great-granduncle, Noah and Solomon Grant, held British commissions during the final French-and-Indian or Seven Years' War (1756-63) when both were killed in the same campaign. His grandfather Noah served all through the Revolutionary War. Financial reverses and the death of his grandmother broke up the family; and his father, Jesse Grant, was given the kindest of homes by Judge Tod of Ohio. Jesse, being as independent as he was grateful, turned his energies into the first business at hand, which happened to be a tannery at Deerfield owned by the father of that wild enthusiast John Brown. A great reader, an able contributor to the Western press, and a most public-spirited citizen, Jesse Grant was a good father to his famous son, who was born on April 27, 1822, at Point Pleasant, Clermont County, Ohio. Young Grant hated the tannery, but delighted in everything connected with horses; so he looked after the teams. One day, after swapping horses many miles from home, he found himself driving a terrified bolter that he only just managed to stop on the edge of a big embankment. His grown-up companion, who had no stomach for any more, then changed into a safe freight wagon. But Ulysses, tying his bandanna over the runaway's eyes, stuck to the post of danger.

After passing through West Point without any special distinction, except that he came out first in horsemanship, Grant was disappointed at not receiving the cavalry commission which he would have greatly preferred to the infantry one he was given instead. Years later, when already a rising general, he vainly yearned for a cavalry brigade. Otherwise he had curiously little taste for military life; though at West Point he thought the two finest men in the world were Captain C. F. Smith, the splendidly smart Commandant, and, even more, that magnificently handsome giant, Winfield Scott, who came down to inspect the cadets. Some years after having served with credit all through the Mexican War (when, like Lee, he learnt so much about so many future friends and foes) he left the army, not to return till he and Sherman had seen Blair and Lyon take Camp Jackson. After wisely declining to reënter the service under the patronage of General John Pope, who was full of self-importance about his acquaintance with the Union leaders of Illinois, Grant wrote to the Adjutant-General at Washington offering to command a regiment. Like Sherman, he felt much more diffident about the rise from ex-captain of regulars to colonel commanding a battalion than some mere civilians felt about commanding brigades or directing the strategy of armies. He has himself recorded his horror of sole responsibility as he approached what might have been a little battlefield on which his own battalion would have been pitted against a Southern one commanded by a Colonel Harris. "My heart kept getting higher and higher until it felt as though it was in my throat. I would have given anything then to have been back in Illinois; but I had not the moral courage to halt and consider what to do. When we reached a point from which the valley below was in full view ... the troops were gone. My heart resumed its place. It occurred to me at once that Harris had been as much afraid of me as I had been of him. This was a view of the question I never forgot."

Grant's latent powers developed rapidly. Starting with a good stock of military knowledge he soon added to it in every way he could. He had the insight of genius. Above all, he had an indomitable will both in carrying out practicable plans in spite of every obstacle and in ruthlessly dismissing every one who failed. Not tall, not handsome, in no way striking at first sight, he looked the leader born only by reason of his square jaw, keen eye, and determined expression. Lincoln's conclusive answer to a deputation asking for Grant's removal simply was, "he fights." And, when mounted on his splendid charger Cincinnati, Grant even looked what he was—"a first-class fighting man."

Grant marched straight across the narrow neck of land between the forts, which were only twelve miles apart. Foote of course had to go round by the Ohio—fifteen times as far. His vanguard, the dauntless *Carondelet*, now commanded by Henry Walke, arrived on the twelfth and fired the first shots at the fort, which stood on a bluff more than a hundred feet high and mounted fifteen heavy guns in three tiers of fire. Grant's infantry was already in position round the Confederate entrenchments; and when his soldiers heard the naval guns they first gave three rousing cheers and then began firing hard, lest the sailors should get ahead of them again. Birge's sharpshooters, the snipers of those days, were particularly keen. They never drilled as a battalion, but simply assembled in bunches for orders, when Birge would ask: "Canteens full? Biscuits for all day?" After which he would sing out: "All right, boys, hunt your holes"; and off they would go to stalk the enemy with their long-range rifles.

Early next morning Grant sent word to Walke that he was establishing the rest of his batteries and that he was ready to take advantage of any diversion which the *Carondelet* could make in his favor. Walke then fired hard for two hours under cover of a wooded point. The fort fired back equally hard; but with little effect except for one big solid shot which stove in a casemate, knocked down a dozen men, burst the steam heater, and bounded about the engine room "like a wild beast pursuing its prey." Forty minutes later the *Carondelet* was again in action, firing hard till dark. Late that night Foote arrived with the rest of the flotilla.

The fourteenth was another naval day. Foote's flotilla advanced gallantly, the four ironclads leading in line abreast, the two wooden gunboats half a mile astern. The ironclads closed in to less than a quarter-mile and hung on like bulldogs till the Confederates in the lowest battery were driven from their guns. But the plunging fire from the big guns on the bluff crashed down with ever increasing effect. Davits were smashed like matches, boats knocked into kindling wood, armor dented, started, ripped, stripped, and sent splashing overboard as if by strokes of lightning. Before the decks could be re-sanded there was so much blood on them that the gun crews could hardly work for slipping. Presently the *Pittsburgh* swung round, ran foul of the *Carondelet*, and dropped downstream. The pilot of the *St. Louis* was killed, and Foote, who stood beside him, wounded. The wheel-ropes of the *St. Louis*, like those of the *Louisville*, were shot away. The whole flotilla then retired, still firing hard; and the Confederates wired a victory to Richmond.

Both sides now redoubled their efforts; for Donelson was a great prize and the forces engaged were second only to those at Bull Run. Afloat and ashore, all ranks and ratings on both sides together, there were fifty thousand men present at the investment from first to last. The Confederates began with about twenty thousand, Grant with fifteen thousand. But Grant had twenty-seven thousand fit for duty at the end, in spite of all his losses. He was fortunate in his chief staff officer, the devoted and capable John A. Rawlins, afterwards a general and Secretary of War. Two of his divisional commanders, Lew Wallace and, still more, C. F. Smith, the old Commandant of Cadets, were also first-rate. But the third, McClernand, here began to follow those distorting ideas which led to his dismissal later on. The three chief Confederates ranked in reverse order of efficiency: Floyd first and worst, cantankerous Pillow next, and Buckner best though last.

The Federal prospect was anything but bright on the evening of the fourteenth. Foote had just been repulsed; while McClernand had fought a silly little battle on his own account the day before, to the delight of the Confederates and the grievous annoyance of Grant. The fifteenth dawned on a scene of midwinter discomfort in the Federal lines, where most of the rawest men had neither great-coats nor blankets, having thrown them away during the short march from Fort Henry, regardless of the fact that they would have to bivouac at Donelson. Thus it was in no happy frame of mind that Grant slithered across the frozen mud to see what Foote proposed; and, when Foote explained that the gunboats would take ten days for indispensable repairs, Grant resigned himself to the very unwelcome idea of going through the long-drawn horrors of a regular winter siege.

But, to his intense surprise, the enemy saved him the trouble. At first, when they had a slight preponderance of numbers, they stood fast and let Grant invest them. Now that he had the preponderance they tried to cut their way out by the southern road, upstream, where McClernand's division stood guard. As Grant came ashore from his interview with Foote an aide met him with the news that McClernand had been badly beaten and that the enemy was breaking out. Grant set spurs to his horse and galloped the four muddy miles to his left, where that admirable soldier, C. F. Smith, was as cool and wary as ever, harassing the enemy's new rear by threatening an assault, but keeping his division safe for whatever future use Grant wanted. Wallace had also done the right thing, pressing the enemy on his own front and sending a brigade to relieve the pressure on McClernand. These two generals were in conversation during a lull in the battle when Grant rode up, calmly returned their salutes, attentively listened to their reports, and then, instead of trying the Halleckian expedient of digging in farther back before the enemy could make a second rush, quietly said: "Gentlemen, the position on the right must be retaken."

Grant knew that Floyd was no soldier and that Pillow was a stumbling-block. He read the enemy's mind like an open book and made up his own at once by the flash of intuition which told him that their men were mostly as much demoralized by finding their first attempt at escape more than half a failure as even McClernand's were by being driven back. He decided to use Smith's fresh division for an assault in rear, while McClernand's, stiffened by Wallace's, should re-form and hold fast. Before leaving the excited officers and men, who were talking in groups without thinking of their exhausted ammunition, he called out cheerily "Fill your cartridge boxes quick, and get into line. The enemy is trying to escape and he must not be permitted to do so." McClernand's division, excellent men, but not yet disciplined soldiers, responded at once to the touch of a master hand; and as Grant rode off to Smith's he had the satisfaction of seeing the defenseless groups melt, change, and harden into well-armed lines.

Smith, ready at all points, had only to slip his own division from the leash. Buckner, who was to have covered the Confederate escape, was also ready with the guns of Fort Donelson and the rifles of defenses that "looked too thick for a rabbit to get through." Smith, knowing his unseasoned men would need the example of a commander they could actually see, rode out in front of his center as if at a formal review. "I was nearly scared to death," said one of his followers, "but I saw the old man's white moustache over his shoulder, and so I went on." As the line neared the Confederate abatis a sudden gust of fire seemed to strike it numb. In an instant Smith had his cap on the point of his sword. Then, rising in his stirrups to his full gigantic height, he shouted in stentorian tones: "No flinching now, my lads! Here—this way in! Come on!" In, through, and out the other side they went, Smith riding ahead, holding his sword and cap aloft, and seeming to bear a charmed life amid that hail of bullets. Up the slope he rode, the Confederates retiring before him, till, unscathed, he reached the deadly crest, where the Union colors waved defiance and the Union troops stood fast.

Floyd, being under special indictment at Washington for misconduct as Secretary of War, was so anxious to escape that he turned over the command to Pillow, who declined it in favor of Buckner. That night Floyd and Pillow made off with all the river steamers; Forrest's cavalry floundered past McClernand's exposed flank, which rested on a shallow backwater; and Buckner was left with over twelve thousand men to make what terms he could. Next morning, the sixteenth, he wrote to Grant proposing the appointment of commissioners to agree upon terms of surrender. But Grant had made up his mind that compromise was out of place in civil war and that absolute defeat or victory were the only alternatives. So he instantly wrote back the famous letter which quickly earned him the appropriate nickname—suggested by his own initials—of Unconditional Surrender Grant.

Hd Qrs., Army in the Field
Camp near Donelson Feb'y 16th 1882

Gen. S. B. Buckner,
Confed. Army.

Sir: Yours of this date proposing armistice, and appointment of Commissioners to settle terms of capitulation is just received. No terms except an unconditional and immediate surrender can be accepted. I propose to move immediately upon your works

I am, Sir, very respectfully,
Your obt. sert.,
U. S. GRANT
Brig. Gen.

Grant and Buckner were old army friends; so their personal talk was very pleasant at the little tavern where Buckner and his staff had just breakfasted off corn bread and coffee, which was all the Confederate stores afforded.

Donelson at once became, like Grant, a name to conjure with. The fact that the Union had at last won a fight in which the numbers neared, and the losses much exceeded, those at Bull Run itself, the further fact that this victory made a fatal breach in the defiant Southern line beyond the Alleghanies, and the delight of discovering another, and this time a genuine, hero in "Unconditional Surrender Grant," all combined to set the loyal North aflame with satisfaction, pride, and joyful expectation. Great things were expected in Virginia, where the invasion had not yet begun. Great things were expected in the Gulf, where Farragut had not yet tried the Mississippi. And great things were expected to result from Donelson itself, whence the Union forces were to press on south till they met other Union forces pressing north. The river campaign was then to end in a blaze of glory.

Donelson did have important results. Johnston, who had already abandoned Bowling Green for Nashville, had now to abandon Nashville, with most of its great and very sorely needed stores, as well as the rest of Tennessee, and take up a new position along the rails that ran from Memphis to Chattanooga, whence they forked northeast to Richmond and Washington and southeast to Charleston and Savannah. Columbus was also abandoned, and the only points left to the Confederates anywhere near the old line were Island Number Ten in the Mississippi and the Boston Mountains in Arkansas.

But the triumphant Union advance from the north did not take place in '62. Grant was for pushing south as fast as possible to attack the Confederates before they had time to defend their great railway junction at Corinth. But Halleck was too cautious; and misunderstandings, coupled with division of command, did the rest. Halleck was the senior general in the West. But the three, and afterwards four, departments into which the West was divided were never properly brought under a single command. Then telegrams went wrong at the wire-end advancing southwardly from Cairo, the end Grant had to use. A wire from McClellan on the sixteenth of February was not delivered till the third of March. Next day Grant was thunderstruck at receiving this from Halleck: "Place C. F. Smith in command of expedition and remain yourself at Fort Henry. Why do you not obey my orders to report strength and positions of your command?" And so it went on till McClellan authorized Halleck to place Grant under arrest for insubordination. Then the operator at the wire-end suddenly deserted, taking a sheaf of dispatches with him. He was a clever Confederate.

Explanations followed; and on the seventeenth of March Grant rejoined his army, which was assembling round Pittsburg Landing on the Tennessee, near the future battlefield of Shiloh, and some twenty miles northeast of Corinth.

Meanwhile Van Dorn and Sterling Price, thinking it was now or never for Missouri, decided to attack Curtis. They had fifteen against ten thousand men, and hoped to crush Curtis utterly by catching him between two fires. But on the seventh of March the Federal left beat off the flanking attack of McCulloch and McIntosh, both of whom were killed. The right, furiously assailed by the Confederate Missourians under Van Dorn and Price, fared badly and was pressed back. Yet on the eighth Curtis emerged victorious on the hard-fought field that bears the double name of Elkhorn Tavern and Pea Ridge. This battle in the northwest corner of Arkansas settled the fate of Missouri.

A month later the final attack was made on Island Number Ten. Foote's flotilla had been at work there as early as the middle of March, when the strong Confederate batteries on the island and east shore bluffs were bombarded by ironclads and mortarboats. Then the Union General John Pope took post at New Madrid, eight miles below the island, on the west shore, which the Confederates had to evacuate when he cut their line of communications farther south. They now held only the island and the east shore opposite, with no line of retreat except the Mississippi, because the land line on the east shore was blocked by swamps and flanked by the Union armies in western Tennessee.

On the night of the fourth of April the *Carondelet* started to cut this last line south. She was swathed in hawsers and chain cables. Her decks were packed tight with every sort of gear that would break the force of plunging shot; and a big barge, laden with coal and rammed hay, was lashed to her port side to protect her magazine. Twenty-three picked Illinoisian sharpshooters went aboard; while pistols, muskets, cutlasses, boarding-pikes, and hand grenades were placed ready for instant use. The escape-pipe was led aft into the wheel-house, so as to deaden the noise; and hose was attached to the boilers ready to scald any Confederates that tried to board. Then, through the heart of a terrific thunderstorm, and amid a furious cannonade, the *Carondelet* ran the desperate gauntlet at full speed and arrived at New Madrid by midnight.

The Confederates were now cut off both above and below; for the position of Island Number Ten was at the lower point of a V-shaped bend in the Mississippi, with Federal forces at the two upper points. But the Federal troops could not close on the Confederates without crossing over to the east bank; and their transports could not run the gauntlet like the ironclads. So the Engineer Regiment of the West cut out a water road connecting the two upper points of the V. This admirable feat of emergency field engineering was effected by sawing through three miles of heavy timber to the nearest bayou, whence a channel was cleared down to New

ah. But he heard the roar of battle. His excellent successor, W. H.
ace, was killed; and battalions, brigades, and even divisions, soon
inextricably mixed together. There was now the same confusion on
nfederate side, where Johnston was wounded by a bullet from the
's Nest. It was not in itself a mortal wound. But, knowing how vital
nt was, he went on encouraging his men till, falling from the saddle,
carried back to die.

nt still felt confident; though he had seen the worst in the rear as well
est at the front. Two of his brand-new battalions, the very men who
rds fought like heroes, when they had learned the soldier's work,
n like hares. "During the day," says Grant, "I rode back as far as the
d met General Buell, who had just arrived. There probably were as
s four or five thousand stragglers lying under cover of the river bluff,
tricken. As we left the boat Buell's attention was attracted by these
saw him berating them and trying to shame them into joining their
nts. He even threatened them with shells from the gunboats nearby.
to no effect. Most of these men afterward proved themselves as
as any of those who saved the battle from which they had deserted."

half-past five, after twelve hours' fighting, Grant at last succeeded
ing a new and shorter line, a mile behind that morning's front, but
t any dangerous gaps. There were three reorganized divisions—
an's, McClernand's, and Hurlbut's, one fresh division under Nelson,
trong land battery of over twenty field guns helping the two ironclad
ats in the defense of Pittsburg Landing. The Confederate effectives,
d by heavy losses and by as many stragglers as the Federals, were
ced by five thousand fresh men on guard at the Landing. Beauregard,
ad succeeded Johnston, then stopped the battle for the day, with the
retiring next morning to Corinth. But, before his orders reached it,
tle-worn right made a desperate, fruitless, and costly attack on the
sely strengthened Landing.

at night the rain came down in torrents; and the Confederates sought
in the tents the Federals had abandoned. They found little rest there,
narassed all through the bleak dark by the big shells that the gunboats
among them.

dawn Grant, now reinforced by twenty-five thousand fresh men
Buell and Lew Wallace, took the offensive. Beauregard, hopelessly
mbered and without a single fresh man, retired on Corinth,
ficiently covered by Bragg's rearguard, which held the Federals back
urs near the crucial point of Shiloh Church.

Madrid. Then the transports went through in perfect safety and took Pope's advanced guard aboard. The ironclad *Pittsburg* had come down, through another thunderstorm, this same morning of the seventh; and when the island garrison saw their position completely cut off they surrendered to Foote. Next day Pope's men cut off the greater part of the Confederates on the mainland. Thus fell the last point near Johnston's original line along the southern borders of Missouri and Kentucky.

Just before it fell Johnston made a desperate counterattack from his new line at Corinth, in northwest Mississippi, against Grant's encroaching force at Shiloh, fifteen miles northeast, on the Tennessee River.

Writing "A. S. Johnston, 3d April, 62, *en avant*" on his pocket map of Tennessee, the Confederate leader, anguished by the bitter criticism with which his unavoidable retreat had been assailed, cast the die for an immediate attack on Grant before slow Halleck reinforced or ready Buell joined him. Johnston's lieutenants, Beauregard and Bragg, had obtained ten days for reorganization; and their commands were as ready as raw forces could be made in an extreme emergency. They hoped to be joined by Van Dorn, whose beaten army was working east from Pea Ridge. But on the second they heard that Buell was approaching Grant from Nashville; and on the third Johnston's advanced guard began to move off. Van Dorn arrived too late.

The march, which it was hoped to complete on the fourth, was not completed till the fifth. The roads were ankle-deep in clinging mud, the country densely wooded and full of bogs and marshes. The forty thousand men were not yet seasoned; and, though full of enthusiasm, they neither knew nor had time to learn march discipline. Moreover, Johnston allowed his own proper plan of attacking in columns of corps to be changed by Beauregard into a three-line attack, each line being formed by one complete corps. This meant certain and perhaps disastrous confusion. For in an attack by columns of corps the firing line would always be reinforced by successive lines of the same corps; while attacking by lines of corps meant that the leading corps would first be mixed up with the second, and then both with the third.

In the meantime Grant was busier with his own pressing problems of organization for an advance than with any idea of resisting attack. He lacked the prevision of Winfield Scott and Lee, both of whom expected from the first that the war would last for years. His own expectation up to this had been that the South would collapse after the first smashing blow, and that its western armies were now about to be dealt such a blow. He was not unmindful of all precautions; for he knew the Confederates were stirring on his front. Yet he went downstream to Savannah without making sure that his army was really safe at Shiloh.

Pittsburg Landing was at the base of the Shiloh position. But the point at which, by the original orders, Buell was to join was Savannah, nine miles north along the Tennessee. So Grant had to keep in touch with both. He had not ignored the advantage of entrenching. But the best line for entrenching was too far from good water; and he thought he chose the lesser of two evils when he devoted the time that might have been used for digging to drilling instead. His army was raw as an army; many of the men were still rawer recruits; and, as usual, the recruiting authorities had sent him several brand-new battalions, which knew nothing at all, instead of sending the same men as reinforcements to older battalions that could "learn 'em how." Grant's total effectives at first were only thirty-three thousand. This made the odds five to four in favor of Johnston's attack. But the rejoining of Lew Wallace's division, the great reinforcement by Buell's troops, and the two ironclad gunboats on the river, raised Grant's final effective grand total to sixty thousand. The combined grand totals therefore reached a hundred thousand—double the totals at Donelson and far exceeding those at Bull Run.

After a horrible week of cold and wet the sun set clear and calm on Saturday, the eve of battle. The woods were alive with forty thousand Confederates all ready for their supreme attack on the thirty-three thousand Federals on their immediate four-mile front. Grant's front ran, facing south, between Owl and Lick Creeks, two tributaries that joined the Tennessee on either side of Pittsburg Landing. Buell's advance division, under Nelson, was just across the Tennessee. But Grant was in no hurry to get it over. His reassuring wire that night to Halleck said: "The main force of the enemy is at Corinth. I have scarcely the faintest idea of an attack (general one) being made upon us." But the skirmishing farther south on Friday had warned Grant, as well as Sherman and the vigilant Prentiss, that Johnston might be trying a reconnaissance in force—the very thing that Beauregard wished the Confederates to do.

Long before the beautiful dawn of Sunday, the fateful sixth of April, Prentiss had thrown out from the center a battalion which presently met and drove in the vanguard of the first Confederate line of assault. The Confederate center soon came up, overwhelmed this advanced battalion, and burst like a storm on the whole of Prentiss's division. Then, above the swelling roar of multitudinous musketry, rose the thunder of the first big guns. "Note the hour, please, gentlemen," said Johnston; and a member of his staff wrote down: "5:14 A.M."

Johnston's admirable plan was, first, to drive Gr... Creek, then drive it clear of Pittsburg Landing, wl... ironclads were guarding the ferry. This, combined with... assault on the rest of Grant's line, would huddle the re... the cramped angle between Owl Creek and the Tennes... surrender. But there were three great obstacles to this:... the "Hornet's Nest" in the center, and the gunboats a... still for the Confederates, Buell was now too close... earlier Johnston had wired from Corinth to the Gover... "Hope engagement before Buell can form junction." B... march had lost him one whole priceless day.

The Confederate attack was splendidly gallant and... regardless of loss. The ground was confusing to both si... of ups and downs, of underbrush, woods, fields, a... criss-cross paths, small creeks, ravines, and swamp... commanding height or any outstanding features excep... the river, and the Pittsburg Landing.

At the first signs of a big battle Grant hurried to th... a note to Buell, whom he was to have met at Savanna... Crump's Landing on the way, to see Lew Wallace and... this, and not the Pittsburg Landing, was the point of att... field of Shiloh, calm and determined as ever, he was re... how well Sherman was holding his raw troops in har... important point of Shiloh itself, next to Owl Creek.

But elsewhere the prospect was not encouraging, t... under arms very fast and most of them fought very w... lines kept pressing on like the rising tide of an angry s... against all obstructing fronts and swirling round the di... The blue lines, for the most part, resisted till the swift g... to cut them off. Half of Prentiss's remaining men were... afternoon and forced to surrender with their chief, whose... own, was worthy of all praise. Back and still back the blu... the encroaching gray, each losing heavily by sheer hard f... and streams of stragglers running towards the rear.

Sherman, like others, gave ground, but still held... except for the stragglers he could not control. In the ce... division, with Hurlbut's in support, and all that was... defended themselves so desperately that their enemies ca... the Hornet's Nest. Here the fight swayed back and fort... ghastly losses on both sides. C. F. Smith himself was o...

Shiloh was the fiercest battle ever fought in the River War. The losses were over ten thousand a side in killed and wounded; while a thousand Confederates and three thousand Federals were captured. It was a Confederate failure; but hardly the kind of victory the Federals needed just then, before the consummate triumph of Farragut at New Orleans. It brought together Federal forces that the Confederates could not possibly withstand, even on their new line east from Memphis. But it did not raise the Federal, or depress the Confederate, morale.

Four days after the battle Halleck arrived at Pittsburg Landing and took command of the combined armies. He was soon reinforced by Pope; whereupon he divided the whole into right and left wings, center, and reserve, each under its own commander. Grant was made second in command of the whole. But, as Halleck dealt directly with his other immediate subordinates, Grant simply became the fifth wheel of the Halleckian slow-coach, which, after twenty days of preparation, began, with most elaborate precautions, its crawl toward Corinth.

Grant's position became so nearly unbearable that he applied more than once for transfer to some other place. But this was refused. So he strove to do his impossible duty till the middle of July, when his punishment for Shiloh was completed by his promotion to command a depleted remnant of Halleck's Grand Army. It is not by any means the least of Grant's claims to real greatness that, as a leader, he was able to survive his most searching trials: the surprise at Shiloh, the misunderstandings and arrest that followed Shiloh, the slur of being made a fifth-wheel second-in-command, the demoralizing strain of that "most anxious period of the war" when his depleted forces were thrown back on the defensive, and the eight discouraging months of Sisyphean offensive which preceded his triumph at Vicksburg. No one who has not been in the heart of things with fighting fleets or armies can realize what it means to all ranks when there is, or even is supposed to be, "something wrong" with the living pivot on which the whole force turns. And only those who have been behind the scenes of war's all-testing drama can understand what it means for even an imagined "failure" to "come back."

Corinth was of immense importance to both sides, as it commanded the rails not only east and west, from the Tennessee to Memphis, but north and south, from the Ohio to New Orleans and Mobile. Though New Orleans was taken by Farragut on the twenty-fifth of April, the rails between Vicksburg and Port Hudson remained in Confederate hands till next year; while Mobile remained so till the year after that.

Beauregard collected all the troops he could at Corinth. Yet, even with Van Dorn's and other reinforcements, he had only sixty thousand effectives against Halleck's double numbers. Moreover, the loss of three States and many battles had so shaken the Confederate forces that they stood no chance whatever against Halleck's double numbers in the open. All the same, Halleck burrowed slowly forward like a mole, entrenching every night as if the respective strengths and victories had been reversed.

After advancing nearly a mile a day Halleck closed in on Corinth. He was so deeply entrenched that no one could tell from appearances which side was besieging the other. Towards the end of May many Federal railwaymen reported that empty trains could be heard running into Corinth and full trains running out. But, as the Confederates greeted each arriving "empty" with tremendous cheers, Halleck felt sure that Beauregard was being greatly reinforced. The Confederate bluff worked to admiration. On the twenty-sixth Beauregard issued orders for complete evacuation on the twenty-ninth. On the thirtieth Halleck drew up his whole grand army ready for a desperate defense against an enemy that had already gone a full day's march away.

In the meantime the Federal flotilla had been fighting its way down the Mississippi, under (the invalided) Foote's very capable successor, Flag-Officer Charles Henry Davis. The Confederates had very few naval men on the river, but many of their Mississippi skippers were game to the death. They rammed Federal vessels on the tenth of May at Fort Pillow, eighty miles above Memphis. Eight of their fighting craft were strongly built and heavily armored, though very deficient in speed. The Federal flotilla was very well manned by first-class naval ratings, and was reinforced early in June by seven fast new rams, commanded by their designer, Colonel Charles Ellet, a famous civil engineer.

At sunrise on the lovely sixth of June the Federal flotilla, having overcome the Confederate posts farther north and being joined by Ellet's rams, lay near Memphis. The Confederates came upstream to the attack, expecting to ram the gunboats in the stern as they had at Fort Pillow. But Ellet suddenly darted down on the eight Confederate ironclads, caught one of them on the broadside, sank her, and disabled two others. The action then became general. The overmatched Confederates kept up a losing battle for more than an hour, in full view of many thousands of ardent Southerners ashore. The scene, at its height, was appalling. The smoke, belching black from the funnels and white from the guns, made a suffocating pall overhead; while the dark, squat, hideous ironclad hulls seemed to have risen from a submarine inferno to stab each other with livid tongues of flame—so deadly close the two flotillas fought. When the awful hour was over the

Confederates were not only defeated but destroyed; and a wail went up from the thousands of their anguished friends, as if the very shores were mourning.

For the next month Grant held the command at Memphis. Then, on the eleventh of July, Halleck was recalled to Washington as General-in-Chief of the whole army; while Pope was transferred to Virginia. The Federal invasion of Virginia under that "Young Napoleon," McClellan, had not been a success against Lee and Stonewall Jackson. Nor did it improve with Pope at the front and Halleck in the rear, as we shall presently see; though Halleck had declared that Pope's operations at Island Number Ten were destined to immortal fame, and Pope himself admitted his own greatness in sundry proclamations to the world.

The campaign now entered its second phase. The Virginian wing (of the whole front reaching from the Mississippi to the sea) was checked this summer; and was to remain more or less checked for many a long day. The river wing, under the general direction of Halleck, had also reached its limit for '62 about the same time, after having conquered Kentucky and western Tennessee as well as the Mississippi down to Memphis.

This river wing was now depleted of some excellent troops and again divided into quite separate commands. Buell commanded the Army of the Ohio. Grant commanded his own Army of the Tennessee and Rosecrans's Army of the Mississippi. Buell's scene of action lay between the tributary streams—Ohio, Cumberland, and Tennessee—with Chattanooga as his ultimate objective. Grant's scene of action lay along the southward rails and Mississippi, with Vicksburg as his ultimate objective.

The Confederates were of course set on recovering complete control of the line of Southern rails that made direct connections between the Mississippi Valley and the sea: crossing the western tributaries of the St. Francis and White Rivers; then running east from Memphis, through Grand Junction, Corinth, and Iuka, to Chattanooga; thence forking off northeast, through Knoxville, to Washington, Richmond, and Norfolk; and southeast to Charleston and Savannah. Confederate attention had originally been fixed on Corinth and Chattanooga. But General O. M. Mitchel's abortive raid, just after Shiloh, had also drawn it to the part between. The Federals therefore found their enemy alert at every point.

Braxton Bragg, Beauregard's successor and Buell's opponent, basing himself on Chattanooga, tried to drive his line of Confederate reconquest through the heart of Tennessee and thence through mid-Kentucky, with the Ohio as his ultimate objective. His colleagues near the Mississippi, Van

Dorn and Sterling Price, meanwhile tried to effect the reconquest of the Memphis-Corinth rails that Grant and Rosecrans were holding.

All main offensives, on both sides, ultimately failed in this latter half of the river campaign of '62. So nothing but the bare fact that they were attempted needs any notice here.

In August, about the time that Lee and Jackson were maneuvering in Virginia to bring on the Second Bull Run, Price and Bragg began their respective advances against Grant and Buell. Buell was at Murfreesboro, defending Nashville. Bragg, screened by the hills of eastern Tennessee, made for the Ohio at Louisville and Cincinnati. Pivoting on his left he wheeled his whole army round and raced for Louisville. Buell enjoyed the advantage of rails over roads and of interior lines as well. But Bragg had stolen several marches on him at the start and he only won by a head.

The Union Government, now thoroughly alarmed, sent Thomas to supersede Buell. But Thomas declined to take over the command, and on the eighth of October Buell fought Bragg at Perryville. There was no tactical defeat or victory; but Bragg retired on Chattanooga. The Government now urged Buell to enter east Tennessee. He protested that lack of transport and supplies made such a move impossible. William S. Rosecrans then replaced him. Buell was never employed again. He certainly failed fully to appreciate the legitimate bearing of statesmanship on strategy; but, for all that, he was an excellent organizer and a good commander.

In the meantime Grant had been experiencing his "most anxious period of the war." During this anxious period, which lasted from July to October, Rosecrans defeated Price at Iuka. This happened on the nineteenth of September. Van Dorn then joined Price and returned to the attack but was defeated by Rosecrans at Corinth on the fourth of October. The Confederates, who had come near victory on the third, retired in safety, because Grant still lacked the means of resuming the offensive.

As soon as he had the means Grant marched his army south for Vicksburg. There were three converging forces: Grant's from Grand Junction, Sherman's from Memphis, and a smaller one from Helena in Arkansas. But the Confederate General, J. C. Pemberton, who had replaced Van Dorn, escaped the trap they tried to set for him. He was strongly entrenched on the south side of the Tallahatchie, north of Oxford, on the Mississippi Central rails. While Grant and Sherman converged on his front, the force from Helena rounded his rear and cut the rails. But the damage was quickly repaired; and Pemberton retired south toward Vicksburg before Grant and Sherman could close and make him fight.

Then Grant tried again. This time Sherman advanced on board of Mississippi steamers, with the idea of meeting the Union expedition coming up from New Orleans. But Van Dorn cut Grant's long line of land communications at Holly Springs, forcing Grant back for supplies and leaving Sherman, who had made his way up the Yazoo, completely isolated. Grant fared well enough, so far as food was concerned; for he found such abundant supplies that he at once perceived the possibility of living on the country without troubling about a northern base. He spent Christmas and New Year at Holly Springs, and then moved back to Memphis.

In the meantime Sherman's separated force had come to grief. On the twenty-ninth of December its attempt to carry the Chickasaw Bluffs, just north of Vicksburg, was completely frustrated by Pemberton; for Sherman could not deploy into line on the few causeways that stood above the flooded ground.

On the eleventh of January this first campaign along the Mississippi was ended by the capture of Arkansas Post. McClernand was the senior there. But Sherman did the work ashore as D. D. Porter did afloat.

Meanwhile Bragg had brought the campaign to a close among the eastern tributaries by a daring, though abortive, march on Nashville. Rosecrans, now commanding the army of the Cumberland, stopped and defeated him at Stone's River on New Year's Eve.

The "War in the West," that is, in those parts of the Southwest which lay beyond the navigable tributaries of the Mississippi system, was even more futile at the time and absolutely null in the end. Its scene of action, which practically consisted of inland Texas, New Mexico, and Arizona, was not in itself important enough to be a great determining factor in the actual clash of arms. But Texas supplied many good men to the Southern ranks; and the Southern commissariat missed the Texan cattle after the fall of Vicksburg in '63. New Mexico might also have been a good deal more important than it actually was if it could have been made the base of a real, instead of an abortive, invasion of California, the El Dorado of Confederate finance.

We have already seen what happened on February 15, 1861, when General Twiggs handed over to the State authorities all the army posts in Texas. On the first of the following August Captain John R. Baylor, who had been forming a little Confederate army under pretext of a big buffalo hunt, proclaimed himself Governor of New Mexico (south of 34°) and established his capital at Mesilla. In the meantime the Confederate Government itself had appointed General H. H. Sibley to the command of a brigade for the conquest of all New Mexico. Not ten thousand men were engaged in this campaign, Federals and Confederates, whites and Indians, all together; but a decisive Confederate success might have been pregnant of future victories farther west. Some Indians fought on one side, some on the other; and some of the wilder tribes, delighted to see the encroaching whites at loggerheads, gave trouble to both.

On February 21, 1862, Sibley defeated Colonel E. R. S. Canby at Valverde near Fort Craig. But his further advance was hindered by the barrenness of the country, by the complete destruction of all Union stores likely to fall into his hands, and by the fact that he was between two Federal forts when the battle ended. On the twenty-eighth of March there was a desperate fight in Apache Cañon. Both sides claimed the victory. But the Confederates lost more men as well as the whole of their supply and ammunition train. After this Sibley began a retreat which ended in May at San Antonio. His route was marked by bleaching skeletons for many a long day; and from this time forward the conquest of California became nothing but a dream.

The "War in the West" was a mere twig on the Trans-Mississippi branch; and when the fall of Vicksburg severed the branch from the tree the twig simply withered away.

The sword that ultimately severed branch and twig was firmly held by Union hands before the year was out; and this notwithstanding all the Union failures in the last six months. Grant and Porter from above, Banks and Farragut from below, had already massed forces strong enough to make the Mississippi a Union river from source to sea, in spite of all Confederates from Vicksburg to Port Hudson.

CHAPTER V
LINCOLN: WAR STATESMAN

Lincoln was one of those men who require some mighty crisis to call their genius forth. Though more successful than Grant in ordinary life, he was never regarded as a national figure in law or politics till he had passed his fiftieth year. He had no advantages of birth; though he came of a sturdy old English stock that emigrated from Norfolk to Massachusetts in the seventeenth century, and though his mother seems to have been, both intellectually and otherwise, above the general run of the Kentuckians among whom he was born in 1809. His educational advantages were still less. Yet he soon found his true affinities in books, as afterwards in life, not among the clever, smart, or sentimental, but among the simple and the great. He read and reread Shakespeare and the Bible, not because they were the merely proper things to read but because his spirit was akin to theirs. This meant that he never was a bookworm. Words were things of life to him; and, for that reason, his own words live.

He had no artificial graces to soften the uncouth appearance of his huge, gaunt six-foot-four of powerful bone and muscle. But he had the native dignity of straightforward manhood; and, though a champion competitor in feats of strength, his opinion was always sought as that of an impartial umpire, even in cases affecting himself. He "played the game" in his frontier home as he afterwards played the greater game of life-or-death at Washington. His rough-hewn, strong-featured face, shaped by his kindly humor to the finer ends of power, was lit by a steady gaze that saw yet looked beyond, till the immediate parts of the subject appeared in due relation to the whole. Like many another man who sees farther and feels more deeply than the rest, and who has the saving grace of humor, he knew what yearning melancholy was; yet kept the springs of action tense and strong. Firm as a rock on essentials he was extremely tolerant about all minor differences. His policy was to live and let live whenever that was possible. The preservation of the Union was his master-passion, and he was ready for any honorable compromise that left the Union safe. Himself a teetotaller, he silenced a temperance delegation whose members were accusing Grant of drunkenness by saying he should like to send some of his other generals a keg of the same whisky if it would only make them fight.

When he took arms against the sea of troubles that awaited him at Washington he had dire need of all his calm tolerance and strength. To add to his burdens, he was beset by far more than the usual horde of office-seekers. These men were doubly ravenous because their party was so new to power. They were peculiarly hard to place with due regard for all the elements within the coalition. And each appointment needed most discriminating care, lest a traitor to the Union might creep in. While the guns were thundering against Fort Sumter, and afterwards, when the Union Government was marooned in Washington itself, the vestibules, stairways, ante-rooms, and offices were clogged with eager applicants for every kind of civil service job. And then, when this vast human flood subsided, the "interviewing" stream began to flow and went on swelling to the bitter end. These war-time interviewers claimed most of Lincoln's personal attention just when he had the least to spare. But he would deny no one the chance of receiving presidential aid or comfort and he gladly suffered many fools for the chance of relieving the sad or serious others. Add to all this the ceaseless work of helping to form public opinion, of counteracting enemy propaganda, of shaping Union policy under ever-changing circumstances, of carrying it out by coalition means, and of exercising civil control over such vast armed forces as no American had hitherto imagined: add these extra burdens, and we can begin to realize what Lincoln had to do as the chief war statesman of the North.

A sound public opinion is the best embattlement of any home front. So Lincoln set out to help in forming it. War on a national scale was something entirely new to both sides, and especially unwelcome to many people in the North, though the really loyal North was up at Lincoln's call. Then came Bull Run; and Lincoln's renewed determination, so well expressed in Whitman's words: "The President, recovering himself, begins that very night—sternly, rapidly sets about the task of reorganizing his forces, and placing himself in positions for future and surer work. If there was nothing else of Abraham Lincoln for history to stamp him with, it is enough to send him with his wreath to the memory of all future time, that he endured that hour, that day, bitterer than gall—indeed a crucifixion day—that it did not conquer him that he unflinchingly stemmed it, and resolved to lift himself and the Union out of it."

Bull Run was only the beginning of troubles. There were many more rocks ahead in the stormy sea of public opinion. The peace party was always ready to lure the ship of state out of its true course by using false lights, even when certain to bring about a universal wreck in which the "pacifists" would suffer with the rest. But dissensions within the war party were worse, especially when caused by action in the field. Frémont's dismissal in November, '61, caused great dissatisfaction among three kinds of people: those who thought him a great general because he knew how to pose as one and really had some streaks of great ability, those who were fattening on the army contracts he let out with such a lavish hand, and those who hailed him as the liberator of the slaves because he went unwarrantably far beyond what was then politically wise or even possible. He was the first Unionist commander to enter the Northern Cave of Adullam, already infested with Copperhead snakes.

There he was joined by McClellan exactly a year later; and there the peace-at-current-prices party continued to nurse and cry their grievances till the war was over. McClellan's dismissal was a matter of dire necessity because victory was impossible under his command. But he was a dangerous reinforcement to the Adullamites; for many of the loyal public had been fooled by his proclamations, the press had written him up to the skies as the Young Napoleon, and the great mass of the rank and file still believed in him. He took the kindly interest in camp comforts that goes to the soldier's heart; and he really did know how to organize. Add his power of passing off tinsel promises for golden deeds, and it can be well understood how great was the danger of dismissing him before his defects had become so apparent to the mass of people as to have turned opinion decisively against him. We shall presently meet him in his relation to Lincoln during the Virginian campaign, and later on in his relation to Lee. Here we may leave him with the reminder that he was the Democratic candidate for President in '64, that he was still a mortal danger to the Union, even though he had rejected the actual wording of his party's peace plank.

The turn of the tide at the fighting front came in '63; but not at the home front, where public opinion of the most vocal kind was stirred to its dregs by the enforcement of the draft. The dime song books of the Copperhead parts of New York expressed in rude rhymes very much the same sort of apprehension that was voiced by the official opposition in the Presidential campaign of '64.

> Abram Lincoln, what yer 'bout?
> Stop this war, for it's played out.

Another rhyme, called "The Beauties of Conscription," was a more decorous expression of such public opinion.

And this, the "People's Sovereignty,"
Before a despot humbled!

. . . .

Well have they cashed old Lincoln's drafts,
Hurrah for the Conscription!

. . . .

Is not this war—this MURDER—for
The negro, *nolens volens?*

So, carrying out their ideas to the same sort of logical conclusion, the New York mob of '63 not only burnt every recruiting office they found undefended but burnt the negro orphan asylum and killed all the negroes they could lay their hands on.

Public opinion did veer round a little with the rising tide of victory in the winter of '63 and '64. But, incredible as it may seem to those who think the home front must always reflect the fighting front, the nadir of public opinion in the North was reached in the summer of '64, when every expert knew that the resources of the South were nearing exhaustion and that the forces of the North could certainly wear out Lee's dwindling army even if they could not beat it. The trumpet gave no uncertain sound from Lincoln's lips. "In this purpose to save the country and its liberties no class of people seem so nearly unanimous as the soldiers in the field and the sailors afloat. Do they not have the hardest of it? Who should quail while they do not?" But the mere excellence of a vast fighting front means a certain loss of the nobler qualities in the home front, from which so many of the staunchest are withdrawn. And then war-weariness breeds doubts, doubts breed fears, and fears breed the spirit of surrender.

There seemed to be more Copperheads in the conglomerate opposition than Unionists ready to withstand them. The sinister figure of Vallandigham loomed large in Ohio, where he openly denounced the war in such disloyal terms that the military authorities arrested him. An opposition committee, backed by the snakes in the grass of the secret societies, at once wrote to Lincoln demanding release. Lincoln thereupon offered release if the committee would sign a declaration that, since rebellion existed, and since the armed forces of the United States were the constitutional means of suppressing rebellion, each member of the committee would support the war till rebellion was put down. The committee refused to sign. More people then began to see the self-contradictions of the opposition, and most of those "plain people" to whom Lincoln consciously appealed were touched to the heart by his pathetic question: "Must I shoot the simple-minded soldier boy who deserts, while I must not touch a hair of the wily agitator who induces him to desert?"

But there was still defection on the Union side, and among many "plain people" too; for Horace Greeley, the best-known Union editor, lost his nerve and ran away. And Greeley was not the only Union journalist who helped, sometimes unwittingly, to pervert public opinion. The "writing up" of McClellan for what he was not, though rather hysterical, was at least well meant. But the reporters who "wrote down" General Cox, because he would not make them members of his staff in West Virginia, disgraced their profession. The lies about Sherman's "insanity" and Grant's "intoxication" were shamelessly excused on the plea that they made "good stories." Sherman's insanity, as we have seen already, existed only in the disordered imagination of blabbing old Simon Cameron. Grant, at the time these stories were published, was strictly temperate.

Amid all the hindrances—and encouragements, for the Union press generally did noble service in the Union cause—of an uncensored press, and all the complexities of public opinion, Lincoln kept his head and heart set firmly on the one supreme objective of the Union. He foresaw from the first that if all the States came through the war United, then all the reforms for which the war was fought would follow; but that if any particular reform was itself made the supreme objective, then it, and with it all the other reforms, would fail, because only part of the Union strength would be involved, whereas the whole was needed. Moreover, he clearly foresaw the absolute nature of a great civil war. Foreign wars may well, and often do, end in some sort of compromise, especially when the home life of the opponents can go on as before. But a great civil war cannot end in compromise because it radically changes the home life of one side or the other. Davis stood for "Independence or extermination"; Lincoln simply for the Union, which, in his clear prevision, meant all that the body politic could need for a new and better life. He accepted the word "enemy" as descriptive of a passing phase. He would not accept such phraseology as Meade's, "driving the invader from our soil." "Will our generals," he complained, "never get that idea out of their heads? The whole country is our soil."

He was a life-long advocate of Emancipation, first, with compensation, now as part of the price to be paid for rebellion. Emancipation, however, depended on the Union, not the Union on it. His Proclamation was ready in the summer of '62. But to publish it in the midst of defeat would make it look like an act of despair. In September, when the Confederates had to recross the Potomac after Antietam, the Proclamation was given to the world. Its first effect was greater abroad than at home; for now no foreign government could say, and rightly say, that the war, not being fought on account of slavery, might leave that issue still unsettled. This was a most important point in Lincoln's foreign policy, a policy which had been haunted by the fear of recognition for the South or the possibility of war with either the French or British, or even both together.

Lincoln's Cabinet was composed of two factions, one headed by Seward, the Secretary of State, the other by Chase, the Secretary of the Treasury. Both the fighting services were under War Democrats: the Army under Stanton, the Navy under Welles. All these ministers began by thinking that Lincoln had the least ability among them. Seward and Welles presently learnt better. Stanton's exclamation at Lincoln's death speaks for itself "Now he belongs to the ages!" But Chase never believed that Lincoln could even be his equal. Chase and the Treasury were a thorn in the side of the Government; Chase because it was his nature, the Treasury because its notes fell to thirty-nine cents in the dollar during the summer of '64. Welles, hard-working and upright, was guided by an expert assistant. Stanton, equally upright and equally hardworking, made many mistakes. And yet, when all is said and done, Stanton was a really able patriot who worked his hardest for what seemed to him the best.

Such were the four chief men in that Cabinet with which Lincoln carried out his Union policy and over which he towered in what became transcendent statesmanship—the head, the heart, the genius of the war. He never, for one moment, changed his course, but kept it fixed upon the Union, no matter what the winds and tides, the currents and cross-currents were. Thus, while so many lesser minds were busy with flotsam and jetsam of the controversial storm, his own serener soul was already beyond the far horizon, voyaging toward the one sure haven for the Ship of State.

But Lincoln was more than the principal civilian war statesman: he was the constitutional Commander-in-Chief of all the Union forces, afloat and ashore. He was responsible not only for raising, supplying, and controlling them, but for their actual command by men who, in the eyes of the law, were simply his own lieutenants. The problem of exercising civil control without practicing civilian interference, always and everywhere hard, and especially hard in a civil war, was particularly hard in his case, in view of public opinion, the press, his own war policy, and the composition of his Cabinet. His solution was by no means perfect; but the wonder is that he reached it so well in spite of such perverting factors. He began with the mere armed mob that fought the First Bull Run beset with interference. He ended with Farragut, Grant, and Sherman, combined in one great scheme of strategy that included Mobile, Virginia, and the lower South, and that, while under full civil control, was mostly free from interference with its naval and military work—except at the fussy hands of Stanton.

The fundamental difference between civil control, which is the very breath of freedom, and civilian interference, which means the death of all efficiency, can be quite simply illustrated by supposing the proverbial Ship of State to be a fighting man-of-war. The People are the owners, with all an owner's rights; while their chosen Government is their agent, with all an agent's delegated power. The fighting Services, as the word itself so properly implies, are simply the People's servants, though they take their orders from the Government. So far, so good, within the limits of civil control, under which, and which alone, any national resources—in men, money, or material—can lawfully be turned to warlike ends. But when the ship is fitting out, still more when she is out at sea, and most of all when she is fighting, then she should be handled only by her expert captain with his expert crew. Civilian interference begins the moment any inexpert outsider takes the captain's place; and this interference is no less disastrous when the outsider remains at home than when he is on the actual spot.

Lincoln and Stanton were out of their element in the strategic fight with Lee and Stonewall Jackson, as the next chapter abundantly proves. But they will bear, and more than bear, comparison with Davis and Benjamin, their own special "opposite numbers." Benjamin, when Confederate Secretary of War in '62, nearly drove Jackson out of the service by ordering him to follow the advice of some disgruntled subordinates who objected to being moved about for strategic reasons which they could not understand. To make matters worse, Benjamin sent this precious order direct to Jackson without even informing his immediate superior, "Joe" Johnston, or even Lee himself. Thus discipline, the very soul of armies, was attacked from above and beneath by the man who should have been its chief upholder. Luckily for the South things were smoothed over, and Benjamin learnt something he should have known at first.

Davis had none of Lincoln's diffidence about his own capacity for directing the strategy of armies. He had passed through West Point and commanded a battalion in Mexico without finding out that his fitness stopped there. He interfered with Lee and Jackson, sometimes to almost a disabling extent. He forced his enmity on "Joe" Johnston and superseded him at the very worst time in the final campaign. He interfered more than ever just when Lee most required a free hand. And when he did make Lee a real Commander-in-Chief the Southern cause had been lost already. Lincoln's war statesmanship grew with the war. Davis remained as he was.

Lincoln had to meet the difficulties that always occur when professionals and amateurs are serving together. How much Lincoln, Stanton, professionals, and amateurs had to do with the system that was evolved under great stress is far too complex for discussion here. Suffice it to say this: Lincoln's clear insight and openness of mind enabled him to see the universal truth, that, other things being equal, the trained and expert professional must excel the untrained and inexpert amateur. But other things are never precisely equal; and a war in which the whole mass-manhood is concerned brings in a host of amateurs. Lincoln was as devoid of prejudice against the regular officers as he was against any other class of men; and he was ready to try and try again to find a satisfactory commander among them, in spite of many failures. The plan of campaign proposed by General Winfield Scott (and ultimately carried out in a modified form) was dubbed by wiseacre public men the "Anaconda policy"; witlings derided it, and the people were too impatient for anything except "On to Richmond!" Scott, unable to take the field at seventy-five, had no second-in-command. Halleck was a very poor substitute later on. In the meantime McDowell was chosen and generously helped by Lincoln and Stanton. But after Bull Run the very people whose impatience made victory impossible howled him down.

Then the choice fell on McClellan, whose notorious campaign fills much of our next chapter. There we shall see how refractory circumstances, Stanton's waywardness among them, forced Lincoln to go beyond the limits of civil control. Here we need only note McClellan's personal relations with the President. Instead of summoning him to the White House Lincoln often called at McClellan's for discussion. McClellan presently began to treat Lincoln's questions as intrusions, and one day sent down word that he was too tired to see the President. Lincoln had told a friend that he would hold McClellan's stirrups for the sake of victory. But he could not abdicate in favor of McClellan or any one else.

It was none of Lincoln's business to be an actual Commander-in-Chief. Yet night after weary night he sat up studying the science and art of war, groping his untutored way toward those general principles and essential human facts which his native genius enabled him to reach, but never quite understanding—how could he?—their practical application to the field of strategy. His supremely good common sense saved him from going beyond his depth whenever he could help it. His Military Orders were forced upon him by the extreme pressure of impatient public opinion. He told Grant "he did not know but they were all wrong, and he did know that some of them were."

McClellan was not the only failure in Virginia. Burnside and Hooker also failed against Lee and Jackson. All three suffered from civilian interference as well as from their own defects. At last, in the third year of the war, a victor appeared in Meade, a good, but by no means great, commander. In the fourth year Lincoln gave the chief command to Grant, whom he had carefully watched and wisely supported through all the ups and downs of the river campaigns.

Grant's account of his first conference alone with Lincoln is eloquent of Lincoln's wise war statesmanship:

He stated that he had never professed to be a military man or to know how campaigns should be conducted, and never wanted to interfere in them.... All he wanted was some one who would take the responsibility and act, and call on him for all the assistance needed, pledging himself to use all the power of the government in rendering such assistance.... He pointed out on the map two streams which empty into the Potomac, and suggested that the army might be moved on boats and landed between the mouths of these streams. We would then have the Potomac to bring our supplies and the tributaries would protect our flanks while we moved out. I listened respectfully, but did not suggest that the same streams would protect Lee's flanks while he was shutting us up. I did not communicate my plans to the President; nor did I to the Secretary of War or to General Halleck.

Trust begot trust; and some months later Grant showed war statesmanship of the same magnificent kind. McClellan had become the Democratic candidate for President, to the well-founded alarm of all who put the Union first. In June, when Grant and Lee were at grips round Richmond, Lincoln was invited to a public meeting got up in honor of Grant with only a flimsy disguise of the ominous fact that Grant, and not Lincoln, might be the Union choice. Lincoln sagaciously wrote back: "It is impossible for me to attend. I approve nevertheless of whatever may tend to strengthen and sustain General Grant and the noble armies now under his command. He and his brave soldiers are now in the midst of their great trial, and I trust that at your meeting you will so shape your good words that they may turn to men and guns, moving to his and their support." The danger to the Union of taking Grant away from the front moved Lincoln deeply all through that anxious summer of '64, though he never thought Grant would leave the front with his work half done. In August an officious editor told Lincoln that he ought to take a good long rest. Lincoln, however, was determined to stand by his own post of duty and find out from Grant, through their common friend, John Eaton, what Grant's own views of such ideas were. This is Eaton's account of how Grant took it:

We had been talking very quietly. But Grant's reply came in an instant and with a violence for which I was not prepared. He brought his clenched fists down hard on the strap arms of his camp chair. "They can't do it. They can't compel me to do it." Emphatic gesture was not a strong point with Grant. "Have you said this to the President?" "No," said Grant, "I have not thought it worth while to assure the President of my opinion. I consider it as important for the cause that he should be elected as that the army should be successful in the field."

When Eaton brought back his report Lincoln simply said, "I told you they could not get him to run till he had closed out the rebellion."

On the twenty-third of this same gloomy August, lightened only by the taking of Mobile, Lincoln asked his Cabinet if they would endorse a memorandum without reading it. They all immediately signed. After his reëlection in November he read it out: "This morning, as for some days past, it seems exceedingly probable that this Administration will not be reëlected. Then it will be my duty to so coöperate with the President-elect as to save the Union between the election and the inauguration, as he will have secured his election on such ground that he cannot possibly save it afterwards." He added that he would have asked McClellan to throw his whole influence into getting enough recruits to finish the war before the fourth of March. "And McClellan," was Seward's comment, "would have said 'Yes, yes,' and then done nothing."

Lincoln's reëlection was helped by Farragut's victory in August, Sherman's in September, and Sheridan's raid through the Shenandoah Valley in October. But it was also helped by that strange, vivifying touch which passes, no one knows how, from the man who best embodies a supremely patriotic cause to the masses of his fellow patriots, and then, at some great crisis, when they scale heights which he has long since trod, comes back in flood and carries him to power.

Lincoln stories were abroad; the true were eclipsing the false; and all the true ones gained him increasing credit. Naval reformers, and many others too, enjoyed the homely wit with which he closed the first conference about such a startlingly novel craft as the plans for the *Monitor* promised: "Well, Gentlemen, all I have to say is what the girl said when she put her foot into the stocking: 'It strikes me there's something in it.'" The army enjoyed the joke against the three-month captain whom Sherman threatened to shoot if he went home without leave. The same day Lincoln, visiting the camp, was harangued by this prospective deserter in presence of many another man disheartened by Bull Run. "Mr. President: this morning I spoke to Colonel Sherman and he threatened to shoot me, Sir!" Lincoln looked the two men over, and then, in a stage whisper every listener could hear, said: "Well, if I were you, and he threatened to shoot me, I wouldn't trust him; for I'm sure he'd do it." Both Services were not only pleased with the "rise" Lincoln took out of a too inquisitive politician but were much reassured by its model discretion. This importunate politician so badgered Lincoln about the real destination of McClellan's transports that Lincoln at last promised to tell everything he could if the politician would promise not to repeat it. Then, after swearing the utmost secrecy, the politician got the news: "They are going to sea."

The whole home front as well as the Services were touched to the heart by tales of Lincoln's kindness in his many interviews with the war-bereaved; and letters like these spoke for themselves to every patriot in the land:

Executive Mansion, November 21, 1864.

Mrs. Bixby, Boston, Massachusetts.

Dear Madam: I have been shown in the files of the War Department a statement of the Adjutant-General of Massachusetts that you are the mother of five sons who have died gloriously on the field of battle. I feel how weak and fruitless must be any words of mine which should attempt to beguile you from the grief of a loss so overwhelming. But I cannot refrain from tendering to you the consolation that may be found in the thanks of the Republic they died to save. I pray that our heavenly Father may assuage the anguish of your bereavement, and leave you only the cherished memory of the loved and lost, and the solemn pride that must be yours to have laid so costly a sacrifice upon the altar of freedom.

Yours very sincerely and respectfully,
Abraham Lincoln.

Nor did the Lincoln touch stop there. It even began to make its quietly persuasive way among the finer spirits of the South from the very day on which the Second Inaugural closed with words which were the noblest consummation of the prophecy made in the First. This was the prophecy: "The mystic chords of memory, stretching from every battlefield and patriot grave to every living heart and hearthstone, all over this broad land, will yet swell the chorus of the Union, when again touched, as surely they will be, by the better angels of our nature." And this the consummation: "With malice toward none, with charity for all, with firmness in the right, as God gives us to see the right, let us strive on to finish the work we are in, to bind up the nation's wounds, to care for him who shall have borne the battle and for his widow and his orphan—to do all which may achieve and cherish a just and lasting peace among ourselves and with all nations."

CHAPTER VI
LEE AND JACKSON: 1862-3

Most Southerners remained spellbound by the glamour of Bull Run till the hard, sharp truths of '62 began to rouse them from their flattering dream. They fondly hoped, and even half believed, that if another Northern army dared to invade Virginia it would certainly fail against their entrenchments at Bull Run. If, so ran the argument, the North failed in the open field it must fail still worse against a fortified position.

The Southern generals vainly urged their Government to put forth its utmost strength at once, before the more complex and less united North had time to recover and begin anew. They asked for sixty thousand men at Bull Run, to be used for a vigorous counterstroke at Washington. They pointed out the absurdity of misusing the Bull Run (or Manassas) position as a mere shield, fixed to one spot, instead of making it the hilt of a sword thrust straight at the heart of the North. Robert E. Lee, now a full general in the Confederate Army and adviser to the President, grasped the whole situation from the first and urged the right solution in the official way. Stonewall Jackson, still a junior general, was in full accord with Lee, as we know from the confidential interview (at the end of October, '61) between him and his divisional commander, General G. W. Smith, who made it public many years later. The gist of Jackson's argument was this: "McClellan won't come out this year with his army of recruits. We ought to invade now, not wait to be invaded later on. If Davis would concentrate every man who can be spared from all other points and let us invade before winter sets in, then McClellan's recruits couldn't stand against us in the field. Let us cross the upper Potomac, occupy Baltimore, and, holding Maryland, cut the communications of Washington, force the Federal Government out of it, beat McClellan if he attacks, destroy industrial plants liable to be turned to warlike ends, cut the big commercial lines of communication, close the coal mines, seize the neck of land between Pittsburg and Lake Erie, live on the country by requisition, and show the North what it would cost to conquer the South." On asking Smith if he agreed, Smith answered: "I will tell you a secret; for I am sure it won't be divulged. These views were rejected by the Government during the conference at Fairfax Court House at the beginning of the month." Jackson thereupon shook Smith's hand, saying, "I am sorry, very sorry," and, mounting Little Sorrel without another word, rode sadly away.

Jefferson Davis probably, and some of his Cabinet possibly, understood what Lee, "Joe" Johnston, Beauregard, Smith, and Jackson so strongly urged. But they feared the outcry that would assuredly be raised by people in districts denuded of troops for the grand concentration elsewhere. So they remained passive when they should have been active, and, trying to strengthen each separate part, fatally weakened the whole.

Meanwhile the North was collecting the different elements of warlike force and changing its Secretary of War. Cameron was superseded by Stanton on the fifteenth of January. Twelve days later Lincoln issued the first of those military orders which, as we have just seen, he afterwards told Grant that the impatience of the loyal North compelled him to issue, though he knew some were certainly, and all were possibly, wrong. This first order was one of the certainly wrong. McClellan's unready masses were to begin an unlimited mud march through the early spring roads of Virginia on the twenty-second of February, in honor of Washington's birthday. A reconnoitering staff officer reported the roads as being in their proper places; but he guessed the bottom had fallen out. So McClellan was granted some delay.

His grand total was now over two hundred thousand men. The Confederate grand total was estimated at a hundred and fifteen thousand by the civilian detectives whom the Federal Government employed to serve in place of an expert intelligence staff. The detective estimate was sixty-five thousand men out. The real Confederate strength at this time was only fifty thousand. There was little chance of getting true estimates in any other way, as the Federal Government had no adequate cavalry. Most of the few cavalry McClellan commanded were as yet a mere collection of men and horses, quite unfit for reconnoitering and testing an enemy's force.

McClellan's own plan, formed on the supposition that the Confederates held the Bull Run position with at least a hundred thousand men, involved the transfer of a hundred and fifty thousand Federals by sea from Washington to Fortress Monroe, on the historic peninsula between the York and James rivers. Then, using these rivers as lines of communication, his army would take Richmond in flank. Lincoln's objection to this plan was based on the very significant argument that while the Federal army was being transported piecemeal to Fortress Monroe the Confederates might take Washington by a sudden dash from their base at Centreville, only thirty miles off. This was a valid objection; for Washington was not only the

Federal Headquarters but the very emblem of the Union cause—a sort of living Stars and Stripes—and Washington lost might well be understood to mean almost the same as if the Ship of State had struck her colors.

On the ninth of March the immediate anxiety about Washington was relieved. That day came news that the *Monitor* had checkmated the *Merrimac* in Hampton Roads and that "Joe" Johnston had withdrawn his forces from the Bull Run position and had retired behind the Rappahannock to Culpeper. On the tenth McClellan began a reconnoitering pursuit of Johnston from Washington. Having found burnt bridges and other signs of decisive retirement, he at last persuaded the reluctant Lincoln to sanction the Peninsula Campaign. On the seventeenth his army began embarking for Fortress Monroe, ten thousand men at a time, that being all the transports could carry. For a week the movement of troops went on successfully; while the Confederates could not make out what was happening along the coast. Everything also seemed quite safe, from the Federal point of view, in the Shenandoah Valley, where General Banks commanded. And both there and along the Potomac the Federals were in apparently overwhelming strength; even though the detectives doing duty as staff officers still kept on doubling the numbers of all the Confederates under arms.

Suddenly, on the twenty-third, a fight at Kernstown in the Shenandoah Valley gave a serious shock to the victorious Federals, not only there but all over the semicircle of invasion, from West Virginia round by the Potomac and down to Fortress Monroe. The fighting on both sides was magnificent. Yet Kernstown itself was a very small affair. Little more than ten thousand men had been in action: seven thousand Federals under Shields against half as many Confederates under Stonewall Jackson. The point is that Jackson's attack, though unsuccessful, was very disconcerting elsewhere. From Kernstown the area of disturbance spread like wildfire till the tactical victory of seven thousand Federals had spoilt the strategy of thirty times as many. Shields reported: "I set to work during the night to bring together all the troops within my reach. I sent an express after Williams's division, requesting the rear brigade, about twenty miles distant, to march all night and join me in the morning. I swept the posts in rear of almost all their guards, hurrying them forward by forced marches, to be with me at daylight." Banks, now on his way to Washington, halted in alarm at Harper's Ferry. McClellan, perceiving that Jackson's little force was more than a mere corps of observation, approved Banks and added: "As soon as you are strong enough push Jackson hard and drive him well beyond Strasburg," that is, west of the Massanuttons, where Frémont could close in and finish him. Lincoln had already been thinking of transferring nine thousand men from McClellan to Frémont. Kernstown decided it; so off they went to West

Virginia. Still fearing an attack on Washington, Lincoln halted McDowell's army corps, thirty-seven thousand strong, on the march overland to join McClellan on the Peninsula, and kept them stuck fast round Centreville, near Bull Run. And so McClellan's Peninsular force was suddenly reduced by forty-six thousand men.

April was a month of maneuvers and suspense. By the end of it McClellan, based on Fortress Monroe, had accumulated a hundred and ten thousand men. The Confederates on the Peninsula, holding Yorktown, numbered fifty thousand. McClellan sadly missed McDowell, whose corps was to have taken the fort at Gloucester Point that prevented the Federal gunboats from turning the enemy's lines at Yorktown. McDowell moved south to Fredericksburg, leaving a small force near Manassas Junction to connect him with the garrison of Washington. The Confederates could spare only twelve thousand men to watch him. Meanwhile Banks occupied the Shenandoah Valley, having twenty thousand men at Harrisonburg and smaller forces at several points all round, from southwest to northeast, each designed to form part of the net that was soon to catch Jackson. Beyond Banks stood Frémont's force in West Virginia, also ready to close in. Jackson's complete grand total was less than that of Banks's own main body. Yet, with one eye on Richmond, he lay in wait at Swift Run Gap, crouching for a tiger-spring at Banks. Virginia was semicircled by superior forces. But everywhere inside the semicircle the Confederate parts all formed one strategic whole; while the Federal parts outside did not. Moreover, the South had already decided to call up every available man; thus forestalling the North by more than ten months on the vital issue of conscription.

In May the preliminary clash of arms began on the Peninsula. The Confederates evacuated the Yorktown lines on the third. On the fifth McClellan's advanced guard fought its way past Williamsburg. On the seventh he began changing his base from Fortress Monroe to White House on the Pamunkey. Here on the sixteenth he was within twenty miles of Richmond, while all the seaways behind him were safe in Union hands. The fate not only of Richmond but of the whole South seemed trembling in the scales. The Northern armies had cleared the Mississippi down to Memphis. The Northern navy had taken New Orleans, the greatest Southern port. And now the Northern hosts were striking at the Southern capital. McClellan with double numbers from the east, McDowell with treble numbers from the north, and the Union navy, with more than fourfold strength on all the navigable waters, were closing in. The Confederate Government had even decided to take the extreme step of evacuating Richmond, hoping to prolong the struggle elsewhere. The official records had been packed. Davis had made all arrangements for the flight of his family. And from Drewry's Bluff, eight miles south of Richmond, the masts of the foremost Federal vessels could be seen coming up the James, where, on the eleventh, the *Merrimac*, having grounded, had been destroyed by her own commander.

But the General Assembly of Virginia, passionately seconded by the City Council, petitioned the Government to stand its ground "till not a stone was left upon another." Every man in Richmond who could do a hand's turn and who was not already in arms marched out to complete the defenses of the James at Drewry's Bluff. Senators, bankers, bondmen and free, merchants, laborers, and ministers of all religions, dug earthworks, hauled cannon, piled ammunition, or worked, wet to the waist, at the big boom that was to stop the ships and hold them under fire. The Government had changed its mind. Richmond was to be held to the last extremity. And the Southern women were as willing as the men.

In the midst of all this turmoil Lee calmly reviewed the situation. He saw that the Federal gunboats coming up the James were acting alone, as the disconnected vanguard of what should have been a joint advance, and that no army was yet moving to support them. He knew McClellan and Banks and read them like a book. He also knew Jackson, and decided to use him again in the Shenandoah Valley as a menace to Washington. Writing to him on the sixteenth of May, the very day McClellan reached White House, only twenty miles from Richmond, he said: "Whatever movement you make against Banks, do it speedily, and, if successful, drive him back towards the Potomac, and create the impression, as far as possible, that you design threatening that line." Moreover, out of his own scanty forces, he sent Jackson two excellent brigades. Thus, while the great Federal civilians who knew nothing practical of war were all agog about Richmond, a single point at one end of the semicircle, the great Confederate strategist was forging a thunderbolt to relieve the pressure on it by striking the Federal center so as to threaten Washington. The fundamental idea was a Fabian defensive at Richmond, a vigorous offensive in the Valley, to produce Federal dispersion between these points and Washington; then rapid concentration against McClellan on the Chickahominy.

The unsupported Federal gunboats were stopped and turned back at the boom near Drewry's Bluff. McClellan, bent on besieging Richmond in due form, crawled cautiously about the intervening swamps of the oozy Chickahominy. McDowell, who could not advance alone, remained at Fredericksburg. Shields stood behind him, near Catlett's Station, to keep another eye on nervous Washington.

In the meantime Stonewall Jackson, still in the Shenandoah, had fought no battles since his tactical defeat at Kernstown on the twenty-third of March had proved such a pregnant strategic victory elsewhere. But late in April he had a letter from Lee, telling of the general situation and suggesting an attack on Banks. Banks, however, still had twenty thousand men at Harrisonburg, with twenty-five thousand more in or within call of the Valley. Jackson's complete grand total was less than eighteen thousand. The odds against him therefore exceeded five against two; and direct attack was out of the question. But he now began his maneuvers anew and on a bolder scale than ever. He had upset the Federal strategy at Kernstown, when there were less than eight thousand Confederates in the Valley. What might he not do with ten thousand more? His wonderful Valley Campaign, famous forever in the history of war, gives us the answer.

He had five advantages over Banks. First, his own expert knowledge and genius for war, backed by a dauntless character. Banks was a very able man who had worked his way up from factory hand to Speaker of the House of Representatives and Governor of Massachusetts. But he had neither the knowledge, genius, nor character required for high command; and he owed his present position more to his ardor as a politician than to his ability as a general. Jackson's second advantage was his own and his army's knowledge of the country for which they naturally fought with a loving zeal which no invaders could equal. The third advantage was in having Turner Ashby's cavalry. These were horsemen born and bred, who could make their way across country as easily as the "footy" Federals could along the road. In answer to a peremptory order a Federal cavalry commander could only explain: "I can't catch them. They leap fences and walls like deer. Neither our men nor our horses are so trained." The fourth advantage was in discipline. Jackson habitually spared his men more than his officers, and his officers more than himself, whenever indulgence was possible. But when discipline had to be sternly maintained he maintained it sternly, throughout all ranks, knowing that the flower of discipline is self-sacrifice, from the senior general down, and that the root is due subordination, from the junior private up. After the Conscription Act had come into force a few companies, who were time-expired as volunteers, threw down their arms and told their colonel they wouldn't serve another day. On hearing this officially Jackson asked: "Why does Colonel Grigsby refer to me to learn how to deal with mutineers? He should shoot them where they stand." The rest of the regiment was then paraded with loaded arms, facing the mutineers, who were given the choice of complete submission or instant death. They chose submission. That was the last mutiny under Stonewall Jackson. Both sides suffered from straggling, the Confederates as much as the Federals. But Confederate stragglers rejoined the better of the two; and in downright desertion the Federals were the worse, simply because their own peace party was by far the stronger. The final advantage brings us back to strategy, on which the whole campaign was turning. Lee and Jackson worked the Confederates together. Lincoln and Stanton worked the Federals apart.

On the last of April Jackson slipped away from Swift Run Gap while Ewell quietly took his place and Ashby blinded Banks by driving the Federal cavalry back on Harrisonburg. Jackson's men were thoroughly puzzled and disheartened when they had to leave the Valley in full possession of the enemy while they ploughed through seas of mud towards Richmond. What was the matter? Were they off to Richmond? No; for they presently wheeled round. "Old Jack's crazy, sure, this time." Even one of his staff officers thought so himself, and put it on paper, to his own confusion afterwards. The rain came down in driving sheets. The roads became mere drains for the oozing woods. Wheels stuck fast; and Jackson was seen heaving his hardest with an exhausted gun team. But still the march went on—slosh, slosh, squelch; they slogged it through. *Close up, men!—close up in rear!— close up, there, close up!*

On the fourth of May Jackson got word from Edward Johnson, commanding his detached brigade near Staunton, that Milroy, commanding Frémont's advanced guard, was coming on from West Virginia. Jackson at once seized the chance of smashing Milroy by railing in to Staunton before Banks or Frémont could interfere. This would have been suicidal against a great commander with a well-trained force. But Banks, grossly exaggerating Jackson's numbers, was already marching north to the railhead at New Market, where he would be nearer his friends if Jackson swooped down. Detraining at Staunton the Confederates picketed the whole neighborhood to stop news getting out before they made their dash against Milroy. On the seventh they moved off. The cadets of the Virginia Military Institute, where Jackson had been a professor for so many years, had just joined to gain some experience of the real thing, and as they stepped out in their smart uniforms, with all the exactness of parade-ground drill, they formed a marked contrast to the gaunt soldiers of the Valley, half fed, half clad, but wholly eager for the fray.

That night Milroy got together all the men he could collect at McDowell, a little village just beyond the Valley and on the road to Gauley Bridge in West Virginia. He sent posthaste for reinforcements. But Frémont's men were divided too far west, fearing nothing from the Valley, while Banks's were thinking of a concentration too far north.

In the afternoon of the eighth, Milroy attacked Jackson with great determination and much skill. But after a stern encounter, in which the outnumbered Federals fought very well indeed, the Confederates won a decisive victory. The numbers actually engaged—twenty-five hundred Federals against four thousand Confederates—were even smaller than at Kernstown. But this time the Confederates won the tactical victory on the spot as well as the strategic victory all over the Valley; and the news cheered Richmond at what, as we have seen already, was its very darkest hour. The night of the battle Jackson sent out strong working parties to destroy all bridges and culverts and to block all roads by which Frémont could reach the Valley. In some places bowlders were rolled down from the hills. In one the trees were felled athwart the path for a mile. A week later Jackson was back in the Valley at Lebanon Springs, while Frémont was blocked off from Banks, who was now distractedly groping for safety and news.

The following day, the famous sixteenth, we regain touch with Lee, who, as mentioned already, then wrote to Jackson about attacking Banks in order to threaten Washington. This dire day at Richmond, the day McClellan reached White House, was also the one appointed by the Southern Government as a day of intercession for God's blessing on the Southern arms. None kept it more fervently, even in beleaguered Richmond, than pious Jackson in the Valley. Then, like a giant refreshed, he rose for swift and silent marches and also sudden hammer-strokes at Banks.

Confident that all would now go well, Washington thought nothing of the little skirmish at McDowell, because it apparently disturbed nothing beyond the Shenandoah Valley. The news from everywhere else was good; and Federals were jubilant. So were the civilian strategists, particularly Stanton, who, though tied to his desk as Secretary of War, was busy wire-pulling Banks's men about the Valley. Stanton ordered Banks to take post at Strasburg and to hold the bridges at Front Royal with two detached battalions. This masterpiece of bungling put the Federals at Front Royal in the air, endangered their communications north to Winchester, and therefore menaced the Valley line toward Washington. But Banks said nothing; and Stanton would have snubbed him if he had.

On the twenty-third of May a thousand Federals under Colonel Kenly were sweltering in the first hot weather of the year at Stanton's indefensible position of Front Royal when suddenly a long gray line of skirmishers emerged from the woods, the Confederate bugles rang out, and Jackson's battle line appeared. Then came a crashing volley, which drove in the Federal pickets for their lives. Colonel Kenly did his best. But he was outflanked and forced back in confusion. A squadron of New York cavalry came to the rescue; but were themselves outflanked and helpless on the road against the Virginian horsemen, who could ride across country. Kenly had just made a second stand, when down came the Virginians, led by Colonel Flournoy at racing speed over fence and ditch, scattering the Federal cavalry like chaff before the wind and smashing into the Federal infantry. Two hundred and fifty really efficient cavalry took two guns (complete with limbers, men, and horses), killed and wounded a hundred and fifty-four of their opponents, and captured six hundred prisoners as well—and all with a loss to themselves of only eleven killed and fifteen wounded.

Ashby's cavalry, several hundreds strong, pushed on and out to the flanks, cutting the wires, destroying bridges, and blocking the roads against reinforcements from beyond the Valley. Three hours after the attack a dispatch-rider dashed up to Banks's headquarters at Strasburg. But Banks refused to move, saying, when pressed by his staff to make a strategic retreat on Winchester, "By God, sir, I will not retreat! We have more to fear from the opinions of our friends than from the bayonets of our enemies!" The Cabinet backed him up next day by actually proposing to reinforce him at Strasburg with troops from Washington and Baltimore. Nevertheless he was forced to fly for his life to Winchester. His stores at Strasburg had to be abandoned. His long train of wagons was checked on the way, with considerable loss. And some of his cavalry, caught on the road by horsemen who could ride across country, were smashed to pieces.

Jackson pressed on relentlessly to Winchester with every one who could march like "foot cavalry," as his Valley men came to be called. On the twenty-fifth, the third day of unremitting action, he carried the Winchester heights and drove Banks through the town. Only the Second Massachusetts, which had already distinguished itself during the retreat, preserved its formation. Ten thousand Confederate bayonets glittered in the morning sun. The long gray lines swept forward. The piercing rebel yell rose high. And the people, wild with joy, rushed out of doors to urge the victors on.

By the twenty-sixth, the first day on which Stanton's reinforcements from Baltimore and Washington could possibly have fought at Strasburg, the Confederates had reached Martinsburg, fifty miles beyond it. Banks had already crossed the Potomac, farther on still. The newsboys of the North were crying, *Defeat of General Banks! Washington in danger!* Thirteen Governors were calling for special State militia, for which a million men were volunteering, spare troops were hurrying to Harper's Ferry, a reserve corps was being formed at Washington, the Federal Government was assuming control of all the railroad lines, and McClellan was being warned that he must either take Richmond at once or come back to save the capital. Nor did the strategic disturbance stop even there; for the Washington authorities ordered McDowell's force at Fredericksburg to the Valley just as it was coming into touch with McClellan.

On the twenty-eighth Jackson might have taken Harper's Ferry. But the storm was gathering round him. A great strategist directing the Federal forces could have concentrated fifty thousand men, by sunset on the first of June, against Jackson's Army of the Valley, which could not possibly have mustered one-third of such a number. McDowell arrived that night at Front Royal. He had vainly protested against the false strategy imposed by the Government from Washington, and he was not a free agent now. Yet, even so, his force was at least a menace to Jackson, who had only two chances of getting away to aid in the defeat of McClellan and the saving of Richmond. One was to outmarch the converging Federals, gain interior lines along the Valley, and defeat them there in detail. The other was to march into friendly Maryland, trusting to her Southern sentiments for help and reinforcements. He decided on the Valley route and marched straight in between his enemies.

His fortnight's work, from the nineteenth of May to the first of June, inclusive, is worth summing up. In these fourteen days he had marched 170 miles, routed 12,500 men, threatened an invasion of the North, drawn McDowell off from Fredericksburg, taken or destroyed all Federal stores at Front Royal, Winchester, and Martinsburg, and brought off safely a convoy seven miles long. Moreover, he had done all this with the loss of only six hundred, though sixty thousand enemies lay on three sides of his own sixteen thousand men.

His remaining problem was harder still. It was how to mystify, tire out, check short, and then immobilize the converging Federals long enough to let him slip secretly away in time to help Johnston and Lee against McClellan. Jackson, like his enemies, moved through what has been well called the Fog of War—that inevitable uncertainty through which all commanders must find their way. But none of his enemies equaled him in knowledge, genius, or character for war.

The first week in June saw desperate marches in the Valley, with the outnumbering Federals hot-foot on the trail of Jackson, who turned to bay one moment and at the next was off again. On the sixth the Federals got home against his rear guard. It began to waver, and Ashby ordered the infantry to charge. As he gave the order his horse fell dead. In a flash he was up, waving his sword and shouting: "Charge, for God's sake, charge!" The Confederate line swept forward gallantly. But, just as it left the wood, Ashby was shot through the heart. His men avenged him. Yet none could fill his place as a born leader of irregular light horse.

Next morning the hounds were hot upon the scent again: Shields and Frémont converging on Jackson, whom they would run to earth somewhere north of Staunton. But on the eighth and ninth Jackson turned sharply and bit back, first at Frémont close to Cross Keys, then at Shields near Port Republic. Each was caught alone, just before their point of junction, and each was defeated in detail as well.

Fully to appreciate Jackson's strategy we must compare the strategical and tactical numbers concerned throughout this short but momentous Valley Campaign. The strategic numbers are those at the disposal of the commander within the theater of operations. The tactical numbers are those actually present on the field of battle, whether engaged or not. At McDowell the Federals had 30,000 in strategic strength against 17,000 Confederates; yet the Confederates got 6000 on to the field of battle against no more than 2500. At Winchester the Federal strategic strength was 60,000 against 16,000; yet the Confederate tactical strength was every man of the 16,000 against 7500 — only one-eighth of Banks's grand total. At Cross Keys the strategic strengths were 23,000 Federals against 13,000 Confederates; yet 12,750 Federals were beaten by 8000 Confederates. Finally, at Port Republic, the Federals, with a strategic strength of 22,000 against the Confederate 12,700, could only bring a tactical strength of 4500 to bear on 6000 Confederates. The grand aggregate of these four remarkable actions is well worth adding up. It comes to this in strategic strength: 135,000 Federals against 58,700 Confederates. Yet in tactical strength the odds are reversed; for they come to this: 36,000 Confederates against only 27,250 Federals. Therefore Stonewall Jackson, with strategic odds of nearly seven to three against him, managed to fight with tactical odds of four to three in his favor.

While Jackson was fighting in the Valley the Confederates at Richmond were watching the nightly glow of Federal camp fires. McClellan had 30,000 men north of the Chickahominy, waiting for McDowell to come back from his enterprise against Jackson, and 75,000 south of it. What could the 65,000 Confederates do, except hold fast to their lines? TO RICHMOND 4-1/2 MILES: so read the sign-post at the Mechanicsville bridge, and there stood the nearest Federal picket. Johnston and Lee knew, however, that McClellan's alarmist detectives swore to a Confederate army three times its actual strength at this time; and there was reason to hope that the consequent moral ascendancy would help the shock of an attack suddenly made on one of McClellan's two wings while the flooded Chickahominy flowed between them and its oozy swamps bewildered his staff.

Hearing that McDowell need not be feared, Johnston attacked at daylight on the thirty-first of May. The battle of Seven Pines (known also as Fair Oaks) was not unlike Shiloh. The Federals were taken by surprise on the first day and only succeeded in holding their own by hard fighting and with a good deal of loss. A mistake was made by the Confederate division told off for the attack on the key to the Federal front (an attack which, if completely successful, would have split the Federals in two) and the main bodies were engaged before this fatal error could be rectified. So the surprised Federals gradually recovered from the first shock and began to feel and use their hitherto unrealized strength. On the second day (the first of June) Johnston, who had been severely wounded, was plainly defeated and compelled to fall back on Richmond again.

On the morrow of this defeat Lee was appointed to "the immediate command of the armies in eastern Virginia and North Carolina." Davis was not war statesman enough to make him Commander-in-Chief till '65—four years too late. Johnston did not reappear till he tried to relieve Vicksburg from the determined attacks of Grant in '63.

The twelfth of June will be remembered forever in the annals of cavalry for Stuart's first great ride round McClellan's host. With twelve hundred troopers and two horse artillery guns he stole out beyond the western flank of the Federals and reached Taylorsville that evening, twenty-two miles north of Richmond. Next day he rode right in among the Federal posts in rear, discovering that McClellan's right stretched little north of the Chickahominy, that it was not fortified, and that it did not rest on any strong natural feature, such as a swampy stream. This was exactly the information Lee required. So far, so good. The Federals met with up to this time had simply been ridden down. But now the whole country was alarmed and McClellan had forces out to cut Stuart off on his return, while General Cooke (Stuart's father-in-law) began to pursue him from Hanover Court House.

Then Stuart took the boldest step of all, deciding to go clear round the rest of the Federal army. At Tunstall's Station on the York River Railroad he routed the guard, tore up the track, destroyed the stores and wagons, cut the wires, burnt the bridge, and replenished his supplies. Thence southeast, by the Williamsburg road, his column marched under a full summer moon, the people running out of doors, wild with joy at his daring. At sunrise he reached the Chickahominy, only to find it flooded, full of timber, and spanned by nothing better than a broken bridge. But, using the materials of a warehouse to make a footway, the troopers crossed in single file, leading their chargers, which swam. Waving his hand to the Federals, who had just arrived too late, Stuart pushed on the remaining thirty-five miles to Richmond, rounding the Federal flank within range of Federal gunboats on the James.

This magnificent raid not only procured in three days information that McClellan's civilian detectives could not have procured in three years but raised Confederate morale and depressed the Federals correspondingly.

Moreover, it drove the first nail into McClellan's coffin. For in October, just after another Stuart raid, the following curious incident occurred on board the *Martha Washington* when Lincoln was returning from an Alexandria review which had cheered him up considerably, coming, as it did, after Lee had failed in Maryland. By way of answering the very pertinent question— "Mr. President, how about McClellan?"—Lincoln simply drew a ring on the deck, quietly adding: "When I was a boy we used to play a game called 'Three times round and out.' Stuart has been round McClellan twice. The third time McClellan will be out."

Stuart rode ahead of his troopers, straight to Lee, who immediately wrote to Jackson suggesting that the Army of the Valley, while keeping the Federals alarmed to the last about an attack on the line of the Potomac, might secretly slip away and join a combined attack on McClellan. Jackson, who had of course foreseen this, was ready with every blind known to the art of war. Even his staff and generals knew nothing of their destination. The first move was so secret that the enemy never suspected anything till it was too late, while friends thought there was to be another surprise in the Valley. The second move led various people to suspect a march on Washington— no bad news to leak out; and nothing but misleading items did leak out. The Army of the Valley moved within a charmed circle of cavalry which prevented any one from going forward, ahead of the advance, and swept before it all stragglers through whom the news might leak out by the rear. On the twenty-third of June, only eight days after Stuart had reported his raid to Lee, Jackson attended Lee's conference at the same place, Richmond. The Valley Army was then on its thirty-mile march from Frederick's Hall to Ashland, where it arrived on the twenty-fifth, fifteen miles north.

McClellan had over a hundred thousand men. Lee had less than ninety thousand, even after Jackson had joined him. To attack McClellan's strongly fortified front, with its almost impregnable flanks, would have been suicide. But McClellan's farther right, commanded by that excellent officer, FitzJohn Porter, lay north of the Chickahominy, with its own right open for junction with McDowell. So Lee, knowing McClellan and the state of this Federal right, decided on the twenty-fourth to attack Porter and threaten McClellan's communications not only with McDowell to the north but with White House, the Federal base twenty miles northeast. This was an exceedingly bold move, first, because McClellan had plenty of men to take Richmond during Lee's march north, secondly, because it meant the convergence of separate forces on the field of battle (Jackson being at Ashland, fifteen miles from Richmond) and, thirdly, because the Confederates were inferior in armament and in supplies of all kinds as well as in actual numbers. Magruder, who had held the Yorktown lines so cleverly with such inferior forces, was to hold Richmond (on both sides of the James) with thirty-five thousand men against McClellan's seventy-five thousand, while Lee and Jackson converged on Porter's twenty-five thousand with over fifty thousand.

Then followed the famous Seven Days, beginning on the twenty-sixth of June near the signpost at the Mechanicsville bridge—TO RICHMOND 4-1/2 MILES—and ending at Harrison's Landing on the second of July. On the twenty-sixth the attack was made with consummate strategic skill. But it was marred by bad staff work, by the great obstructions in Jackson's path, and by A. P. Hill's premature attack with ten thousand men against Porter's admirable front at Beaver Dam Creek. Hill's men moved down their own side of the little valley in dense masses till every gun and rifle on Porter's side was suddenly unmasked. No scythe could have mowed the leading Confederates better. Two thousand went down in the first few minutes, and the rest at once retreated.

Porter fell back on Gaines's Mill, where, after being reinforced, he took up a strong position on the twenty-seventh. Again there was failure in combining the attack. Jackson found obstructions that even he could not overcome quickly enough. Hill attacked again with the utmost gallantry, wave after wave of Confederates rushing forward only to melt away before the concentrated fire of Porter's reinforced command.

But at last the Confederates—though checked and roughly handled—converged under Lee's own eye; and an inferno of shot and shell loosened and shook the steadfast Federal defense. Lee and Jackson, though far apart, gave the word for the final charge at almost the same moment. As Jackson's army suddenly burst into view and swept forward to the assault the joyful news was shouted down the ranks: "The Valley men are here!" Thereupon Lee's men took up the double-quick with "Stonewall Jackson! Jackson! Jackson!" as their battle cry. The Federals fought right valiantly till their key-point suddenly gave way, smashed in by weight of numbers; for Lee had brought into action half as many again as Porter had, even with his reinforcements. On the gallantly defended hill the long blue lines rocked, reeled, and broke to right and left all but the steadfast regulars, whose infantry fell back in perfect order, whose cavalry made a desperate though futile attempt to stay the rout by charging one against twenty, and whose four magnificent batteries, splendidly served to the very last round, retired unbroken with the loss of only two guns. Then the Confederate colors waved in triumph on the hard-won crest against the crimson of the setting sun.

The victorious Confederates spent the twenty-eighth and twenty-ninth in finding the way to McClellan's new base. His absolute control of all the waterways had enabled him to change his base from White House on the Pamunkey to Harrison's Landing on the James. When the Confederates discovered his line of retreat by the Quaker Road they pressed in to cut it. On the thirtieth there was severe fighting in White Oak Swamp and on Frayser's Farm. But the Federals passed through, and made a fine stand on Malvern Hill next day. Finally, when they turned at bay on the Evelington Heights, which covered Harrison's Landing, they convinced their pursuers that it would be fatal to attack again; for now Northern sea-power was visibly present in flotillas of gunboats, which made the flanks as hopelessly strong as the front.

McClellan therefore remained safely behind his entrenchments, with the navy in support. He had to his own credit the strategic success of having foiled Lee by a clever change of base; and to the credit of his army stood some first-rate fighting besides some tactical success, especially at Malvern Hill. Nevertheless the second invasion of Virginia was plainly a failure; though by no means a glaring disaster, like the first invasion at Bull Run.

McClellan, again reinforced, still professed his readiness to take Richmond under conditions that suited himself. But the most promising Northern force now seemed to be Pope's Army of Virginia, coming down from the line of the Potomac, forty-seven thousand strong, composed of excellent material, and heralded by proclamations which even McClellan could never excel. John Pope, Halleck's hero of Island Number Ten, came from the West to show the East how to fight. "I presume that I have been called here to lead you against the enemy, and that speedily. I hear constantly of taking strong positions and holding them—of lines of retreat and bases of supplies. Let us discard such ideas. Let us study the probable line of retreat of our opponents, and leave our own to take care of themselves." His Army of Virginia contained Frémont's (now Sigel's) corps, as well as those of Banks and McDowell—all experts in the art of "chasing Jackson."

Jackson was soon ready to be chased again. The Confederate strength had been reduced by the Seven Days and not made good by reinforcement; so Lee could spare Jackson only twenty-four thousand men with whom to meet the almost double numbers under Pope. But Jackson's men had the better morale, not only on account of their previous service but because of their rage to beat Pope, who, unlike other Northerners, was enforcing the harshest rules of war. His lieutenant, General von Steinwehr, went further, not only seizing prominent civilians as hostages (to be shot whenever he chose to draw his own distinctions between Confederate soldiers and guerillas) but giving his German subordinates a liberty that some of them knew well how to turn into license. This, of course, was most exceptional;

for nearly all Northerners made war like gentlemen. Unhappily, those who did not were bad enough and numerous enough to infuriate the South.

Halleck, who had now become chief military adviser to the Union Government, was as cautious as McClellan and had so little discernment that he thought Pope a better general than Grant. Lincoln, Stanton, and Halleck put their heads together; and an order soon followed which had the effect of relieving the pressure on Richmond and giving the initiative to Lee. Halleck ordered McClellan to withdraw from Harrison's Landing, take his Army of the Potomac round by sea to Aquia Creek, and join Pope on the Rappahannock—an operation requiring the whole month of August to complete.

Lee lost no time. His first move was to get Pope's advanced troops defeated by Jackson, who brought more than double numbers against Banks at Cedar Run on the ninth of August. The Federals fought magnificently, nine against twenty thousand men. After the battle Jackson marched across the Rapidan, and Halleck wisely forbade Pope from following him, even though the first of Burnside's men (now the advanced guard of McClellan's army) had arrived at Aquia and were marching overland to Pope. Then followed some anxious days at Federal Headquarters. Jackson vanished; and Pope's cavalry, numerous as it was, wore itself out trying to find the clue. McClellan was still busy moving his men from Harrison's Landing to Fortress Monroe, whence detachments kept sailing to Aquia. What would Lee do now?

On the thirteenth he began entraining Longstreet's troops for Gordonsville. On the fifteenth he conferred with his generals. And on the seventeenth, from the lookout on Clark's Mountain, he saw Pope's unsuspecting army camped round Slaughter Mountain within fifteen miles of the united Confederates. Halleck had just given Pope the fatal order to "fight like the devil" till McClellan came up. Pope was full of confidence. And there he lay, in a bad strategic and worse tactical position, and with slightly inferior numbers, just within reach of Jackson and Lee. Pope was, however, saved from immediate disaster by an oversight on the part of Stuart. In ordering Fitzhugh Lee's cavalry brigade to rendezvous at Verdierville that night Stuart forgot to make the order urgent and the missing brigade came in late. Stuart, anxious to see the enemy's position for himself, rode out and was nearly taken prisoner. His dispatch-box fell into Pope's hands, with a memorandum of Jackson's reinforcements. Jackson was for attacking next day in any case and groaned aloud when Lee decided not to, owing to the failure of cavalry combination in front and the belated supplies in the rear. Pope retired safely on the eighteenth, and on the nineteenth a thick haze hid his rear from Lee's lookout.

Lee was now in a very difficult position, apparently face to face with what would soon be the joint forces of Pope, McClellan, and probably another corps from Washington: the whole well fed, well armed, and certainly more than twice as strong as the united Confederates. But Jackson and Stuart multiplied their forces by skillful maneuvers and mystifying raids, and presently Stuart had his revenge for the affront he had suffered on the seventeenth. On the tempestuous night of the twenty-second he captured Pope's dispatches. On the twenty-fourth, at Jefferson, Lee and Jackson discussed the situation with these dispatches before them. Dr. Hunter McGuire, the Confederate staff-surgeon, noticed that Jackson was unusually animated, drawing curves in the sand with the toe of his boot while Lee nodded assent. Perhaps it was Jackson who suggested the strategic idea of that wonderful last week in August. However that may have been, Lee alone was responsible for its adoption and superior direction.

With a marvelous insight into the characters of his opponents, a consummate knowledge of the science and art of war, and—quite as important—an exact appreciation of the risks worth running, Lee actually divided his 55,000 men in face of Pope's 80,000, of 20,000 more at Washington and Aquia, and of 50,000 available reinforcements. Then, by the well-deserved results obtained, he became one of the extremely few really great commanders of all time.

The "bookish theorick" who, with all the facts before him, revels in the fond delights of retrospective prophecy, will never understand how Lee succeeded in this enterprise, except by sheer good luck. Only those who themselves have groped their perilous way through the dense, distorting fog of war can understand the application of that knowledge, genius, and character for war which so rarely unite in one man.

Lee sent Jackson north, to march at utmost speed under cover of the Bull Run Mountains, to cross them at Thoroughfare Gap, and to cut Pope's line at Manassas, where the enormous Federal field base had been established. Unknown to Pope, Longstreet then slipped into Jackson's place, so as to keep Pope in play till the raid on Manassas and threat against Washington would draw him northeast, away from McClellan at Aquia. The final move of this profound, though very daring, plan was to take advantage of the Federal distractions and consequent dispersions so as to effect a junction on the field of battle against a conquerable force.

Jackson moved off by the first gray streak of dawn on the twenty-fifth, and that day made good the six-and-twenty miles to Salem Church. Screened by Stuart's cavalry, and marching through a country of devoted friends on such an errand as a commonplace general would never suspect, Jackson stole this march on Pope in perfect safety. The next day's march was far more dangerous. Roused while the stars were shining the men moved off in even greater wonder as to their destination. But when the first flush of dawn revealed the Bull Run Mountains, with the well-known Thoroughfare Gap straight to their front, they at once divined their part of Lee's stupendous plan: a giant raid on Manassas, the Federal base of superabundant supplies. The news ran down the miles of men, and with it the thrill that presaged victory. Mile after mile was gained, almost in dead silence, except for the clank of harness, the rumble of wheels, the running beat of hoofs, and that long, low, ceaselessly rippling sound of multitudinous men's feet. Hungry, ill-clad, and worn to their last spare ounce, the gaunt gray ranks strained forward, slipped from their leash at last and almost in sight of their prey. So far they were undiscovered. But the Gap was only ten miles by airline from Pope's extreme right, and the tell-tale cloud of dust, floating down the mountain side above them, must soon be sighted, signaled, noted, and attended to. Only speed, the speed of "foot-cavalry," could now prevail, and not a man must be an inch behind. *Close up, men, close up! — Close up there in rear! — Close up! Close up!*

By noon the head of the column had already crossed those same communications which Pope had told his army to disregard in favor of the much more interesting enemy line of retreat. Little did he think that the man he had come to chase was about to burn the bridge at Bristoe Station and thus cut the line between the Federal front at Warrenton and the Federal base at Manassas. All went well with Jackson, except that some news escaped to Washington and Warrenton sooner than he expected. A Federal train dashed on to Washington before the rails could be torn up. The next two trains were both derailed and wrecked. But the fourth put all brakes down and speeded back to Warrenton. Jackson quickly took up a very strong position on the north side of Broad Run, behind the burnt railway bridge, and sent Stuart's troopers with two battalions of "foot-cavalry" to raid the base at Manassas, replenish the exhausted Confederate supplies, and do the northward scouting.

The situation of the rival armies on the night of the twenty-seventh forms one of the curiosities of war. Jackson was concentrating round Manassas Junction. Lee was following Jackson's line of march, but was still beyond Thoroughfare Gap. Between them stood part of Pope's army, the whole of which occupied an irregular quadrilateral formed by lines joining the following points: Warrenton Junction, Bristoe Station, Gainesville, and Thoroughfare Gap. Thirty miles northeast were the twenty thousand Federals who joined Pope too late. Thirty miles southeast the rear of

McClellan's forces were still massing at Aquia. In Pope's opinion Jackson was clearly trapped and Lee cut off.

But when Pope began to close his cumbrous net the following day Jackson had disappeared again. Orders and counter-orders thereupon succeeded each other in bewildering confusion. McClellan could be left out: and a very good thing too, thought Pope, who wanted the victory all to himself, and whose own army greatly outnumbered Lee's and Jackson's put together. But Washington was nervous again; it contained the reinforcements; and it had suddenly become indispensable to Pope as an immediate base of supplies now that the base at Manassas had been so completely destroyed. Pope's troops therefore mostly drew east during the twenty-eighth, forming by nightfall a long irregular line, facing west, with its right beyond Centreville and its extreme left held by Banks's mauled divisions south of Catlett's Station. Meanwhile Jackson had slipped into place in the curve of Bull Run, facing southeast, with his left near Stone Bridge, his back to Sudley Springs, and his right open to junction with Lee, who was waiting for daylight to force the Gap against the single division left there on guard.

During the afternoon, while Jackson's tired men were lying sound asleep in their ranks, Jackson himself was roused to see captured orders which showed that some Federals were crossing his front. Reading these orders to his divisional commanders he immediately ordered one to attack and another to support. If the Federals concerned were exposing an unguarded flank they should be attacked at a disadvantage. If they were screening larger forces trying to join the reinforcements from Washington or Aquia, then they should be attacked so as to distract Pope's attention and draw him on before the Federal union became complete, though not before Lee had reached the new Bull Run position the following day. The attack was consequently made from the woods around Groveton not too long before dark. It resulted in a desperate frontal fight, neither side knowing what the other had in its rear or on its flanks. Again the Federals were outnumbered: twenty-eight against forty-five hundred men in action. But again they fought with the utmost resolution and drew off in good order. The strategic advantage, however, was wholly Confederate; for Pope, who thought Jackson must now be falling back to the Gap, at once began confusedly trying to concentrate for pursuit on the twenty-ninth—the very thing that suited Lee and Jackson best.

Early that morning the two-days' Battle of Second Manassas (or Second Bull Run) began with Pope's absurd attempt to pursue an army drawn up in line of battle. Moreover, Jackson's position was not only strong in itself but well adapted for giving attackers a shattering surprise. The left rested on Bull Run at Sudley Ford. The center occupied the edge of the flat-topped

Stony Ridge. A quarter-mile in front of it, and some way lower down, were the embankments and cuttings of an unfinished railroad. On the right was Stuart's Hill, where Lee was to join by sending Longstreet in. The approaches in rear were hidden from the eyes of an enemy in front. The cuttings and embankments made excellent field works for the defense. And the forward edge of the Ridge was wooded enough to let counter-attackers mass under cover and then run down to surprise the attackers by manning the cuttings and embankments.

Sigel's Germans, supported by the splendid Pennsylvanians under Reynolds, advanced from the Henry Hill to hold Jackson till Pope could come up and finish him. The numbers were about even, with slight odds in favor of Jackson. But the shock was delivered piecemeal. Each part was roughly handled and driven back in disorder. And by the time Reynolds had come to the front Lee's advanced guard was arriving. Then eighteen thousand Federals marched in from Centreville under Reno, Kearny, and "fighting Joe Hooker," of whom we shall hear again. Pope came up in person with the rest of his available command, rode along his line, and explained the situation as founded on his ignorance and colored by his fancy. At this very moment Longstreet came up on Jackson's right. Reynolds went into action against what he thought was Jackson's extended right but what was really Longstreet's left. Meanwhile the Centreville troops attacked near Bull Run. But that dashing commander, Philip Kearny, was held up by Jackson's concentrated guns; so Hooker and Reno advanced alone, straight for the railroad line. The Confederates behind it poured in a tremendous hail of bullets, and the long dry grass caught fire. But nothing stopped Hooker till bayonets were crossed on the rails and the Confederate line was broken. Then the Confederate reserves charged in and drove the Federals back. No sooner was this seen than, with a burst of cheering, another blue line surged forward. Again the Confederate front was broken, but again their reserves drove back the Federals. And so the fight went on, with stroke and counterstroke, till, at a quarter past five, twelve hours after Pope's first men had started from the Henry Hill, his thirty thousand attackers found themselves unable to break through.

Pope wished to make one more effort to round up Jackson's supposedly open right. But Porter quite properly sent back word that it was far too strong for his own ten thousand. In reply Pope angrily ordered an immediate attack. But it was now too dark, and the battle ended for the day.

Strangely enough, Lee was also having trouble with his subordinate on the same flank at the same time, but with this difference, that Porter was right while Longstreet was wrong. Lee saw his chance of rolling up Pope's left and ordered Longstreet to do it. But, after reconnoitering the ground, Longstreet came back to say the chance was "not inviting." Again Lee ordered an attack. But Longstreet wasted time, looking for needlessly favorable ground till long after dark. Meanwhile the Federals were also feeling their way forward over the same ground to get into a good flanking position for next day's battle. So the two sides met; and it was past midnight when Longstreet settled down. Lee wanted a sword thrust. Longstreet gave a pin prick. We shall meet Longstreet again, in the same character of obstructive subordinate, at Gettysburg. But he was, for the most part, a very good officer indeed; and the South, with its scanty supply of trained leaders, could not afford to make changes like the North. The fault, too, was partly Lee's; for his one weak point with good but wayward subordinates was a tendency to let his sensitive consideration for their feelings overcome his sterner insight into their defects.

At noon on the fatal thirtieth of August, Pope, self-deluded and self-sufficient as before, dismayed his best officers by ordering his sixty-five thousand men to be "immediately thrown forward in pursuit of the enemy," whose own fifty thousand were now far readier than on the previous day.

Then the dense blue masses marched to their doom. Twenty thousand bayonets shone together from Groveton to Bull Run. Forty thousand more supported them on the slopes in rear, while every Federal gun thundered forth protectingly from the heights behind. The Confederate batteries were pointed out as the objective of attack. Not one glint of steel appeared between these batteries and the glittering Federal host. To the men in the ranks and to Pope himself victory seemed assured. But no sooner had that brave array come within rifle range of the deserted railroad line than, high and clear, the Confederate bugles called along the hidden edges of the flat-topped Ridge; when instantly the great gray host broke cover, ran forward as one man, and held the whole embankment with a line of fire and steel.

A shock of sheer amazement ran through the Federal mass. Then, knightly as any hero of romance, a mounted officer rode out alone, in front of the center, and, with his sword held high, continued leading the advance, which itself went on undaunted. The Confederate flank batteries crossed their fire on this devoted center. Bayonets flashed out of line in hundreds as their owners fell. Colors were cut down, raised high, cut down again. But still that gallant horse and man went on, unswerving and untouched. Even the sweeping volleys spared them both, though now, as the Federals closed, these volleys cut down more men than the cross-fire of the guns. At last the unscathed hero waved his sword and rode straight up the deadly embankment, followed by the charging line. "Don't kill him! Don't kill him!" shouted the admiring Confederates as his splendid figure stood, one glorious moment, on the top. The next, both horse and man sank wounded, and were at once put under cover by their generous foes.

For thirty-five dire minutes the fight raged face to face. One Federal color rose, fell, and rose again as fast as living hands could take it from the dead. Over a hundred men lay round it when the few survivors drew back to re-form. Pope fed his front line with reserves, who advanced with the same undaunted gallantry, but also with the same result. As if to make this same result more sure he never tried to win by one combined assault, wave after crashing wave, without allowing the defense to get its second wind; but let each unit taste defeat before the next came on. Federal bravery remained. But Federal morale was rapidly disintegrating under the palpable errors of Pope. Misguided, misled, and mishandled, the blue lines still fought on till four, by which time every corps, division, and brigade had failed entirely.

Then, at the perfect moment and in the perfect way, Lee's counterstroke was made: the beaten Federals being assailed in flank as well as front by every sword, gun, bayonet, and bullet that could possibly be brought to bear. Only the batteries remained on the ridge, firing furiously till the Federals were driven out of range. The infantry and cavalry were sent in— wave after wave of them, without respite, till the last had hurled destruction on the foe.

As at the First Bull Run, so here, the regulars fell back in good order, fighting to the very end. But the rest of Pope's Army of Virginia was no longer an organized unit. Even strong reinforcements could do nothing for it now. On the second of September, three days after the battle, its arrival at Washington, heralded by thousands of weary stragglers, threw the whole Union into gloom.

The first counter-invasion naturally followed. Southern hopes ran high. Bragg's invasion of Kentucky seemed to be succeeding at this time. The trans-Mississippi line still held at Vicksburg and Port Hudson. Richmond had been saved. Washington was menaced. And most people on both sides thought so much more of the land than of the sea that the Federal victories along the coast and up the Mississippi were half forgotten for the time being; and so was the strangling blockade. Lee, of course, saw the situation as a whole; and, as a whole, it was far from bright. But though the counter-invasion was now a year too late it seemed worth making. Maryland was full of Southern sympathizers; and campaigning there would give Virginia a chance to recuperate, while also preventing the North from recovering too quickly from its last reverse. Thus it was with great expectations that the Confederates crossed the Potomac singing *Maryland, my Maryland!*

But Maryland did not respond to this appeal. The women, it is true, were mostly Southern to the core and ready to serve the Confederate cause in every way they could. But the men, reflecting more, knew they were in the grip of Northern sea-power. Nor could they fail to notice the vast difference between the warlike resources of the North and South. Northern armies had been marching through for many months, well fed, well armed, and superabundantly supplied. The Confederates, on the other hand, were fewer in numbers, half starved, in ragged clothing, less well armed, and far less abundantly supplied in every way. A Northerner who fell sick could generally count on the best of medical care, not to mention a profusion of medical comforts. But the blockade kept medicines and surgical instruments out of the Southern ports; and the South could make few of her own. So, to be very sick or badly wounded meant almost a sentence of death in the South. Eighteen months of war had disillusioned Maryland. The expected reinforcements never came.

Lee had again divided his army in the hope of snatching victory by means of better strategy. On the thirteenth of September Jackson was bombarding the Federals at Harper's Ferry, Longstreet was at Hagerstown, and Stuart was holding the gaps of South Mountain.

The same day McClellan, whose whole army was at Frederick, received a copy of Lee's orders. They had been wrapped round three cigars and lost by a careless Confederate staff officer. Had McClellan forced the gaps immediately, maneuvered with reasonable skill, and struck home with every available man, he might have annihilated Lee. But he let the thirteenth pass quietly; and when he did take the passes on the fourteenth it cost him a good deal, as the Confederate infantry had reinforced Stuart. On the fifteenth Jackson took Harper's Ferry. On the sixteenth he joined Lee at Antietam. And on the seventeenth, when the remaining availables had also joined Lee, McClellan made up his mind to attack. "Ask me for anything but time," said the real Napoleon. The "Young Napoleon" did not even need the asking.

Antietam (so called from the Antietam Creek) or Sharpsburg (so called from the Confederate headquarters there) was one of the biggest battles of the Civil War; and it might possibly have been the most momentous. But, as things turned out, it was in itself an indecisive action, spoilt for the Federals, first, by McClellan's hesitating strategy, and then by his failure to press the attack home at all costs, with every available man, in an unbroken succession of assaults. He had over 80,000 men with 275 guns against barely 40,000 with 194 guns of inferior strength. But though the Federals fought with magnificent devotion, and though the losses were very serious on both sides, the tactical result was a mutual checkmate. The strategic result, however, was a Confederate defeat; for, with his few worn veterans, Lee had no chance whatever of keeping his precarious hold on a neutral Maryland.

October was a quiet month, each side reorganizing without much interference from the other, except for Stuart's second raid round the whole embattled army of McClellan. This time Stuart took nearly two thousand men and four horse artillery guns. Crossing the Potomac at McCoy's Ford on the tenth he reached Chambersburg that night, destroyed the Federal stores, took all the prisoners he wanted, cut the wires, obstructed the rails, and went on with hundreds of Federal horses. Next day he circled the Federal rear toward Gettysburg, turned south through Emmitsburg, and crossed McClellan's line of communications with Washington at Hyattstown early on the twelfth. By this time the Federal cavalry were riding themselves to exhaustion in vain pursuit; while many other forces were trying to close in and cut him off. But he reached the mouth of the Monocacy and crossed White's Ford in safety, fighting off all interference. The information he brought back was of priceless value. Lee now learned that McClellan was not falling back on Washington but being reinforced from there, and that consequently no new Peninsula Campaign was to be feared at present. This alone was worth the effort, risk, and negligible loss. Stuart had marched a hundred and twenty-six miles on the Federal side of the Potomac—eighty of them without a single halt; and he had been fifty-six hours inside the Federal lines, mostly within four riding hours of McClellan's own headquarters.

This second stinging raid roused the loyal North to fury; and by November a new invasion of Virginia was in full swing on the old ground, with McClellan at Warrenton, Lee at Culpeper, and Jackson in the Valley.

But McClellan's own last chance had gone. Late at night on the seventh he was sitting alone in his tent, writing to his wife, when Burnside asked if he could come in with General C. P. Buckingham, the confidential staff officer to the War Department. After some forced conversation Buckingham handed McClellan a paper ordering his supersession by Burnside. McClellan simply said: "Well, Burnside, I turn the command over to you." The eighth and ninth were spent in handing over; and on the tenth McClellan made his official farewell. Next day he was entraining at Warrenton Junction when the men, among whom he was immensely popular, broke ranks and swarmed round his car, cursing the Government and swearing they would follow no one but their "Old Commander." McClellan, with all his faults in the field, was a good organizer, an extremely able engineer, a very brave soldier, a very sympathetic comrade in arms, and a regular father to his men, whose personal interests were always his first care. The moment was critical. McClellan, had he chosen, might have imitated the Roman generals who led the revolts of Prætorian Guards. But he stepped out on the front platform of the car, held up his hand, and, amid tense silence, asked the men to "stand by General Burnside as you have stood by me." The car they had uncoupled to prevent his departure was run up and coupled again; and then, amid cheers of mournful farewell, they let him go.

General Ambrose E. Burnside was expected to smash Lee, take Richmond, and end the war at once. He was a good subordinate, but quite unfit for supreme command, which he accepted only under protest. Moreover, he was not supported as he should have been by the War Department, nor even by the Headquarter Staff. While changing his position from Warrenton to Fredericksburg he was hampered by avoidable delays. So when he reached Falmouth he found Lee had forestalled him on the opposing heights of Fredericksburg itself.

The disastrous thirteenth of December was dull, calm, and misty. But presently the sun shone down with unwonted warmth; the mists rolled up like curtains; and there stood 200,000 men, arrayed in order of battle: 80,000 Confederates awaiting the onslaught of 120,000 Federals.

On came the solid masses of the Federals, eighty thousand strong, with forty in support, amid the thunder of five hundred attacking and defending guns. The sunlight played upon the rising tide of Federal bayonets as on sea currents when they turn inshore. The colors waved proudly as ever; and to the outward eye the attack seemed almost strong enough to drive the stern and silent gray Confederates clear off the crest. But the indispensable morale was wanting. For this was the end of a long campaign, full of drawn battles and terrible defeats. Burnside was an unpopular substitute for McClellan; he was not in any way a great commander; and he was acting under pressure against his own best judgment. His army knew or felt all this; and he knew they knew or felt it. The Federals, for all their glorious courage, felt, when the two fronts met at Fredericksburg, that they were no more than sacrificial pawns in the grim game of war. After much useless slaughter they reeled back beaten. But they could and did retire in safety, skillfully "staffed" by their leaders and close to their unconquerable sea.

Lee could make no counterstroke. The Confederate Government had not dared to let him occupy the far better position on the line of the North Anna, from which a vigorous counterstroke might have almost annihilated a beaten attacker, who would have been exposed on both flanks, beyond the sure protection of the sea. Thus fear of an outcry against "abandoning" the country between Fredericksburg and the North Anna caused the Southern politicians to lose their chance at home. But without a decisive victory they could not hope for foreign intervention. So losing their chance at home made them lose it abroad as well.

Burnside was dazed by his defeat and the appalling loss of life in vain. But after five weeks of most discouraging inaction he tried to surprise Lee by crossing the Rappahannock several miles higher up. On the twentieth and twenty-first of that miserable January the Federal army ploughed its dreary way through sloughs of gluey mud under torrents of chilling rain. Then, when the pace had slackened to a funereal crawl, and the absurdly little chance of surprising Lee had vanished altogether, this despairing "Mud March" came to its wretched end. Four days later Burnside was superseded by one of his own subordinates, General Joseph Hooker, known to all ranks as "Fighting Joe Hooker."

Fredericksburg, the spell of relaxing winter quarters beside the fatal Rappahannock, and then the fatal "Mud March," combined to lower Federal morale. Yet the mass of the men, being composed of fine human material, quickly recovered under "Fighting Joe Hooker," who knew what discipline meant. Numbers and discipline tell. But disciplined numbers were not the only or even the greatest menace to the South. For here, as farther west, the Confederate Government was beginning to be foolish just as the Federal Government showed signs of growing wise. Lincoln and Stanton were giving Joe Hooker a fairly free hand just when Davis and Seddon (his makeshift minister of war) were using Confederate forces as puppets to be pulled about by Cabinet strings from Richmond. Here again (as later on at Chattanooga) Longstreet was sent away on a useless errand just when he was needed most by Lee. Good soldier though he was in many ways he was no such man as Stonewall Jackson; and, in this one year, he failed his seniors thrice.

It is true enough that the April situation of 1863 might well shake governmental nerves; for Richmond was being menaced from three points—north, southeast, and south: Fredericksburg due north, Suffolk southeast, Newbern south. Newbern in North Carolina was a long way off. But its possession by an active enemy threatened the rail connection from Richmond south to Wilmington, Charleston, and Savannah, the only three Atlantic ports through which the South could get supplies from overseas. Suffolk was nearer. It covered the landward side of Norfolk, which, with Fortress Monroe, might become the base of a new Peninsula Campaign. But Fredericksburg was nearest; nearest to Richmond, nearest to Washington, nearest to the main Southern force; and not only nearest but strongest, in every way strongest and most to be feared. "Fighting Joe Hooker" was there, with a hundred and thirty thousand men, already stirring for the spring campaign that was to wipe out memories of Fredericksburg, make short work of Lee, and end the war at Richmond.

Yet Longstreet cheerfully marched off, pleased with his new command, to see what he could do to soothe the Government by winning laurels for himself at Suffolk. On the seventeenth, just two weeks before the supreme test came on Lee's weakened army at Chancellorsville, Longstreet reported to Seddon that Suffolk would cost three thousand men, if taken by assault, or three days' heavy firing if subdued by bombardment. Shrinking from such expenditure of life or ammunition, Davis, Seddon, and Longstreet fell back on a siege, which, preventing all junction with Lee, might well have cost the ruin of their cause.

Lee and Jackson then prepared to make the best of a bad business along the Rappahannock, and to snatch victory once more, if possible, from the very jaws of death. The prospect was grimmer than before. Hooker was a better fighter than McClellan and wiser than Burnside or Pope. Moreover, after two years of war, the Union Government had at last found out that civilian detectives knew less about armies than expert staff officers know, and that cavalry which was something more than mere men on horses could collect a little information too. Hooker knew Lee's strength as well as his own. So he decided to hold Lee fast with one part of the big Federal army, turn his flank with another, and cut his line of supply and retreat with Stoneman's ten thousand sabers as well. The respective grand totals were 130,000 Federals against 62,000 Confederates.

So far, so good; so very good indeed that Hooker and his staff were as nearly free from care on May Day as headquarter men can ever be in the midst of vital operations. Hooker had just reason to be proud of the Army of the Potomac and of his own work in reviving it. He had, indeed, issued one bombastic order of the day in which he called it "the finest on the planet." But even this might be excused in view of the popular call for encouraging words. What was more to the point was the reëstablishment of Federal morale, which had been terribly shaken after the great Mud March. Hooker's sworn evidence (as given in the official *Report of Committee on the Conduct of the War*) speaks for itself: "The moment I was placed in command I caused a return to be made of the absentees of the army, and found the number to be 2922 commissioned officers and 81,964 non-commissioned officers and privates. They were scattered all over the country, and the majority were absent from causes unknown."

On the twenty-eighth of April Stuart saw the redisciplined Federals in motion far up the Rappahannock, while next day Jackson saw others laying pontoons thirty miles lower down, just on the seaward side of Fredericksburg. Lee took this news with genial calm, remarking to the aide: "Well, I heard firing and was beginning to think it was time some of your lazy young fellows were coming to tell me what it was about. Tell your good general he knows what to do with the enemy just as well as I do." On the thirtieth it became quite clear that Hooker was bent on turning Lee's left and that he had divided his army to do so. Jackson wished to attack Sedgwick's 35,000 Federals still on the plains of Fredericksburg. But Lee convinced him that the better way would be to hold these men with 10,000 Confederates in the fortified position on the confronting heights while the remaining 52,000 should try to catch Hooker himself between the jaws of a trap in the forest round Chancellorsville, where the Federal masses would be far more likely to get out of hand. It was an extremely daring maneuver to be setting this trap when Sedgwick had enough men to storm the heights of Fredericksburg, when Stoneman was on the line of communication with the south, and when Hooker himself, with superior numbers, was gaining Lee's rear. But Lee had Jackson as his lieutenant, not Longstreet, as he was to have at Gettysburg.

Hooker's movements were rapid, well arranged, and admirably executed up to the evening of the first of May, when, finding those of the enemy very puzzling among the dense woods, he chose the worst of three alternatives. The first and best, an immediate counter-attack, would have kept up his army's morale and, if well executed, revealed his own greater strength. The second, a continued advance till he reached clearer ground, might have succeeded or not. The third and worst was to stand on his defense, a plan which, however sound in other places, was fatal here, because it not only depressed the spirits of his army but gave two men of genius the initiative against him in a country where they were at home and he was not. The absence of ten thousand cavalry baffled his efforts to get trustworthy information on the ground, while the dense woods baffled his balloons from above. On the second of May he still thought the initiative was his, that the Confederates were retreating, and that his own jaws were closing on them instead of theirs on him.

Meanwhile, owing to miscalculations of the space that had to be held in force, his right was not only thrown forward too far but presented a flank in the air. This was the flank round which Stonewall Jackson maneuvered with such consummate skill that it was taken on three sides and rolled up in fatal confusion. Its commander, the very capable General O. O. Howard, who perceived the mistake he could not correct, tried hard to stay the rout. But, as his whole reserve had been withdrawn by Hooker to join an attack elsewhere, his lines simply melted away.

The three days' battle that followed (ending on the fifth of May) was bravely fought by the bewildered Federals. Yet all in vain. Hooker was caught like a bull in a net; and the more he struggled the worse it became. At 6 P.M. on the second the cunning trap was sprung when a single Confederate bugle rang out. Instantly other bugles repeated the call at regular intervals through miles of forest. Then, high and clear on the silent air of that calm May evening, the rebel yell rose like the baying of innumerable hounds, hot on the scent of their quarry, with Jackson leading on. Nothing could stop the eager gray lines, wave after wave of them pressing through the woods; not even the gallant fifty guns that fought with desperation in defense of Hazel Grove, where Hooker was rallying his men.

For two days more the tide of battle ebbed and flowed; but always against the Federals in the end, till, broken, bewildered, and disheartened, they retired as best they could. Lee was unable to pursue. Longstreet's men were still missing; and so were many supplies that should have been forwarded from Richmond. There the Government clung to the fond belief that this mere victory had won the war, and that pursuit was useless. Thus Lee's last chance of crushing the invaders was taken from him by his friends.

At the same time the Southern cause suffered another irreparable loss; but in this case at the purely accidental hands of Southern men. Jackson's staff, suddenly emerging from a thicket as the first night closed in, was mistaken for Federal cavalry and shot down. Jackson himself was badly wounded in three places and carried from the field. He never heard the rebel yell again. Next Sunday, when the staff-surgeon told him that he could not possibly live through the night, he simply answered: "Very good, very good; it is all right." Presently he asked Major Pendleton what chaplain was preaching at headquarters. "Mr. Lacy, sir; and the whole army is praying for you." "Thank God," said Jackson, "they are very kind to me." A little later, rousing himself as if from sleep, he called out: "Order A. P. Hill to prepare for action! Pass the infantry to the front! Tell Major Hawks—" There his strength failed him. But after a pause he said quietly, "Let us cross over the river and rest under the shade of the trees." And with these words he died.

CHAPTER VII
GRANT WINS THE RIVER WAR: 1863

We have seen already how the River War of '62 ended in a double failure of the Federal advance on Vicksburg: how Grant and Sherman, aided by the flanking force from Helena in Arkansas, failed to catch Pemberton along the Tallahatchie; and then how Sherman alone, moving down the Mississippi, was defeated by Pemberton at Chickasaw Bayou, just outside of Vicksburg.

Leaving Memphis for good, Grant took command in the field again on the thirtieth of January. His army was strung out along seventy miles of the Mississippi just north of Vicksburg, so hard was it to find enough firm ground. The first important move was made when, in Grant's own words, "the entire Army of the Tennessee was transferred to the neighborhood of Vicksburg and landed on the opposite or western bank of the river at Milliken's Bend."

Grant, everywhere in touch with Admiral D. D. Porter's fleet and plentifully supplied with water transport of all kinds, thus commanded the peninsula or tongue of low land round which the mighty river took its course in the form of an elongated U right opposite Vicksburg. His farthest north base was still at Cairo; and the whole line of the Mississippi above him was effectively held by Union forces afloat and ashore. Four hundred miles south lay Farragut and Banks, preparing for an attack on Port Hudson and intent on making junction with the Union forces above.

Two bad generals stood very much in Grant's way, one on either side of him in rank—McClernand, his own second-in-command, and Banks, his only senior in the Mississippi area. McClernand presently found rope enough to hang himself. Our old friend Banks, who had not yet learnt the elements of war, though schooled by Stonewall Jackson, never got beyond Port Hudson, and so could not spoil Grant's command in addition to his own. Fortunately, besides Sherman and other professional soldiers of quite exceptional ability, Grant had three of the best generals who ever came from civil life: Logan, Blair, and Crocker. Logan shed all the vices, while keeping all the virtues, of the lawyer when he took up arms. Blair knew how to be one man as an ambitious politician and another as a general in the field.

Crocker was in consumption, but determined to die in his boots and do his military best for the Union service first. The personnel of the army was mostly excellent all through. The men were both hardy and handy as a rule, being to a large extent farmers, teamsters, railroad and steamboat men, well fitted to meet the emergencies of the severe and intricate Vicksburg campaign.

Throughout this campaign the army and navy of the Union worked together as a single amphibious force. Grant's own words are no mere compliment, but the sober statement of a fact. "The navy, under Porter, was all it could be during the entire campaign. Without its assistance the campaign could not have been successfully made with twice the number of men engaged. It could not have been made at all, in the way it was, with any number of men, without such assistance. The most perfect harmony reigned between the two arms of the Service. There never was a request made, that I am aware of, either of the Flag-Officer or any of his subordinates, that was not promptly complied with." And what is true of Porter is at least as true of Farragut, who was the greater man and the senior of every one afloat.

Grant could take Vicksburg only by reaching good ground, and the only good ground was below and in rear of the fortress. There was no foothold for his army on the east bank of the Mississippi anywhere between Memphis and Vicksburg. This meant that he must either start afresh from Memphis and try again to push overland by rail or cross the swampy peninsula in front of him and circle round his enemy. A retirement on Memphis, no matter how wise, would look like another great Union defeat and consequently lower a public morale which, depressed enough by Fredericksburg, was being kept down by the constant naval reverses that opened '63. Circling the front was therefore very much to be preferred from the political point of view. On the other hand, it was beset by many alarming difficulties; for it meant starting from the flooded Mississippi and working through the waterlogged lowlands, across the peninsula, till a foothold could be seized on the eastern bank below Vicksburg. Moreover, this circling attack, though feasible, might depress the morale of the troops by the way. Burnside's disastrous "Mud March" through the January sloughs of Virginia, made in the vain hope of outflanking Lee, had lowered the morale of the army almost as much as Fredericksburg itself had lowered the morale of the people.

Through the depth of winter the army toiled "in ineffectual efforts," says Grant, "to reach high land above Vicksburg from which we could operate against that stronghold, and in making artificial waterways through which a fleet might pass, avoiding the batteries to the south of the town, in case the other efforts should fail." A wetter winter had never been known. The whole complicated network of bends and bayous, of creeks, streams, runs, and tributary rivers, was overflowing the few slimy trails through the spongy forest and threatening the neglected levees which still held back the encroaching waters. There was nothing to do, however, but to keep the men busy and the enemy confused by trying first one line and then another for two weary months. By April, writes Grant, "the waters of the Mississippi having receded sufficiently to make it possible to march an army across the peninsula opposite Vicksburg, I determined to adopt this course, and moved my advance to a point below the town."

Meanwhile, far below, Farragut and Banks were at work round Port Hudson: Farragut to good effect; Banks as usual. On the fourteenth of March Farragut started up the river with seven men-of-war and wanted the troops to make a demonstration against Port Hudson from the rear while the fleet worked its way past the front. But, just as Farragut was weighing anchor, Banks, who had had ample time for preparation, sent word to say he was still five miles from Port Hudson. "He'd as well be at New Orleans," muttered Farragut, "for all the good he's doing us."

Six of the vessels were lashed together in pairs, the heavier ones next the enemy, the lighter ones secured well aft so as to mask the fewest guns. This arrangement also gave each pair the advantage of having twin screws. Farragut's flagship, the *Hartford*, leading the line-ahead, suffered least from the dense smoke on that damp, calm, moonless night. But the others were soon groping blindly up the tortuous channel. The *Hartford* herself took the ground for a critical moment. But, with her own screw going ahead and that of the *Albatross* going astern, she drew clear and won through. Not so, however, the other five ships. Only the *Hartford* and *Albatross* reached the Red River. Yet even this was of great importance, as it completely cut off Port Hudson from all chance of relief. Farragut went on up the Mississippi to see Grant, destroying all riverside stores on the way. Grant was delighted, and, in the absence of Porter, who was up the Yazoo, sent Farragut an Ellet ram and some sorely needed coal.

Grant's seventh (and first successful) effort to get a foothold (from which to carry out one of the boldest and most brilliant operations recorded in the history of war) began with a naval operation on the sixteenth of April, when Porter ran past the Vicksburg batteries by night. Though Porter had the four-knot current in his favor he needed all his skill and moral courage to take a regular flotilla round the elongated U made by the Mississippi at Vicksburg, with such a bend as to keep vessels under more or less distant fire for five miles, and under much closer fire for nearly nine. At the bend the vessels could be caught end-on. For nearly five miles after that they were subject to a plunging fire. Porter led the way on board the flagship *Benton*. He had seven ironclads, of which three were larger vessels and four were gunboats built by Eads, a naval constructor with orignal ideas and great executive ability. One ram and three transports followed. Coal barges were lashed alongside or taken in tow. Some of these were lost and one transport was sunk. But the rest got through, though not unscathed. It seemed like a miracle to the tense spectators that any flotilla should survive this dash down a river of death flowing through a furnace. But the ironclads, magnificently handled, stood up to their work unflinchingly, fired back with regulated vigor, and took their terrific pounding without one vital wound.

Porter presently relieved Farragut, who went back to New Orleans. From this time, till after the fall of Vicksburg and Port Hudson, Porter commanded three flotillas, each with a base of its own: first, a flotilla remaining north of Vicksburg for work on the Yazoo; secondly, the main body between Vicksburg and Grand Gulf; thirdly, the Red River flotilla. This combined naval force commanded all lines of communication north, south, and west of Vicksburg, thus enabling Grant to concentrate entirely against the eastern side.

On the thirtieth of April Grant landed with twenty thousand men at Bruinsburg, on the east side of the Mississippi, about sixty miles below Vicksburg. A week later Sherman reinforced him to thirty-three thousand. Before the fall of Vicksburg his total strength reached seventy-five thousand. The Confederate total also fluctuated; but not so much. There were about sixty thousand Confederates in the whole strategic area between Vicksburg and Jackson (fifty miles east) when Grant made his first daring move, and about the same when Vicksburg surrendered. The scene of action was almost triangular; for it lay between the three lines joining Jackson, Haynes's Bluff, Rodney, and Jackson again. The respective lengths of these straight lines are forty, fifty, and seventy miles. But roundabout ways by land and water multiplied these distances, and much fighting and many obstacles vastly increased Grant's difficulties.

An army, however, that had managed to reach Bruinsburg from the north and west was assuredly fit for more hard work of any kind; while a commander who had left a safe base above Vicksburg and landed below, to live on (as well as in) an enemy country till victory should give him a new land line to the north, must, in view of the resultant triumph, be counted among the master-minds of war. Grant's marvelous skill in massing, dividing, forwarding, and concentrating his forces over a hundred miles of intricate passages between Milliken's Bend and Bruinsburg was only excelled by his consummate genius in carrying out this daring operation, forcing his way through his enemies, into full possession of interior lines, between their great garrison of Vicksburg and their field army from Jackson.

He had to create two fronts in spite of his doubled enemy and live on that enemy's country without any land base of his own.

Grant knew the country was quite able to support his army if he could only control enough of it. Bread, beef, and mutton would be almost unobtainable. But chickens, turkeys, and ducks were abundant, while hard-tack would do instead of bread. Bird-and-biscuit of course became unpopular; and after weeks of it Grant was not surprised to hear a soldier mutter "hard-tack" loudly enough for others to take up the cry. By this time, however, he luckily knew that the bread ration was about to be resumed; and when he told the men they cheered as only men on service can—men to whom battles are rare events but rations the very stuff of daily existence. Coffee, bacon, beef, and mutton came next in popular favor when full rations were renewed. So when the Northern land line was reopened towards the end of the siege, and friends came into camp with presents from home, they found, to their amazement, that even the tenderest spring chicken was loathsome to their boys in blue.

Grant set to work immediately on landing. His first objective was Grand Gulf, which he wanted as a field base for further advance. But in order to get it he had to drive away the enemy from Port Gibson, which was by no means easy, even with superior numbers, because the whole country thereabouts was so densely wooded and so intricately watered that concerted movements could only be made along the few and conspicuous roads. On the first of May, however, the Confederates were driven off before their reinforcements could arrive. McClernand bungled brigades and divisions out of mutual support. But Grant personally put things right again.

By the third of May the bridge burnt by the enemy had been repaired and Grant's men were crossing to press them back on Vicksburg, so as to clear Grand Gulf. Grant's supply train (raised by impressing every horse, mule, ox, and wheeled thing in the neighborhood) looked more like comic opera than war. Fine private carriages, piled high with ammunition, and sometimes drawn by mules with straw collars and rope lines, went side by side with the longest plantation wagons drawn by many oxen, or with a two-wheeled cart drawn by a thoroughbred horse.

Before any more actions could be fought news came through that the Federals in Virginia had been terribly beaten by Lee, who was now expected to invade the North. The South was triumphant; so much so, indeed, that its Government thought the war itself had now been won. But Lincoln, Grant, and Lee knew better.

Swiftly, silently, and with a sure strategic touch, Grant marched northeast on Jackson, to make his rear secure before he turned on Vicksburg. On the twelfth he won at Raymond and on the fourteenth at Jackson itself. Here he turned back west again. On the sixteenth he won the stubborn fight of Champion's Hill, on the seventeenth he won again at Big Black River, and on the eighteenth he appeared before the lines of Vicksburg. With the prestige of five victories in twenty days, and with the momentum acquired in the process, he then tried to carry the lines by assault on the spot. But the attack of the nineteenth failed, as did its renewal on the twenty-second. Next day both sides settled down to a six weeks' siege.

The failure of the two assaults was recognized by friend and foe as being a mere check; and Grant's men all believed they had now found the looked-for leader. So they had. Like Lee and Stonewall Jackson in Virginia, Grant, with as yet inferior numbers (but with the immense advantage of sea-power), had seized, held, and acted on interior lines so ably that his forty-three thousand men had out-maneuvered and out-fought the sixty thousand of the enemy, beating them in detail on ground of their own besides inflicting a threefold loss. Grant lost little over four thousand. The Confederates lost nearly twelve thousand, half of whom were captured.

The only real trouble, besides the failure to carry the lines by assault, was with the two bad generals, McClernand and Banks. McClernand had promulgated an order praising his own corps to the skies and conveying the idea that he and it had won the battles. Moreover, he hinted that he had succeeded in the assault while the others had failed. This was especially offensive because Grant, at McClernand's urgent request, had sent reinforcements from other corps to confirm a success that he found nonexistent on the spot, except in McClernand's own words. To crown this, McClernand had sent his official order, with all its misleading statements, to be published in the Northern press; and the whole army was now supplied with the papers containing it. So gross a breach of discipline could not go unpunished; and McClernand was sent back to Springfield in disgrace.

Banks, unfortunately, was senior to Grant and of course independent of Farragut; so he could safely vex them both—Grant, by spoiling the plan of concerting the attacks on Port Hudson and Vicksburg in May; Farragut, by continual failure in coöperation and by leaving big guns exposed to capture on the west bank. But things turned out well, after all. The guns were saved by the naval vessels that beat off a Confederate attack on Donaldsonville; and Grant's army was saved from coming under Banks's command by Banks's own egregious failure in coöperation. This failure thus became a blessing in disguise: a disguise too good for Halleck, whose reprimand from Washington on the twenty-third of May shows what dangers lurked beneath the might-have-been. "The Government is exceedingly disappointed that you and General Grant are not acting in conjunction. It thought to secure that object by authorizing you to assume the entire command as soon as you and General Grant could unite."

In the end the Confederates suffered much more than the Federals from civilian interference; for the orders of their Government came through in time to confuse a situation that was already bad and growing worse. Between Porter afloat and Grant ashore Vicksburg was doomed unless "Joe" Johnston came west with sufficient force to relieve it in time. Johnston did come early enough, but not in sufficient force; so the next best thing was to destroy all stores, abandon Vicksburg, and save the garrison. The Government, however, sent positive orders to hold Vicksburg to the very last gasp. Johnston had meanwhile sent Pemberton (the Vicksburg commander) orders to combine with him in free maneuvering for an attack in the field. But Pemberton's own idea was to await Grant on the Big Black River, where, with Johnston's help, he thought he could beat him. Then followed hesitation, a futile attempt to harmonize the three incompatible schemes; and presently the division of the Confederates into separated armies, driven apart by Grant, whose own army soon dug itself in between them and quickly grew stronger than both.

Grant's lines, facing both opponents, from Haynes's Bluff to Warrenton, were fifteen miles long, which gave him one man per foot when his full strength was reached Pemberton's were only seven; and his position was strong, both towards the river, where the bluffs rose two hundred feet, and on the landward side, where the slopes were sharp and well fortified. Grant closed in, however, and pressed the bombardment home. Except for six 32-pounders and a battery of big naval guns he had nothing but field artillery. Yet the abundance of ammunition, the closeness of the range, and the support of his many excellent snipers, soon gave him the upper hand. Six hundred yards was the farthest the lines were apart. In some places they nearly touched.

All ranks worked hard, especially at engineering, in which there was such a dearth of officers that Grant ordered every West Pointer to do his turn with the sappers and miners as well as his other duty. This brought forth a respectful protest from the enormously fat Chief Commissary, who said he could only be used as a sap-roller (the big roller sappers shove protectingly before them when snipers get their range). The real sap-rollers came to grief when an ingenious Confederate stuffed port-fires with turpentined cotton and shot them into rollers only a few yards off. But after this the Federals kept their rollers wet; and sapped and burrowed till the big mine was fully charged and safe from the Confederate countermine, which had missed its mark.

While trying to blow each other up the men on both sides exchanged amenities and chaff like the best of friends. Each side sold its papers to the other; and the wall-paper newsprint of Vicksburg made a good war souvenir for both. There was a steady demand for Federal bread and Confederate tobacco. When market time was over the Confederates would heave down hand-grenades, which agile Federals, good at baseball, would heave uphill again before they exploded. And woe to the man whose head appeared out of hours; for snipers were always on the watch, especially that prince of snipers, Lieutenant H. C. Foster, renowned as "Coonskin" from the cap he wore. A wonderful stalker and dead shot he was a terror to exposed Confederates at all times; but more particularly towards the end, when (their front artillery having been silenced by Grant's guns) Coonskin built a log tower, armored with railway iron, from which he picked off men who were safe from ordinary fire.

On the twenty-first of June Pemberton planned an escape across the Mississippi and built some rough boats. But Grant heard of this; the flotilla grew more watchful still; and before any attempt at escape could be made the great mine was fired on the twenty-fifth. The whole top of the hill was blown off, and with it some men who came down alive on the Federal side. Among these was an unwounded but terrified colored man, who, on being asked how high he had gone, said, "Dunno, Massa, but t'ink 'bout t'ree mile." An immense crater was formed. But there was no practicable breach; so the assault was deferred. A second mine was exploded on the first of July. But again there was no assault; for Grant had decided to wait till several huge mines could be exploded simultaneously. In the meantime an intercepted dispatch warned him that Johnston would try to help Pemberton to cut his way out. But by the time the second mine was exploded Pemberton was sounding his generals about the chances of getting their own thirty thousand to join Johnston's thirty thousand against Grant's seventy-five thousand. The generals said No. Negotiations then began.

On the third of July Grant met Pemberton under the "Vicksburg Oak," which, though quite a small tree, furnished souvenir-hunters with many cords of sacred wood in after years. Grant very wisely allowed surrender on parole, which somewhat depleted Confederate ranks in the future by the number of men who, returning to their homes, afterwards refused to come back when the exchange of prisoners would have permitted them to do so.

That was a great week of Federal victory—the week including the third, fourth, and eighth of July. On the third Lee was defeated at Gettysburg. On the now doubly "Glorious Fourth" Vicksburg surrendered and the last Confederate attack was repulsed at Helena in Arkansas. On the eighth Port Hudson surrendered. With this the whole Mississippi fell into Federal hands for good. On the first of August Farragut left New Orleans for New York in the battle-scarred *Hartford* after turning over the Mississippi command to Porter's separate care.

Meanwhile the Confederates in Tennessee, weakened by reinforcing Johnston against Grant, had been obliged to retire on Chattanooga. To cover this retirement and make what diversion he could, Bragg sent John H. Morgan with twenty-five hundred cavalry to raid Kentucky, Indiana, and Ohio. Perplexing the outnumbering Federals by his daring, "Our Jack Morgan" crossed the Ohio at Brandenburg, rode northeast through Indiana, wheeled south at Hamilton, Ohio, rode through the suburbs of Cincinnati, reached Buffington Island on the border of West Virginia, and then, hotly pursued by ever-increasing forces, made northeast toward Pennsylvania. On the twenty-sixth of July he surrendered near New Lisbon with less than four hundred men left.

The Confederate main body passed the summer vainly trying to stem the advance of the Army of the Cumberland, with which Rosecrans and Thomas skillfully maneuvered Bragg farther and farther south till they had forced him into and out of Chattanooga. In the meantime Burnside's Army of the Ohio cleared eastern Tennessee and settled down in Knoxville.

But in the middle of September Longstreet came to Bragg's rescue; and a desperate battle was fought at Chickamauga on the nineteenth and twentieth. The Confederates had seventy thousand men against fifty-six thousand Federals: odds of five to four. They were determined to win at any price; and it cost them eighteen thousand men, killed, wounded, and missing; which was two thousand more than the Federals lost. But they felt it was now or never as they turned to bay with, for once, superior numbers. As usual, too, they coveted Federal supplies. "Come on, boys, and charge!" yelled an encouraging sergeant, "they have cheese in their haversacks!" Yet the pride of the soldier stood higher than hunger. General D. H. Hill stooped to cheer a very badly wounded man. "What's your regiment?" asked Hill. "Fifth Confederate, New Orleans, and a damned good regiment it is," came the ready answer.

Rosecrans, like many another man who succeeds halfway up, failed at the top. He ordered an immediate general retreat which would have changed the hard-won Confederate victory into a Federal rout. But Thomas, with admirable judgment and iron nerve, stood fast till he had shielded all the others clear. From this time on both armies knew him as the "Rock of Chickamauga."

The unexpected defeat of Chickamauga roused Washington to immediate, and this time most sensible, action. Grant was given supreme command over the whole strategic area. Thomas superseded Rosecrans. Sherman came down with the Army of the Tennessee. And Hooker railed through from Virginia with two good veteran corps. Meanwhile the Richmond Government was more foolish than the Washington was wise; for it let Davis mismanage the strategy without any reference to Lee. Bragg also made a capital mistake by sending Longstreet off to Knoxville with more than a third of his command just before Grant's final advance. The result was that Bragg found himself with only thirty thousand men at Chattanooga when Grant closed in with sixty thousand, and that Longstreet was useless at Knoxville, which was entirely dependent on Chattanooga. Whoever won decisively at Chattanooga could have Knoxville too. Davis, as the highest authority, and Bragg, as the most responsible subordinate, ensured their own defeat.

Chattanooga was the key to the whole strategic area of the upper Tennessee; for it was the best road, rail, and river junction between the lower Mississippi and the Atlantic ports of the South. It had been held for some time by a Federal garrison which had made it fairly strong. But toward the end of October it was short of supplies; and Hooker had to fight Longstreet at Wauhatchie in the Lookout Valley before it could be revictualed. When Hooker, Thomas, and Sherman were there together under Grant in November it was of course perfectly safe; and the problem changed from defense to attack. The question was how to drive Bragg from his commanding positions on Missionary Ridge and Lookout Mountain. The woods and hills offered concealment to the attack in some places. But Lookout Mountain was a splendid observation post, twenty-two hundred feet high and crested with columns of rock. The Ridge was three miles east, the Mountain three miles south, of Cameron Hill, which stood just west of Chattanooga, commanding the bridge of boats that crossed the Tennessee.

The battle, fought with great determination on both sides, lasted three days—the twenty-third, twenty-fourth, and twenty-fifth of November. Sherman made the flank attack on Missionary Ridge from the north and Thomas the frontal attack from the west. Hooker attacked the western flank of Lookout Mountain.

Thomas did the first day's fighting, which was all preliminary work, by advancing a good mile, taking the Confederate lines on the lower slopes of the Ridge, and changing their defensive features to face the Ridge instead of Chattanooga.

At two the next morning Giles Smith's brigade dropped down the Tennessee in boats and surprised the extreme north pickets placed by Bragg at the mouth of the South Chickamauga to cover the right of the Ridge. By noon Sherman's men were over the Tennessee ready to coöperate with Thomas. Sherman had hidden his camp among the hills on the other side so well that his movements could not be observed, even from the commanding height of Lookout Mountain. The night surprise of Bragg's pickets and the drizzling rain of the morning prevented the Confederates from hearing or seeing anything of Sherman's attack in the early afternoon; so he found himself on the northern flank of Missionary Ridge before Bragg's main body knew what he was doing. When the Confederates did attack it was too late; and the twenty-fourth ended with Sherman entrenched against the flank on even higher ground than Thomas held against the center. Sherman's cavalry had meanwhile moved round the flank, on the lower level and much farther off, to cut Bragg's right rear connection with Chickamauga Station, whence the rails ran east to Cleveland, Knoxville, and Virginia.

Hooker's work this second day was to feel the Confederate force on Lookout Mountain while keeping the touch with Thomas, who kept the touch with Sherman. Mists hid his earlier maneuvers. He closed in successfully, handled his men to admiration, and gained more ground than either he or Grant had expected. Having succeeded so well he changed his demonstration into a regular attack, which became known as the "Battle above the Clouds." Step by step he fought his way up, over breastworks and rifle pits, felled trees and bowlders, through ravines and gullies, till the vanguard reached the giant palisades of rock which ramparted the top. The roar of battle was most distinctly heard four miles away, on Orchard Knob, where Grant and Thomas were anxiously waiting. But nothing could be seen until a sudden breeze blew the clouds aside just as the long blue lines charged home and the broken gray retreated. Then, from thirty thousand watching Federals, went up a cheer that even cannon could not silence.

At midnight Grant sent a word of encouragement to Burnside at Knoxville. He then wrote his orders for what he now hoped would be a completely victorious attack. The twenty-fifth of November broke beautifully clear, and the whole scene of action remained in full view all day long. Fearful of being cut off from their main body on Missionary Ridge the Confederates had left Lookout Mountain under cover of the dark. But by destroying the bridges across the Chattanooga River, which ran through the valley between the Mountain and the Ridge, they delayed Hooker till late that afternoon, thus saving their left from an even worse disaster than the one that overtook their center and their right.

Sherman had desperate work against their right, as Bragg massed every available gun and man to meet him. This massing, however, was just what Grant wanted; for he now expected Hooker to appear on the other flank, which Bragg would either have to give up in despair or strengthen at the expense of the center, which Thomas was ready to charge. But with Hooker not appearing, and Sherman barely holding his own, Grant slipped Thomas from the leash. The two centers then met hand to hand. But there was no withstanding the Federal charge. Back went the Confederates, turning to bay at their second line of defense. Here again they were overborne by well-led superior numbers and soon put to flight. Sheridan, of whom we shall hear again in '64, took up the pursuit. Bragg lost all control of his men. Stores, guns, and even rifles were abandoned. Thousands of prisoners were taken; and most of the others were scattered in flight. The battle, the whole campaign, and even the war in the Tennessee sector, were won.

Vicksburg meant that the trans-Mississippi South would thenceforth wither like a severed branch. Chattanooga meant that the Union forces had at last laid the age to the root of the tree.

CHAPTER VIII
GETTYSBURG: 1863

On the fifth of May we left Lee victorious in Virginia; but with his indispensable lieutenant, Stonewall Jackson, mortally wounded.

Though thoroughly defeated at Chancellorsville, Hooker soon recovered control of the Army of the Potomac and prepared to dispute Lee's right of way. Lee faced a difficult, perhaps an insoluble, problem. Longstreet urged him to relieve the local pressure on Vicksburg by concentrating every available man in eastern Tennessee, not only withdrawing Johnston's force from Grant's rear but also depleting the Confederates in Virginia for the same purpose. Then, combining these armies from east and west with the one already there under Bragg, the united Confederates were to crush Rosecrans in their immediate front and make Cincinnati their great objective. Lee, however, dared not risk the loss of his Virginian bases in the meantime; and so he decided on a vigorous counter-attack, right into Pennsylvania, hoping that, if successful, this would produce a greater effect than any corresponding victory could possibly produce elsewhere.

On the ninth of June a cavalry combat round Brandy Station, in the heart of Virginia, made Hooker's staff feel certain that Lee was again going up the Valley and on to Maryland. At one time, for want of supplies, Lee had to spread out his front along a line running eighty miles northwest from Fredericksburg to Strasburg. Hooker, on the keen alert, implored the Government to let him attack the three Confederate corps in detail. Success against one at least was certain. Lincoln understood this perfectly. But the nerves of his colleagues were again on edge; and no argument could persuade them to adopt the best of all possible schemes of defense by destroying the enemy's means of destroying them. They insisted on the usual shield theory of passive defense, and ordered Hooker to keep between Lee and Washington whatever might happen. This absurd maneuver was of course attended with all the usual evil results at the time. Equally of course, it afterwards drew down the wrath of the wiseacre public on their own representatives. But wiseacre publics never stop to think that many a government is forced to do foolish and even suicidal things in war simply because it represents the ignorance and folly, as well as the wisdom, of all who have the vote.

Yet both the loyal public and its Government had some good reasons to doubt Hooker's ability, even apart from his recent defeat; and Lincoln, wisest of all—except in applying strategy to problems he could not fully understand—felt almost certain that Hooker's character contained at least the seeds of failure in supreme command. "He talks to me like a father," said Hooker, on reading the letter Lincoln wrote when appointing him Burnside's successor. This remarkable letter, dated January 26, 1863, though printed many times, is worth reading again:

I have placed you at the head of the Army of the Potomac. Of course I have done this upon what appears to me to be sufficient reasons, and yet I think it best for you to know that there are some things in regard to which I am not quite satisfied with you. I believe you to be a brave and skillful soldier, which, of course, I like. I also believe you do not mix politics with your profession, in which you are right. You have confidence in yourself, which is a valuable, if not an indispensable, quality. You are ambitious, which, within reasonable bounds, does good rather than harm; but I think that during General Burnside's command of the army you have taken counsel of your ambition, and thwarted him as much as you could, in which you did a great wrong to the country and to a most meritorious and honorable brother officer. I have heard, in such way as to believe it, of your recently saying that both the army and the Government needed a Dictator. Of course it was not for this, but in spite of it, that I have given you the command. Only those generals who gain successes can set up dictatorships. What I now ask of you is military success, and I will risk the dictatorship. The Government will support you to the utmost of its ability, which is neither more nor less than it has done and will do for all commanders. I much fear that the spirit which you have aided to infuse into the army, of criticizing their commander and withholding confidence from him, will now turn upon you. I shall assist you as far as I can to put it down. Neither you nor Napoleon, if he were alive again, could get any good out of an army while such a spirit prevails in it. And now, beware of rashness, but with energy and sleepless vigilance go forward, and give us victories.

Then came Chancellorsville, doubts at Washington, interference by Stanton, ill-judged orders from Halleck, and some not very judicious rejoinders from Hooker himself, who became rather peevish, to Lincoln's alarm. So when, on the twenty-seventh of June, Hooker tendered his resignation, it was promptly accepted. With Lee in Pennsylvania there was no time for discussion: only for finding some one to trust.

Lee, as usual, had divined the political forces working on the Union armies from Washington and had maneuvered with a combination of skill and daring that exactly met the situation. Throwing his left forward (under Ewell) in the Shenandoah Valley he had driven Milroy out of Winchester on the fourteenth of June and next day secured a foothold across the Potomac. Then the rest of his army followed. It was so much stretched out (to facilitate its food supply) that Lincoln again wished to strike it at any vulnerable spot. But the Cabinet in general (and Stanton in particular) were still determined that the Union army should be their passive shield, not their active sword. On the twenty-fourth Ewell was already beginning to semicircle Gettysburg from the Cumberland Valley. On the twenty-eighth, the day on which Meade succeeded Hooker in the Federal command, the Confederate semicircle, now formed by Lee's whole army, stretched from Chambersburg on the west, through Carlisle on the north, to York on the east; while the massed Federals were still in Maryland, near Middletown and Frederick, thirty miles south of Gettysburg, and only forty miles northwest of nervous Washington.

Hooker's successor, George G. Meade, was the fifth defender of Washington within the last ten months. Luckily for the Union, Meade was a sound, though not a great, commander, and his hands were fairly free. Luckily again, he was succeeded in command of the Fifth Corps by George Sykes, the excellent leader of those magnificent regulars who fought so well at Antietam and Second Manassas. The change from interference to control was made only just in time at Washington; for three days after Meade's free hand began to feel its way along the threatened front the armies met upon the unexpected battlefield of Gettysburg.

Lee in Pennsylvania was in the midst of a very hostile population and facing superior forces which he could only defeat in one of two difficult ways: either by a sudden, bewildering, and unexpected attack, like Jackson's and his own at Chancellorsville, or by an impregnable defense on ground that also favored a victorious counter-attack and the subsequent crushing pursuit. But there was no Jackson now; and the nature of the country did not favor the bewildering of Federals who were fighting at home under excellent generals well served by a competent staff and well screened by cavalry. So the "fog of war" was quite as dense round Lee's headquarters as it was round Meade's on the first of July, when Lee found that his chosen point of concentration near Gettysburg was already occupied by Buford's cavalry, with infantry and some artillery in support. The surprise—and no very great surprise—was mutual. The Federals were found where they could stand on their defense in a very strong position if the rest of their army could come up in time. And Lee's only advantage was that, having already ordered concentration round the same position, he had a few hours' start of Meade in getting there.

Each commander had intended to make the other one attack if possible; and Meade of course knew that Lee, with inferior numbers and vastly inferior supplies, could not afford to stay long among gathering enemies in the hostile North without decisive action. The Confederates must either fight or retreat without fighting, and make their choice very soon. So, when the two armies met at Gettysburg, Lee was practically forced to risk an immediate action or begin a retreat that might have ruined Confederate morale.

Gettysburg is one of those battles about which men will always differ. The numbers present, the behavior of subordinates, the tactics employed, were, and still are, subjects of dispute. Above all, there is the vexed question of what Lee should or should not have done. We have little space to spare for any such discussions. We can only refer inquirers to the original evidence (some of which is most conflicting) and give the gist of what seems to be indubitable fact. The numbers were a good seventy thousand Confederates against about eighty thousand Federals. But these are the approximate grand totals; and it must be remembered that the Confederates, having the start, were in superior numbers during the first two days. On each side there was an aggrieved and aggrieving subordinate general, Sickles on the Federal side, Longstreet on the other. But Sickles was by far the less important of the two. In tactics the Federals displayed great judgment, skill, and resolution. The Northern people called Gettysburg a soldiers' battle; and so, in many ways, it was; for there was heroic work among the rank and file on both sides. But it most emphatically was not a soldiers' battle in the sense of its having been won more by the rank and file than by the generals in high command; for never did so many Federal chiefs show to such great advantage. No less than five commanded in succession between morning and midnight on the first day, each meeting the crisis till the next senior came up. They were Buford, Reynolds, Howard, Hancock, Meade. Hunt also excelled in command of the artillery; and this in spite of much misorganization of that arm at Washington. Warren was not only a good commander of the engineers but a good all-round general, as he showed by seizing, on his own initiative, the Little Round Top, without which the left flank could never have been held.

Finally, there is the great vexed question of what Lee should or should not have done. First, it seems clear that (like Farragut and unlike Grant and Jackson) he lacked the ruthless power of making every subordinate bend or break in every time of crisis: otherwise he would have bent or broken Longstreet. Next, it may have been that he was not then at his best.

Concludingly, it may be granted to armchair (and even other) critics that if everything had been something else the results might not have been the same.

Lee, having invaded the North by marching northeast under cover of the mountains and wheeling southeast to concentrate at Gettysburg, found Buford's cavalry suddenly resisting him, as they formed the northwest outpost of Meade's army, which was itself concentrating round Pipe Creek, near Taneytown in Maryland, fifteen miles southeast. Gettysburg was a meeting place of many important roads. It stood at the western end of a branch line connecting with all the eastern rails. And it occupied a strong strategic point in the vitally important triangle formed by Pittsburgh, Philadelphia, and Washington. Thus, like a magnet, it drew the contending armies to what they knew would prove a field decisive of the whole campaign.

The Federal line, as finally held on the third of July, was nearly five miles long. The front faced west and was nearly three miles long. The flanks, thrown back at right angles, faced north and south. Near the north end of the front stood Cemetery Hill, near the south the Devil's Den, a maze of gigantic bowlders. Along the front the ground was mostly ridged, and even the lower ground about the center was a rise from which a gradual slope went down to the valley that rose again to the opposite heights of Seminary Ridge, where Lee had his headquarters only a mile away. The so-called hills were no more than hillocks, the ridges were low, and most slopes were those of a rolling country. But the general contour of the ground, the swelling hillocks on the flanks (Culp's Hill on the right, the Round Tops on the left) and the broad glacis up which attackers must advance against the center, all combined to make the position very strong indeed when held by even or superior numbers.

The first day's fight began when A. P. Hill's Confederates, with Longstreet's following, closed in on Gettysburg from the west to meet Ewell's, who were coming down from the north. Buford's Federal cavalry resisted Hill's advanced brigades successfully till Reynolds had brought the First Corps forward in support and ordered the two other nearest corps to follow at the double quick. Reynolds was killed early in the day; but not before his well trained eye had taken in the situation at a glance and his sure judgment had half committed both armies to that famous field.

The full commitment came shortly after, when Meade sent Hancock forward to command the three corps and Buford's cavalry in their attempt to stem the Confederate advance. Howard was then the senior general on the field, having taken over from Doubleday, who had succeeded

Reynolds. But he at once agreed that such a strong position should be held and that Hancock should proceed to rectify the lines. This was no easy task; for Ewell's Confederates had meanwhile come down from the north and driven in the Federal flank on the already hard-pressed front. The front thereupon gave way and fell back in confusion. But Hancock's masterly work was quickly done and the Federal line was reëstablished so well that the Confederates paused in their attack and waited for the morrow.

The Confederates had got as good as they gave, much to their disgust. Archer, one of their best brigadiers, felt particularly sore when most of his men were rounded up by Meredith's "Iron Brigade." When Doubleday saw his old West Point friend a prisoner he shook hands cordially, saying, "Well, Archer, I *am* glad to see you!" But Archer answered, "Well, I'm not so glad to see *you*—not by a damned sight!" The fact was that the excellent Federal defense had come as a very unpleasing surprise upon the rather too cocksure Confederates. Buford's cavalry and Reynolds's infantry had staunchly withstood superior numbers; while Lieutenant Bayard Wilkeson actually held back a Confederate division for some time with the guns of Battery G, Fourth U. S. Artillery. This heroic youth, only nineteen years of age, kept his men in action, though they were suffering terrible losses, till two converging batteries brought him down.

He was well matched by a veteran of over seventy, John Burns, an old soldier, whom the sound of battle drew from his little home like the trumpet-call to arms. In his swallow-tailed, brass-buttoned, old-fashioned coatee, Burns seemed a very comic sight to the nearest boys in blue until they found he really meant to join them and that he knew a thing or two of war. "Which way are the rebels?" he asked, "and where are our troops? I know how to fight—I've fit before." So he did; and he fought to good purpose till wounded three times.

Late in the evening Meade arrived and inspected the lines by moonlight. Having ordered every remaining man to hasten forward he faced the second day with well-founded anxiety lest Lee's full strength should break through before his own last men were up. His right was not safe against surprise by the Confederates who slept at the foot of Culp's Hill, and his left was in imminent danger from Longstreet's corps. But on the second day Longstreet marked his disagreement with Lee's plans by delaying his attack till Warren, with admirable judgment, had ordered the Round Tops to be seized at the double quick and held to the last extremity. Then, after wasting enough time for this to be done, Longstreet attacked and was repulsed; though his men fought very well. Meanwhile Ewell, whose attack against the right was to synchronize with Longstreet's against the left, was delayed by Longstreet till the afternoon, when he carried Culp's Hill.

This was the only Confederate success; for Early failed to carry Cemetery Hill, the adjoining high ground, which formed the right center, and the rest of the Federal line remained intact; though not without desperate struggles.

The third was the decisive day; and on it Meade rose to the height of his unappreciated skill. This was the first great battle in which all the chief Federals worked so well together and the first in which the commander-in-chief used reserves with such excellent effect, throwing them in at exactly the right moment and at the proper place. But these indispensable qualities were not of the kind that the public wanted to acclaim, or, indeed, of the kind that they could understand.

Meade was determined to clear his flanks. So he began at dawn to attack Ewell on Culp's Hill and kept on doggedly till, after four hours of strenuous fighting, he had driven him off. By this time Meade saw that Lee was not going to press home any serious attack against the Round Tops and Devil's Den on the left. So the main interest of the whole battle shifted to the center of the field, where Lee was massing for a final charge. The idea had been to synchronize three coöperating movements against Meade's whole position. His left was to have been held by a demonstration in force by Longstreet against the Devil's Den and Round Tops, while Ewell held Culp's Hill, which seemed to be at his mercy, and which would flank any Federal retreat. At the same time Meade's center was to have been rushed by Pickett's fresh division supported by three attached brigades. But though the central force was ready before nine o'clock it never stepped off till three; so great was Longstreet's delay in ordering Pickett's advance. Meanwhile the Federals had made Culp's Hill quite safe against Ewell. So all depended now on the one last desperate assault against the Federal center.

This immortal assault is known as Pickett's Charge because it was made by Pickett's division of Longstreet's corps supported by three brigades from Hill's—Wilcox's, Perry's, and Pettigrew's. The whole formed a mass of about ten thousand men. If they broke the Federal line in two, then every supporting Confederate was to follow, while the rest turned the flanks. If they failed, then the battle must be lost.

Hour after hour passed by. But it was not till well past one that Longstreet opened fire with a hundred and forty guns. Hunt had seventy-seven ready to reply. But after firing for half an hour he ceased, wishing to reserve his ammunition for use against the charging infantry. This encouraged the Confederate gunners, who thought they had silenced him. They then continued for some time, preparing the way for the charge, but firing too high and doing little execution against the Federal infantry, who were lying down, mostly under cover. Hunt's guns were more exposed and formed better targets; so some of them suffered severely: none more than those of Battery A, Fourth U.S. Artillery. This gallant battery had three of its limbers blown up and replaced. Wheels were also smashed to pieces and guns put out of action, till only a single gun, with men enough to handle it, was left with only a single officer. This heroic young lieutenant, Alonzo H. Cushing (brother to the naval Cushing who destroyed the *Albemarle*), then ran his gun up to the fence and fired his last round through it into Pickett's men as he himself fell dead.

Pickett advanced at three o'clock, to the breathless admiration of both friend and foe. He had a mile of open ground to cover. But his three lines marched forward as steadily and blithely as if the occasion was a gala one and they were on parade. The Confederate bombardment ceased. The Federal guns and rifles held their fire. Fate hung in silence on those gallant lines of gray. Then the Federal skirmishers down in the valley began fitfully firing; and the waiting masses on the Federal slopes began to watch more intently still. "Here they come! Here comes the infantry!" The blue ranks stirred a little as the men felt their cartridge boxes and the sockets of their bayonets. The calm warnings of the officers could be heard all down the line of Gibbon's magnificent division, which stood straight in Pickett's path. "Steady, men, steady! Don't fire yet!"

For a very few, tense minutes Pickett's division disappeared in an undulation of the ground. Then, at less than point-blank range, it seemed to spring out of the very earth, no longer in three lines but one solid mass of rushing gray, cresting, like a tidal wave, to break in fury on the shore. Instantly, as if in answer to a single word, Hunt's guns and Gibbon's rifles crashed out together, and shot, shell, canister, and bullet cut gaping wounds deep into the dense gray ranks. Still, the wave broke; and, from its storm-blown top, one furious tongue surged over the breastwork and through the hedge of bayonets. It came from Armistead's brigade of stark Virginians. He led it on; and, with a few score men, reached the highwater mark of that last spring tide.

When he fell the tide of battle turned; turned everywhere upon that stricken field; turned throughout the whole campaign; turned even in the war itself.

As Pickett's men fell back they were swept by scythe-like fire from every gun and rifle that could mow them down. Not a single mounted officer remained; and of all the brave array that Pickett led three-fourths fell killed or wounded. The other fourth returned undaunted still, but only as the wreckage of a storm.

Lee's loss exceeded forty per cent of his command. Meade's loss fell short of thirty. But Meade was quite unable to pursue at once when Lee retired on the evening of the fourth. The opposing cavalry, under Pleasonton and Stuart respectively, had fought a flanking battle of their own, but without decisive result. So Lee could screen his retreat to the Potomac, where, however, his whole supply train might have been cut off if its escort under the steadfast Imboden had not been reinforced by every teamster who could pull a trigger.

Gettysburg and Vicksburg, coming together, of course raised the wildest expectations among the general public, expectations which found an unworthy welcome at Government headquarters, where Halleck wrote to Meade on the fourteenth: "The escape of Lee's army has created great dissatisfaction in the mind of the President." Meade at once replied: "The censure is, in my judgment, so undeserved that I most respectfully ask to be immediately relieved from the command of this army." Wiser counsels thereupon prevailed.

Lee and Meade maneuvered over the old Virginian scenes of action, each trying to outflank the other, and each being hampered by having to send reinforcements to their friends in Tennessee, where, as we have seen already, Bragg and Rosecrans were now maneuvering in front of Chattanooga. In October (after the Confederate victory of Chickamauga) Meade foiled Lee's attempt to bring on a Third Manassas. The campaign closed at Mine Run, where Lee repulsed Meade's attempted surprise in a three-day action, which began on the twenty-sixth of November, the morrow of Grant's three days at Chattanooga.

From this time forward the South was like a beleaguered city, certain to fall if not relieved, unless, indeed, the hearts of those who swayed the Northern vote should fail them at the next election.

CHAPTER IX
FARRAGUT AND THE NAVY: 1863-4

The Navy's task in '63 was complicated by the many foreign vessels that ran only between two neutral ports but broke bulk into blockade-runners at their own port of destination. For instance, a neutral vessel, with neutral crew and cargo, would leave a port in Europe for a neutral port in America, say, Nassau in the Bahamas or Matamoras on the Rio Grande. She could not be touched of course at either port or anywhere inside the three-mile limit. But international law accepted the doctrine of continuous voyage, by which contraband could be taken anywhere on the high seas, provided, of course, that the blockader could prove his case. If, for example, there were ten times as many goods going into Matamoras as could possibly be used through that port by Mexico, then the presumption was that nine-tenths were contraband. Presumption becoming proof by further evidence, the doctrine of continuous voyage could be used in favor of the blockaders who stopped the contraband at sea between the neutral ports. The blockade therefore required a double line of operation: one, the old line along the Southern coast, the other, the new line out at sea, and preferably just beyond the three-mile limit outside the original port of departure, so as to kill the evil at its source. Nassau and Matamoras gave the coast blockade plenty of harassing work; Nassau because it was "handy to" the Atlantic ports, Matamoras because it was at the mouth of the Rio Grande, over the shoals of which the Union warships could not go to prevent contraband crossing into Texas, thence up to the Red River, down to the Mississippi (between the Confederate strongholds of Vicksburg and Port Hudson) and on to any other part of the South. But what may be called the high-seas blockade was no less harassing, complicated as it was by the work of Confederate raiders.

The coast blockade of '63 was marked by two notable ship duels and three fights round Charleston, then, as always, a great storm center of the war. At the end of January two Confederate gunboats under Commodore Ingraham attacked the blockading flotilla of Charleston, forced the *Mercedita* to surrender, badly mauled the *Keystone State*, and damaged the *Quaker City*. But, though some foreign consuls and all Charleston thought the blockade had been raised for the time being, it was only bent, not broken.

At the end of February the Union monitor *Montauk* destroyed the Confederate privateer *Nashville* near Fort McAllister on the Ogeechee River in Georgia. In April nine Union monitors steamed in to test the strength of Charleston; but, as they got back more than they could give, Admiral Du Pont wisely decided not to try the fight-to-a-finish he had meant to make next morning. Wassaw Sound in Georgia was the scene of a desperate duel on the seventeenth of June, when the Union monitor *Weehawken* captured the old blockade-runner *Fingal*, which had been converted into the new Confederate ram *Atlanta*. The third week in August witnessed another bombardment of Charleston, this time on a larger scale, for a longer time, and by military as well as naval means. But Charleston remained defiant and unconquered both this year and the next.

Confederate raiders were at work along the trade routes of the world in '63, doing much harm by capture and destruction, and even more by shaking the security of the American mercantile marine. American crews were hard to get when so many hands were wanted for other war work; and American vessels were increasingly apt to seek the safety of a neutral flag.

Slowly, and with much perverse interference to overcome in the course of its harassing duties, the Union navy was getting the strangle-hold that killed the sea-girt South. By '64 the North had secured this strangle-hold; and nothing but foreign intervention or the political death of the Northern War Party could possibly shake it off. The South was feeling its practical enislement as never before. The strong right arm of the Union navy held it fast at every point but three—Wilmington, Charleston, and Mobile; and round these three the stern blockaders grew stronger every day. The Sabine Pass and Galveston also remained in Southern hands; and the border town of Matamoras still imported contraband. But these other three points were closely watched; and the greatly lessened contraband that did get through them now only served the western South, which had been completely severed from the eastern South by the fall of Vicksburg and Port Hudson. The left arm of the Union navy now held the whole line of the Mississippi, while the gripping hand held all the tributary streams—Ohio, Cumberland, and Tennessee—from which the Union armies were to invade, divide, and devastate the eastern South this year.

Several Southern raiders were still at large in '64. But the most famous or notorious three have each their own year of glory. The *Florida* belongs to '63, the *Shenandoah* to '65. So the one great raiding story we have now to tell is that of the *Alabama*, the greatest of them all.

The *Alabama* was a beautiful thousand-ton wooden barkentine, built by the Lairds at Birkenhead in '62, with standing rigging of wire, a single screw driven by two horizontal three-hundred horse power engines, coal room for three hundred and fifty tons, eight good guns, the heaviest a hundred-pound rifle, and a maximum crew of one hundred and forty-nine—all ranks and ratings—under Captain Raphael Semmes, late U. S. N. Semmes was not only a very able officer but an accomplished lawyer, well posted on belligerent and neutral rights at sea.

For nearly two years the *Alabama* roved the oceans of the Old World and the New, taking sixty-six Union vessels valued at seven million dollars, spreading the terror of her name among all the merchantmen that flew the Stars and Stripes, and infuriating the Navy by the wonderful way in which she contrived to escape every trap it set for her. She was designed for speed rather than for fighting, and, with her great spread of canvas, could sometimes work large areas under sail. But, even so, her runs, captures, and escapes formed a series of adventures that no mere luck could have possibly performed with a fluctuating foreign crew commanded by ex-officers of the Navy. Her wanderings took her through nearly a hundred degrees of latitude, from the coast of Scotland to St. Paul Island, south of the Indian Ocean, also through more than two hundred degrees of longitude, from the Gulf of Mexico to the China Sea. She captured "Yankees" within one day's steaming of the New York Navy Yard as well as in the Straits of Sunda. West of the Azores and off the coast of Brazil her captures came so thick and fast that they might have almost been a flock of sheep run down there by a wolf. Finally, to fill the cup of wrath against her, she had sunk a blockader off the coast of Texas, given the slip to a Union man-of-war at the Cape of Good Hope, and kept the Navy guessing her unanswered riddles for two whole years.

Imagine, then, the keen elation with which all hands aboard the U. S. S. *Kearsarge* heard at their berth off Flushing that the *Alabama* was in port at Cherbourg on the Channel coast of France, only one day's sail southwest! And there she was when the *Kearsarge* came to anchor; and every Northern eye was turned to see the ship of which the world had heard so much. The Kearsarges hardly dared to hope that there would be a fight; for they had the stronger vessel, and now the faster one as well. The *Alabama* had been built for speed; but she had knocked about so much without a proper overhaul that her copper sheathing was in rags, while she was more or less strained in nearly every other part. The *Kearsarge*, on the other hand, was in good order, with mantlets of chain cable protecting her vitals, with one-third greater horse power, with fourteen more men in her crew, and with two big pivot guns throwing eleven inch shells with great force at short ranges. Moreover, the *Kearsarge*, with her superior speed and stronger hull, could choose the range and risk close quarters. The Alabamas were also keen to estimate respective strengths. But the French authorities naturally kept the two ships pretty far apart; so the Alabamas never saw the chain mantlets which the Kearsarges had cleverly hidden under a covering of wood that appeared to be flush with the hull.

The Kearsarges had a second and still more elating surprise when they heard the *Alabama* was coming out to fight. Semmes was apparently anxious to show that his raider could be as gallant in fighting a man-of-war as she was effective in sinking merchant vessels; so he wrote his challenge to the Confederate Consul at Cherbourg, who passed it on to the U. S. Consul, who handed it to Captain Winslow, commanding the *Kearsarge*. Still, four days passed without the *Alabama*; and the Kearsarges were giving up hope, when, suddenly, on Sunday morning, the nineteenth of June, just as they had rigged church and fallen in for prayers, out came the *Alabama*. The *Kearsarge* thereupon drew off, so that the *Alabama* could not easily escape to neutral waters if the duel went against her. Cherbourg, of course, was all agog to see the fight; and many thousands of people, some from as far as Paris, watched every move. An English yacht, the *Deerhound*, kept an offing of about a mile, ready to rescue survivors from a watery grave. Its owner, with his wife and family, had intended to stay ashore and go to church. But, when they heard the *Alabama* was really going out, he put the question to the vote around the breakfast-table, whereupon it was carried unanimously that the *Deerhound* should go too.

When the deck-officer of the *Kearsarge* sang out, "*Alabama!*" Captain Winslow put down his prayer-book, seized his speaking-trumpet, and turned to gain a proper offing, while the drum beat to general quarters and the ship was cleared for action, with pivot-guns to starboard. The weather was fine, with a slight haze, little sea, and a light west breeze. Having drawn the *Alabama* far enough to sea, the *Kearsarge* turned toward her again, showing the starboard bow. When at a mile the *Alabama* fired her hundred-pounder. For nearly the whole hour this famous duel lasted the ships continued fighting in the same way—starboard to starboard, round and round a circle from half to a quarter mile across. Each captain stood on the horse-block abreast the mizzen-mast to direct the fight. Semmes presently called to his executive officer: "Mr. Kell, use solid shot! Our shell strike the enemy's side and fall into the water" (after bounding off the iron mantlets Winslow had so cleverly concealed). The *Kearsarge's* gunnery was magnificent, especially from the after-pivot, which Quartermaster William Smith fired with deadly aim, even when three of his gun's crew had been wounded by a shell. These three, strange to say, were the only casualties that occurred aboard the *Kearsarge*. But at sea the stronger side usually suffers much less and the weaker much more than on land. The *Alabama* lost forty: killed, drowned, and wounded.

The Kearsarges soon saw how the fight was going and began to cheer each first-rate shot. "That's a good one! Now we have her! Give her another like the last!" The big eleven-inchers got home repeatedly as the range decreased; so much so that Semmes ordered Kell to keep the *Alabama* headed for the coast the next time the circling brought her bow that way. This would bring her port side into action, which was just what Semmes wanted now, because she had a dangerous list to starboard, where the water was pouring through the shot-holes. Kell changed her course with perfect skill, righting the helm, hoisting the head-sails, hauling the fore-try-sail-sheet well aft, and pivoting to port for a broadside delivered almost as quickly as if there had not been a change at all. But at this moment the engineer came up to say the water had put his fires out and that the ship was sinking. At the same time a strange thing happened. An early shot from the *Kearsarge* had carried away the *Alabama*'s colors; and now the *Alabama*'s own last broadside actually announced her own defeat by "breaking out" the special Stars and Stripes that Winslow had run up his mizzenmast on purpose to break out in case of victory. A cannon ball had twitched the cord that held the flag rolled up "in stops."

Semmes sent his one remaining boat to announce his surrender; threw his sword into the sea; and jumped in with the survivors. The *Deerhound*, on authority from Winslow, had already closed in to the rescue, followed by two French pilot boats and two from the *Kearsarge*; when suddenly the *Alabama*, rearing like a stricken horse, plunged to her doom.

Long before the *Alabama*'s end the Navy had been preparing for the finishing blows against the Southern ports. Farragut had returned to New Orleans in January, '64, hoping for immediate action. But vexatious delays at Washington postponed his great attack till August, when he crowned his whole career by his master-stroke against Mobile. Grant was equally annoyed by this absurd delay, which was caused by the eccentric, and therefore entirely wasteful, Red River Expedition of '64, an expedition we shall ignore otherwise than by pointing out, in this and the succeeding chapters, that it not only postponed the overdue attack on Mobile but spoilt Sherman's grand strategy as well as Farragut's and Grant's. Banks commanded it. But by this time even he had learnt enough of war to know that it was a totally false move. So he boldly protested against it. But Halleck's orders, dictated by the Government, were positive. So there was nothing for it but to suffer a well-deserved defeat while trying to kill the dead and withering branches of Confederate power beyond the Mississippi, in order to "show the flag in

Texas" and say "hands off!" to Mexico and France in the least effective way of all.

During this delay the Confederate ram *Albemarle* came down the Roanoke River, hoping to break through the local blockade in Albemarle Sound and so give North Carolina an outlet to the sea. Two attempts against Newbern, which closed the way out to Pamlico Sound, had failed; but now (the fifth of May) great hopes were set upon the *Albemarle*. At first she seemed impregnable; and the Federal shot and shell glanced harmlessly off her iron sides. But presently Commander Roe of the *Sassacus* (a light-draft, pair-paddle, double-ender gunboat) getting at right angles to her, ordered his engineer to stuff the fires with oiled waste and keep the throttle open. "All hands, lie down!" shouted Roe, as the throbbing engines drove his vessel to the charge. Then came an earthquake shock: the *Sassacus* crashed her bronze beak into the *Albemarle's* side. Both vessels were disabled; a shell from the *Albemarle* burst the boilers of the *Sassacus*, scalding the engineers. But the rest fought off the attempt made by the Albemarles to board. Presently the furious opponents drifted apart; and the *Albemarle*, unable to face her other enemies, took refuge upstream. There, on the twenty-seventh of October, she was heroically attacked and sunk by Lieutenant W. B. Cushing, U. S. N., with a spar torpedo projecting from a little steam launch. Cushing himself swam off through a hail of bullets, worked his way through the woods, seized a skiff belonging to one of the enemy's outposts, and reached the flagship half dead but wholly triumphant.

Between the *Albemarle's* two fights Farragut took Mobile after a magnificent action on the fifth of August. There were batteries ashore, torpedoes across the channel, the *Tennessee* ram and other Confederate vessels waiting on the flank: three kinds of danger to the Union fleet if one false movement had been made. But Farragut's touch was sure. He sent his ironclads through next to the batteries, which were only really dangerous on one side. This protected the wooden ships against the batteries and the ironclads against the torpedoes; for the Confederates had to leave part of the fairway clear in order to use it themselves. Through this narrow channel the four strongly armored monitors led the desperate way, a little ahead and to starboard of the wooden vessels, which followed in pairs, each pair lashed together, with the stronger on the starboard side, next to Fort Morgan.

The Confederates in Fort Morgan, and in the small and distant Fort Powell on the other side, hardly reached a thousand men. Their force afloat was also comparatively small: the ironclad ram *Tennessee* and three side-wheeler gunboats. But the great strength of their position and the many dangers to a hostile fleet combined to make Farragut's attack a very serious operation, even with his four monitors, eight screw sloops, and four smaller vessels. The Union army, which took no part in this great attack, was over five thousand strong, and lost only seven men in the land bombardment later on.

Farragut crossed the bar in the *Hartford* at ten past six in the morning with the young flood tide and a westerly breeze to blow the smoke against Fort Morgan. All his ships ran up the Stars and Stripes not only at the peak, as usual, but at each mast-head as well. Farragut himself at first took post in the port main rigging. But as the smoke of battle rose around him he climbed higher and higher till he got close under the maintop, where a seaman, sent up by Captain Drayton, lashed him on securely.

All went well amid the furious cannonade till the monitor *Tecumseh*, taking the wrong side of the channel buoy in her anxiety to ram the *Tennessee*, ran over the torpedoes, was horribly holed by the explosion, and plunged headforemost to the bottom, her screw madly whirling in the air. Nor was this the worst; for the *Tecumseh's* mistake had thrown the other monitors out of their proper line-ahead, athwart the wooden ships, which began to slow and swing about in some confusion. The Confederates redoubled their fire. Ahead lay the fatal torpedoes. For a moment Farragut could not decide whether to risk an advance at all costs or to turn back beaten. He was a very devout as well as a most determined man; and his simple prayer, "O God, shall I go on?" seemed answered by the echo of his soul, "Go on!" So on he went, not in unreflecting exaltation, but in exaltation based on knowledge and on skill. Like Cromwell, he might well have said, "Trust in the Lord and keep your powder dry!" For he had done all that naval foresight could have done to ensure success. And now, in one lightning flash of genius, he reviewed the situation. He knew the torpedoes of his day were often unreliable, that they exploded only on a special kind of shock, that those which did explode could not be replaced in action, that they were all fixed to their own spots, and that if one ship was blown up her next-astern would get through safely.

The *Brooklyn*, his next-ahead, was in his way. So he ordered the flagship *Hartford* and her lashed-together consort, the double-ender *Metacomet*, to use, the one her screw, the other her paddles, in opposite directions, till he had cleared the *Brooklyn's* stern. As he drew clear and headed for the danger-channel a shout went up from the *Brooklyn's* deck—"'ware torpedoes!" But Farragut, his mind made up, instantly roared back—"Damn the torpedoes!" Then, turning to the *Hartford's* and *Metacomet's* decks, he called his orders down: "Four bells! Captain Drayton, go ahead! Captain Jouett, full speed!" In answer to the order of "four bells" the engines worked their very utmost and the two vessels dashed ahead. Torpedoes knocked against the bottom and some of the primers actually snapped. But nothing exploded; and Farragut won through.

Inside the harbor the *Tennessee* fought hard against the overwhelming Union fleet. But her low-powered engines gave her no chance at quick maneuvers. Three vessels rammed her in succession; and she was forced to surrender.

After this purely naval victory on the fifth of August, General Granger's troops invested Fort Morgan, which, becoming the target of an irresistible converging fire from both land and sea on the twenty-second, surrendered on the twenty-third.

The next objective of a joint expedition was Fort Fisher, which stood at the end of a long, low tongue of land between the sea and Cape Fear River. Fort Fisher guarded the entrance to Wilmington in North Carolina, the port, above all others, from which the Confederate armies drew their oversea supplies. Lee wrote to Colonel Lamb, its commandant, saying that he could not subsist if it was taken. Lamb had less than two thousand men in the fort; but there were six thousand more forming an army of support outside. The Confederates, however, had no naval force to speak of, while the Union fleet, commanded by Admiral Porter, was the largest that had ever yet assembled under the Stars and Stripes. There were nearly sixty fighting vessels of all kinds, including five new ironclads and the three finest new frigates. The guns that were carried exceeded six hundred.

There was also a mine ship, the old *Louisiana*, stuffed chock-a-block with powder to blow in the side of the fort. The Washington wiseacres set great store on this new mine of theirs. It was, of course, to end the war. But naval and military experts on the spot were more than doubtful. On the night of the twenty-third of December the *Louisiana* was safely worked in near the fort by brave Commander Rhind, who fired the slow match and escaped unhurt with his devoted crew of volunteers. A tremendous explosion followed. But, as there was nothing to drive the force of it against the walls, it simply resulted in an enormous flurry of water, mud, sand, earth, and bits of flaming wreckage.

Next morning the fleet bombarded with such success as to silence many of the guns opposed to them. But on Christmas Day General Weitzel reported that an assault would fail; whereupon General Butler concurred and retreated, much to the rage of the fleet, which thought quite otherwise.

In a few days General Terry arrived with the same white troops reinforced by two small colored brigades, making a total of eight thousand men. To these Porter, strongly reinforced, added a naval brigade, two thousand strong, that volunteered to storm the sea face of Fort Fisher. These gallant men had only cutlasses and pistols—except the four hundred marines, who carried bayonets and rifles. They were a scratch lot, from the soldier's point of view, never having been landed together as a single unit till called upon to assault the most dangerous features of the fort. Yet, though they were repulsed with considerable loss, they greatly helped to win the day by obliging the defenders to divide their forces. As Terry's army was, by itself, four or five times stronger than Lamb's entire command the military stormers succeeded in fighting their way through every line of defense and compelling a surrender. They did exceedingly well. But their rear was safe, because Bragg had withdrawn the supporting army for service elsewhere; while, in their front, the enemy defenses had been almost torn out by the roots in many places under the terrific converging fire of six hundred naval guns for three successive days.

When Fort Fisher surrendered on the fifteenth of January (1865) the exhausted South had only one good port and one good raider left: Charleston and the *Shenandoah*.

CHAPTER X
GRANT ATTACKS THE FRONT: 1864

On March 9, 1864, at the Executive Mansion, and in the presence of all the Cabinet Ministers, Lincoln handed Grant the Lieutenant-General's commission which made him Commander-in-Chief of all the Union armies—a commission such as no one else had held since Washington. On April 9, 1865, Grant received the surrender of Lee at Appomattox; and the four years war was ended by a thirteen months campaign.

Victor of the River War in '63, Grant moved his headquarters from Chattanooga to Nashville soon before Christmas. He then expected not only to lead the river armies against Atlanta in '64 but, at the same time, to send another army against Mobile, where it could act in conjunction with the naval forces under Farragut's command.

He consequently made a midwinter tour of inspection: southeast to Chattanooga, northeast to Knoxville and Cumberland Gap, northwest to Lexington and Louisville, thence south, straight back to Nashville. This satisfied him that his main positions were properly taken and held, and that a well-concerted drive would clear his own strategic area of all but Forrest's elusive cavalry.

It was the hardest winter known for many years. The sticky clay roads round Cumberland Gap had been churned by wheels and pitted by innumerable feet throughout the autumn rains. Now they were frozen solid and horribly encumbered by débris mixed up with thousands upon thousands of perished mules and horses. Grant regretted this terrible wastage of animals as much in a personal as in a military way; for, like nearly all great men, his sympathies were broad enough to make him compassionate toward every kind of sentient life. No Arab ever loved his horse better than Grant loved his splendid charger Cincinnati, the worthy counterpart of Traveler, Lee's magnificent gray.

Summoned to Washington in March, Grant, after one scrutinizing look at the political world, then and there made up his steadfast mind that no commander-in-chief could ever carry out his own plans from any distant point; for, even in his fourth year of the war, civilian interference was still being practiced in defiance of naval and military facts and needs, and of some very serious dangers.

Lincoln stood wisely for civil control. But even he could not resist the perverting pressure in favor of the disastrous Red River Expedition, against which even Banks protested. Public and Government alike desired to give the French fair warning that the establishment of an Imperial Mexico, especially by means of foreign intervention, was regarded as a semi-hostile act. There were two entirely different ways in which this warning could be given: one completely effective without being provocative, the other provocative without being in the very least degree effective. The only effective way was to win the war; and the best way to win the war was to strike straight at the heart of the South with all the Union forces. The most ineffective way was to withdraw Union forces from the heart of the war, send them off at a wasteful tangent, misuse them in eccentric operations just where they would give most offense to the French, and then expose them to what, at best, could only be a detrimental victory, and to what would much more likely be defeat, if not disaster.

Yet, to Grant's and Farragut's and every other soldier's and sailor's disgust, this worst way of all was chosen; and Banks's forty thousand sorely needed veterans were sent to their double defeat at Sabine Cross Roads and Pleasant Hill on the eighth and ninth of April, while Porter's invaluable fleet and the no less indispensable transports were nearly lost altogether owing to the long-foretold fall of the dangerous Red River. The one success of this whole disastrous affair was the admirable work of Colonel Joseph Bailey, who dammed the water up just in time to let the rapidly stranding vessels slide into safety through a very narrow sluice.

Even the Red River lesson was thrown away on Stanton, whose interference continued to the bitter end, except when checked by Lincoln or countered by Grant and Sherman in the field. When Grant was starting on his tour of inspection he found that Stanton had forbidden all War Department operators to let commanding generals use the official cipher except when in communication with himself. There were to be no secrets at the front between the commanding generals, even on matters of immediate life and death, unless they were first approved by Stanton at his leisure. The fact that the enemy could use unciphered messages was nothing in his autocratic eyes. Nor did it prick his conscience to change the wording in ways that bewildered his own side and served the enemy's turn.

When Grant took the cipher Stanton ordered the operator to be dismissed. Grant thereupon shouldered the responsibility, saying that Stanton would have to punish him if any one was punished. Then Stanton gave in. Grant saw through him clearly. "Mr. Stanton never questioned his own authority to command, unless resisted. He felt no hesitation in assuming the functions of the Executive or in acting without advising with him.... He was very timid, and it was impossible for him to avoid interfering with the armies covering the capital when it was sought to defend it by an offensive movement against the army defending the Confederate capital. The enemy would not have been in danger if Mr. Stanton had been in the field."

Stanton was unteachable. He never learnt where control ended and disabling interference began. In the very critical month of August, '64, he interfered with Hunter to such an extent that this patriotic general had to tell Grant "he was so embarrassed with orders from Washington that he had lost all trace of the enemy." Nor was that the end of Stanton's interference with the operations in the Shenandoah Valley. Lincoln's own cipher letter to Grant on the third of August shows what both these great men had to suffer from the weak link in the chain between them.

I have seen your despatch in which you say, "I want Sheridan put in command of all the troops in the field, with instructions to put himself south of the enemy, and follow him to the death. Wherever the enemy goes, let our troops go also." This, I think, is exactly right, as to how our forces should move. But please look over the despatches you may have received from here, even since you made that order, and discover, if you can, that there is any idea in the head of any one here of "putting our army *south* of the enemy," or of "following him to the *death*" in any direction. I repeat to you it will neither be done or attempted unless you watch it every day, and hour, and force it.

The experts of the loyal North were partly comforted by knowing that Davis and his ministers had interfered with Jackson, that during the present campaign they made a crucial mistake about Johnston, and that they failed to give Lee the supreme command until it was too late. But no Southern Secretary went quite so far as Stanton, who actually falsified Grant's order to Sheridan at the crisis of the Valley campaign in October. Here are Grant's own words: "This order had to go through Washington, where it was intercepted; and when Sheridan received what purported to be a statement of what I wanted him to do it was something entirely different."

Nor was Stanton the only responsible civilian to interfere with Grant. There was no government press censorship—perhaps, in this peculiar war, there could not be one. So the only safety was unceasing care, even in cases vouched for by civilians of high official standing. When Grant was beginning the great campaign of '64 the Honorable Elihu B. Washburne, afterwards

United States Minister to France, introduced one Swinton as the prospective historian of the war. On this understanding Swinton accompanied the army. One night Grant gave verbal orders to the staff officer on duty. Three days later these orders appeared in a Richmond paper. Shortly afterwards, in the midst of the Wilderness battle, Swinton was found eavesdropping behind a stump during a midnight conference at headquarters. Sent off with a serious warning, he next appeared, in another place, as a prisoner condemned to death for spying. Grant, satisfied that he was not bent on getting news for the enemy in particular, but only for the press in general, released and expelled him with such a warning this time that he never once came back.

The Union forces at the front were about twice the corresponding forces of the South. Sherman, who commanded the river armies after Grant's transfer to Virginia, says: "I always estimated my force at about double, and could afford to lose two to one without disturbing our relative proportion." In Virginia the Army of the Potomac under Meade and the new Army of the James under Butler, both under Grant's immediate command, totaled over a hundred and fifty thousand men against the ninety thousand under Lee. These odds of five to three remained the same when a hundred and ten thousand Federals went into winter quarters against sixty-six thousand Confederates at Petersburg. But, when the naval odds of more than ten to one in favor of the North are added in, the general odds of two to one are reached on this as well as other scenes of action. In reserves the odds were very much greater; for while the South was getting down to its last available man the North began the following year with nearly one million in the forces and two millions on the registered reserve. Thus, even supposing that half the reserves were unfit for active service, the man-power odds against the South were these: two to one in arms at the beginning of the great campaign, five to one at the end of it, and ten to one if the fit reserves were all included. The odds in transportation by land, and very much more so by water, were even greater at corresponding times; while the odds in all the other resources which could be turned to warlike ends were greater still.

The Southern situation, therefore, was not encouraging from the naval and military point of view. The border States had long been lost, then the trans-Mississippi; and now the whole river area was held as a base by the North. Only five States remained effective: Alabama, Georgia, the Carolinas, and Virginia. These formed an irregular oblong of about two hundred thousand square miles between the Appalachians and the sea. There were a good eight hundred Confederate miles from the Shenandoah Valley to Mobile. But the three hundred miles across the oblong, even in its widest part, were everywhere threatened and in some places held by the North. The whole coast was more closely blockaded than ever; and only three ports remained with their defenses still in Southern hands: Wilmington, Charleston, and Mobile. Alabama was threatened by land and sea from the lower Mississippi and the Gulf. Georgia was threatened by Sherman's main body in southeastern Tennessee. The Carolinas were in less immediate danger. But they were menaced both from the mountains and the sea; and if the Union forces conquered Virginia and Georgia, then the Carolinas were certain to be ground into subjugation between Grant's victorious forces on the north and Sherman's on the south.

Grant fixed his own headquarters with the Army of the Potomac at Culpeper Court House, north of the Rapidan. Lee's Army of Northern Virginia was at Orange Court House, over twenty miles south. Grant, taking his own headquarters as the center, regarded Butler's Army of the James as the left wing, which could unite with the center round Richmond and Petersburg. The long right wing ran through the whole of West Virginia, Kentucky, and Tennessee, clear away to Memphis, with its own headquarters at Chattanooga. There Sherman faced Johnston, who occupied a strong position at Dalton, over thirty miles southeast. The great objectives were, of course, the two main Southern armies under Lee and Johnston, with Richmond and Atlanta as the chief positions to be gained.

All other Union forces were regarded as attacking the South from the rear. Wherever coast garrisons could help to tighten the blockade or seriously distract Confederate attention they were left to do so. Wherever they could not they were either depleted for the front or sent there bodily. The principal Union field force attacking from the rear was to have been formed by Banks's forty thousand veterans in conjunction with Farragut's fleet against Mobile. But the Red River Expedition spoilt that combination in the spring and postponed it till August, when Farragut did nearly all the fighting, and the coöperating army was far too late to produce the distracting effect that Grant had originally planned.

General Franz Sigel was sent to the upper Shenandoah Valley, both to guard that approach on Washington and to destroy the resources on which Lee's army so greatly relied. General George Crook was given a mounted column to operate from southern West Virginia against the line of rails running toward Tennessee through the lower end of the Valley.

The most notable new general was Philip H. Sheridan, whom Grant selected for the cavalry command. Sheridan was thirty-three, two years older than his Southern rival, Stuart, and, like him, a young regular officer who rose to well-earned fame the moment his first great chance occurred.

Sherman we have met from the very beginning of the war and followed throughout its course. He was continually rising to more and more responsible command; but it was only now that he became the virtual Commander-in-Chief of all the river armies and the chosen coöperator with Grant on a universal scale. He was of the old original stock, his first American ancestors having emigrated from England in 1634. An old regular, with special knowledge of the South, and in the fullness of his powers at the age of forty-four, he had developed with the war till there was no position which he could not fill to the best advantage of the service.

Grant fixed the fourth of May for the combined advance of all the converging forces of invasion. There were two weak points where the Union armies failed: one in the farthest south, where, as we have so often seen, Banks could not attack Mobile owing to his absence at Red River; the other in the farthest north, where Sigel was badly beaten and replaced by Hunter. Here, after much disabling interference at the hands of Stanton, Hunter was succeeded by Sheridan, whom Grant himself directed with consummate skill. There were also two Confederate thorns in the Federal side: Forrest's cavalry in Sherman's rear, Mosby's cavalry in Grant's. Forrest roved about the river area, snapping up small garrisons, cutting communications, and doing a good deal of damage right up to the Ohio. Mosby, with a much smaller but equally efficient force, actually raided to and fro in Grant's immediate rear; and on one occasion nearly captured Grant himself just on the eve of the opening move. As Grant's unguarded special train from Washington pulled up at Warrenton Junction, where there was only one Union official, Mosby's men had just crossed the track in pursuit of some Federal cavalry.

But neither these two Confederate thorns in the side nor the more serious Federal failures could stop the general advance. Nor yet could Butler's lack of success on the James. Butler had seized and fortified an exceedingly strong defensive position at Bermuda Hundred on a peninsula, with navigable water on both flanks and in rear, and a very narrow neck of land in front. The only trouble was that it was as hard for him to surmount the Confederate front across the same narrow neck as it was for the enemy to surmount his own. He was, in fact, bottled up, with the cork in the enemy's hands. He did send out cavalry from Suffolk to cut the rails south of Petersburg. But no permanent damage was done there. Petersburg itself, which at that time was almost defenseless, was not taken. And in the middle of the month Beauregard attacked Butler so vigorously as to make the Army of the James rather a passive than an active force till it was presently, absorbed by Grant when he arrived before Richmond in June.

Grant felt perfect confidence only in four prime elements of victory: first, in his ability to wear Lee down by sheer attrition if other means failed; next, in his own magnificent army; then in Sherman's; and lastly in Sheridan's cavalry. His supply and transport services were nearly perfect, even in his own most critical eyes. "There never was a corps better organized than was the quartermaster's corps with the Army of the Potomac in 1864." His field engineering and his signal service were also exceedingly good. At every halt the army threw up earth and timber entrenchments with wonderful rapidity and skill. At the same time the telegraph and signal corps was busy laying insulated wires by means of reels on muleback. Parallel lines would be led to the rear of each brigade till quite clear, when their ends would be joined by a wire at right angles, from which headquarters could communicate with every unit at the front. Sherman's army was equally efficient, and Sheridan's cavalry soon proved that sweeping raids could be carried out by one side as well as by the other.

Crossing the Rapidan at the Germanna Ford, Grant marched south through the Wilderness on the fifth of May. The Wilderness was densely wooded; the roads were few and bad; the clearings rare and too small for large units. When Lee attacked from the west and Grant turned to face him the fighting soon became desperate, close, and somewhat confused. Neither side gained any substantial advantage on the first day. Next morning Grant, preparing to attack at five, was forestalled by Lee, who wished to keep him at arm's length till Longstreet came up on the southern flank. Again the opposing armies closed and fought with the greatest determination for over an hour, when the Confederates fell back in some confusion. Then Longstreet arrived and restored the battle till he was severely wounded. After this Lee took command of his right, or southern, wing and kept up the fight all day. Meanwhile Sheridan had countered the Confederate cavalry under Stuart, which had been trying to swing round the same southern flank. The main bodies of infantry swayed back and forth till dark, with the woods and breastworks on fire in several places, and many of the wounded smothering in the smoke.

On the seventh reassuring news came in from Sherman and Butler, Sheridan drove off the Confederate cavalry at Todd's Tavern, and the southward march continued. As Grant and Meade rode south that evening, past Hancock's corps, and the men saw they were heading straight for Richmond, there was such a burst of cheering that the Confederates, thinking it meant a night attack, deluged the intervening woods with a heavy barrage till they found out their mistake.

The race for Richmond continued on the eighth, each army trying to get south of the other without exposing itself to a flank attack. Grant had sent his wagon trains farther east, to move south on parallel roads and keep those nearest Lee quite clear for fighting. This movement at first led Lee to suspect a Federal retirement on Fredericksburg, which caused him to send Longstreet's corps south to Spotsylvania. The woods being on fire, and the men unable to bivouac, the whole corps pushed on to Spotsylvania, thus forestalling Grant, who had intended to get there first himself.

This brought on another tremendous battle in the bush. Lee formed a semicircle, facing north, round Spotsylvania, in a supreme effort to stem, if not throw back, Grant's most determined advance. Grant, on the other hand, indomitably pressed home wave after wave of attack till the evening of the twelfth. The morning of that desperate day was foggy; and the attack was delayed. The Federal objective was a commanding salient, jutting out from the Confederate center, and now weakened by the removal of guns overnight to follow the apparent Federal move toward the south. The gray sentries, peering through the dripping woods, suddenly found them astir. Then wave after wave of densely massed blue dashed to the assault, swarming up and over on both sides, regardless of losses, and fighting hand to hand with a fury that earned this famous salient the name of Bloody Angle. Back and still back went the outnumbered gray, many of whom were surrounded by the swirling currents of inpouring blue. But presently Lee himself came up, and would have led his reinforcements to the charge if a pleading shout of "General Lee to the rear!" had not induced him to desist. Every spare Confederate rushed to the rescue. From right and left and rear the gray streams came, impetuous and strong, united in one main current and dashed against the blue. There, in the Bloody Angle, the battle raged with ever-increasing fury until the rising tide of strife, bursting its narrow bounds, carried the blue attackers back to where they came from. But they were hardly clear of that appalling slope before they reformed, presented an undaunted front once more, and then drew off with stinging resistance to the very last.

After five days of much rain and little fighting Grant made his final effort on the eighteenth. This was meant to be a great surprise. Two corps changed position under cover of the night and sprang their trap at four in the morning. But Lee was again before them, ready and resolute as ever. Thirty guns converged their withering fire on the big blue masses and seemed to burn them off the field. These masses never closed, as they had done six days before; and when they fell back beaten the fortnight's battle in the Wilderness was done.

During it there had been two operations that gave Grant better satisfaction: Sheridan's raid and Sherman's advance. As large bodies of cavalry could not maneuver in the bush Grant had sent Sheridan off on his Richmond Raid ten days before. Striking south near Spotsylvania, Sheridan's ten thousand horsemen rounded Lee's right, cut the rails on either side of Beaver Dam Station, destroyed this important depot on the Virginia Central

Railroad, and then made straight for Richmond. Stuart followed hard, made an exhausting sweep round Sheridan's flank, and faced him on the eleventh at Yellow Tavern, six miles north of Richmond. Here the tired and outnumbered Confederates made a desperate attempt to stem Sheridan's advance. But Stuart, the hero of his own men, and the admiration of his generous foes, was mortally wounded; and his thinner lines, overlapped and outweighed, gave ground and drew off. Richmond had no garrison to resist a determined attack. But Sheridan, knowing he could not hold it and having better work to do, pushed on southeast to Haxall's Landing, where he could draw much-needed supplies from Butler, just across the James. With the enemy aggressive and alert all round him, he built a bridge under fire across the Chickahominy, struck north for the Army of the Potomac, and reported his return to Grant at Chesterfield Station—halfway back to Spotsylvania—on his seventeenth day out.

In the course of this great raid Sheridan had drawn off the Confederate cavalry; fought four successful actions; released hundreds of Union prisoners and taken as many himself; cut rails and wires to such an extent that Lee could only communicate with Richmond by messenger; destroyed enormous quantities of the most vitally needed enemy stores, especially food and medical supplies; and, by penetrating the outer defenses of Richmond, raised Federal prestige to a higher plane at a most important juncture.

Meanwhile Sherman, whose own main body included a hundred thousand men, had started from Chattanooga at the same time as Grant from Culpeper Court House. In Grant's opinion "Johnston, with Atlanta, was of less importance only because the capture of Johnston and his army would not produce so immediate and decisive a result in closing the rebellion as would the possession of Richmond, Lee, and his army." Sherman's organization, supply and transport, engineers, staff, and army generally were excellent. So skillful, indeed, were his railway engineers that a disgusted Confederate raider called out to a demolition party: "Better save your powder, boys. What's the good of blowing up this one when Sherman brings duplicate tunnels along?"

Sherman had double Johnston's numbers in the field. But Johnston, as a supremely skillful Fabian, was a most worthy opponent for this campaign, when the Confederate object was to gain time and sicken the North of the war by falling back from one strongly prepared position to another, inflicting as much loss as possible on the attackers, and forcing them to stretch their line of communication to the breaking point among a hostile population. Two of Sherman's best divisions were still floundering about with the rest of the Red River Expedition. So he had to modify his original plan, which would have taken him much sooner to Atlanta and given him the support of a simultaneous attack on Mobile by a coöperating joint expedition. But he was ready to the minute, all the same.

Dalton, Johnston's first stronghold, was cleverly turned by McPherson's right flank march; whereupon Johnston fell back on Resaca. Here, on the upon the fifteenth of May, the armies fought hard for some hours. But Sherman again outflanked the fortified enemy, who retired to Kingston. Then, after Sherman had made a four days' halt to accumulate supplies, the advance was resumed, against determined opposition and with a good deal of hard fighting for a week in the neighborhood of New Hope Church. The result of the usual outflanking movements was that Johnston had to evacuate Allatoona on the fourth of June. Sherman at once turned it into his advanced field base; while Johnston fell back on another strong and well-prepared position at Kenesaw Mountain.

Grant, favored in a general way by Sherman and in a special way by Sheridan, had meanwhile enjoyed a third advantage, this time on his own immediate front, through the sickness of Lee, who could not take personal command during the last ten days of May. On the twenty-first half of Grant's army marched south while half stood threatening Lee, in order to give their friends a start toward Richmond. This move was so well staffed and screened that perhaps Lee could not have seen his chance quite soon enough in any case. But when he did learn what had happened even his calm self-control gave way to the exceeding bitter cry: "We must strike them! We must never let them pass us again!" On the thirtieth he was horrified at getting from Beauregard (who was then between Richmond and Petersburg) a telegram which showed that the Confederate Government was busy with the circumlocution office in Richmond while the enemy was thundering at the gate. "War Department must determine when and what troops to order from here." Lee immediately answered: "If you cannot determine what troops you can spare, the Department cannot. The result of your delay will be disaster. Butler's troops will be with Grant tomorrow." Lee also telegraphed direct to Davis for immediate reinforcements, which arrived only just in time for the terrific battle of Cold Harbor.

With these three advantages, in addition to the other odds in his favor, Grant seemed to have found the tide of fortune at the flood in the latter part of May. But he had many troubles of his own. No sooner had half his army been badly defeated on the eighteenth than news came that Sigel was in full retreat instead of cutting off supplies from Lee. Then came news of Butler's retreat from Drewry's Bluff, close in to Richmond. Nor was this all; for it was only now that definite news of the Red River Expedition arrived to confirm Grant's worst suspicions and ruin his second plan of helping Farragut to take Mobile. But, as was his wont, Grant at once took steps to meet the crisis.

He ordered Hunter to replace Sigel and go south—straight into the heart of the Valley, asked the navy to move his own base down the Rappahannock from Fredericksburg to Port Royal, and then himself marched on toward Richmond, where Lee was desperately trying to concentrate for battle.

The two armies were now drawing all available force together round the strategic center of Cold Harbor, only nine miles east of Richmond. On the thirty-first Sheridan drove out the enemy detachments there, and was himself about to retire before much superior reinforcements when he got Grant's order to hold his ground at any cost. Nightfall prevented a general assault till the next morning, when Sheridan managed to stand fast till Wright's whole corps came up and the enemy at once desisted. But elsewhere the Confederates did what they could to stave the Federals off from advantageous ground on that day and the next. The day after—the fateful third of June—the two sides closed in death-grips at Cold Harbor.

On this, the thirtieth day of Grant's campaign of stern attrition and would-be-smashing hammer-strokes at Lee, these were his orders for attack: "The moment it becomes certain that an assault cannot succeed, suspend the offensive. But when one does succeed, push it vigorously, and, if necessary, pile in troops at the successful point from wherever they can be taken." The trouble was that Grant was two days late in carrying on the battle so well begun by Sheridan, that Warren's corps was two miles off and entirely disconnected, and that the three remaining corps formed three parts and no whole when the stress of action came.

At dawn Meade's Army of the Potomac (less Warren's corps) began to take post for the grand attack that some, more sanguine than reflecting, hoped would win the war. When it was light the guns burst out in furious defiance, each side's artillery trying to beat the other's down before the crisis of the infantry assault. There was no maneuvering. Each one of Meade's three corps—Hancock's, Wright's, and Smith's (brought over from Butler's command)—marched straight to its front. This led them apart, on diverging lines, and so exposed their flanks as well as their fronts to enemy fire. But though each corps thought its neighbor wrong to uncover its flanks, and the true cause was not discovered till compass bearings were afterwards compared, yet each went on undaunted, gaining momentum with every step, and gathering itself together for the final charge.

Then, surging like great storm-blown waves, the blue lines broke against Lee's iron front. In every gallant case there was the same wild cresting of the wave, the same terrific crash, the same adventurous tongues of blue that darted up as far as they could go alive, the same anguishing recession from the fatal mark, and the same agonizing wreckage left behind. In Hancock's corps the crisis passed in just eight minutes. But in those eight dire minutes eight colonels died while leading their regiments on to a foredoomed defeat. One of these eight, James P. McMahon of New York, alone among his dauntless fellows, actually reached the Confederate lines, and, catching the colors from their stricken bearer, waved them one moment above the parapet before he fell.

Flesh and blood could do no more. Under the withering fire and crossfire of Lee's unshaken front the beaten corps went back, re-formed, and waited. They had not long to wait; for Grant was set on swinging his three hammers for three more blows at least. So again the three assaults were separately made on the one impregnable front; and again the waves receded, leaving a second mass of agonizing wreckage with the first. Yet even this was not enough for Grant, who once more renewed his orders. These orders quickly ran their usual course, from the army to the different corps, from each corps to its own divisions, and from divisions to brigades. But not a single unit stirred. From the generals to the "thinking bayonets" every soldier knew the limit had been reached. Officially the order was obeyed by a front-line fire of musketry, as well as by the staunch artillery, which again gave its infantry the comfort of the guns. But that was all.

Thus ended the battle of Cold Harbor, the last pitched battle on Virginian soil. Grant reported it in three short sentences; and afterwards referred to it in these other three. "I have always regretted that the last assault [*i.e.*, the whole battle of the third of June] was ever made. No advantage whatever was gained to compensate for the heavy loss. Indeed, the advantages, other than those of relative losses, were on the Confederate side." Even these, however, were also on the Confederate side, as Grant lost nearly thirteen thousand, while Lee lost less than eighteen hundred. Cold Harbor undoubtedly lowered Union morale, both at the front and all through the loyal North. It encouraged the Peace Party, revived Confederate hopes, and shook the army's faith in Grant's commandership. Martin McMahon, a Union general, writing many years after the event, of which he was a most competent witness, said: "It was the dreary, dismal, bloody, ineffective close of the lieutenant-general's first campaign with the Army of the Potomac."

Cold Harbor caused a change of plan. Reporting two days later Grant said: "I now find, after thirty days of trial, the enemy deems it of the first importance to run no risks with the armies they now have. Without a greater sacrifice of human life than I am willing to make all cannot be accomplished that I had designed outside of the city [of Richmond]. I have therefore resolved upon the following plan," which, in one word, involved a complete change from a series of pitched battles to a long-drawn open siege.

The battles lasted thirty days, the siege three hundred. Therefore, from this time on for the next ten months, Lee had to keep his living shield between Grant's main body and the last great stronghold of the fighting South, while the rising tide of Northern force, commanding all the sea and an ever-increasing portion of the land, beat ceaselessly against his front and flanks, threw out destroying arms against his ever-diminishing sources of supply, and wore the starving shield itself down to the very bone.

Grant's losses—forty thousand killed and wounded—were all made good by immediate reinforcement; as was his other human wastage from sickness, straggling, and desertion: made good, that is, in the quantities required to wear out Lee, whose thinning ranks could never be renewed; but not made good in quality; for many of the best were dead. The wastage of material is hardly worth considering on the Northern side; for it could always be made good, superabundantly good. But the corresponding wastage on the Southern side was unrenewed and unrenewable. Food, clothing, munitions, medical stores—it was all the same for all the Southern armies: desperate expedients, slow starvation, death.

Consternation reigned at Richmond on the twelfth of June, the day the fitful firing ceased around Cold Harbor. There was danger in the Valley, where Hunter had won success at Staunton, and where Crook's and Averell's Union troops were expected to arrive from West Virginia. Sheridan, too, was off on a twenty-day raid. He cut the Virginia Central rails at Trevilian, did much other damage between Richmond and the Valley, and, toward the end of June, rejoined Grant, who had reached the James nearly a fortnight before. Always trying to overlap Lee's extending right, Grant closed in on Petersburg with the Army of the Potomac while the Army of the James held fast against Richmond. This part of the front then remained comparatively quiet till the end of July.

But the beleaguered Confederates made one last sortie out of the Valley and straight against Washington. At the beginning of July the Valley was uncovered owing to the roundabout flank march that Hunter was forced to make back to his base for ammunition. The enterprising Jubal Early took advantage of this with some veteran troops and made straight for Washington. On the ninth Lew Wallace succeeded in delaying him for one day at the Monocacy by an admirably planned defense most gallantly carried out with greatly inferior numbers and far less veteran men. This gave time for reinforcements to pour into Washington; so that on the twelfth, Early, finding the works alive with men, had to retreat even faster than he came.

In the meantime Grant's extreme right wing was steadily pressing the invasion of Georgia, where we left Sherman and Johnston face to face at Kenesaw in June. Here again the beleaguered Confederates had been making desperate raids or sorties, trying to cut Sherman off from his base in Tennessee and keep back the Federal forces in other parts of the river area. "Our Jack Morgan," whom we left as a prisoner of war after his Ohio raid of '63, had escaped in November, fought Crook and Averell for Saltville and Wytheville in May, and then, leaving southwest Virginia, had raided Kentucky and taken Lexington, but been defeated at Cynthiana and driven back by overwhelming numbers till he again entered southwest Virginia on the twentieth of June. Forrest raided northeastern Mississippi, badly defeated Sturgis at Brice's Cross Roads in June, but was himself defeated by A. J. Smith at Tupelo in July.

Meanwhile Sherman had been tapping Johnston's fifty miles of entrenchments for three weeks of rainy June weather, hoping to find a suitable place into which he could drive a wedge of attack. On the twenty-seventh he tried to carry the Kenesaw lines by assault, but failed at every point, with a loss of twenty-five hundred—three times what Johnston lost.

By a well-combined series of maneuvers Sherman then forced Johnston to fall back or be hopelessly outflanked. Johnston, with equal skill, crossed the Chattahoochee under cover of the strongly fortified bridgehead which he had built unknown to Sherman. But Sherman, with his double numbers, could always hold Johnston with one-half in front while turning his flank with the other. So even the Chattahoochee was safely crossed on the seventeenth of July and the final move against Atlanta was begun. That same night Johnston's magnificent skill was thrown to the winds by Davis, who had ordered the bold and skillful but far too headlong John B. Hood to take command and "fight."

Five days later Hood fought the battle of Atlanta. Just as Sherman was closing in to entrench for a siege Hood attacked his extreme left flank with the utmost resolution, driving it in and completely enveloping it. But Sherman was not to be caught. Knowing that only a part of Hood's army could be sent to this attack while the rest held the lines of Atlanta, Sherman left McPherson's veteran Army of the Tennessee to do the actual fighting, supported, of course, by the movement of troops on their engaged right. McPherson was killed. Logan ably replaced him and won a hard-fought day. Hood's loss was well over eight thousand; Sherman's considerably less than half.

On the twenty-eighth Hood attacked the extreme right, now commanded by General O. O. Howard in succession to McPherson, whose Army of the Tennessee again did most distinguished service, especially Logan's Fifteenth

Corps near Ezra Church. The Confederates were again defeated with the heavier loss. After this the siege continued all through the month of August.

While Hood was trying to keep Sherman off Atlanta Grant was trying to make a breach at Petersburg. Grant gave Meade "minute orders on the 24th [of July] how I wanted the assault conducted," and Meade elaborated the actual plan with admirable skill except in one particular—that of the generals concerned. Burnside was ordered to use his corps for the assault, and he chose Ledlie's division to lead. The mine was on an enormous scale, designed to hold eight tons of powder, though it was only charged with four, and was approached by a gallery five hundred feet long. On the twenty-ninth Grant brought every available man into proper support of Burnside, whose other three divisions were to form the immediate support of Ledlie's grand forlorn hope.

In the early morning of the thirtieth the mine blew up with an earthquaking shock; the enemy round it ran helter-skelter to the rear; a crater like that of a volcano was formed; and a hundred and sixty pieces of artillery opened a furious fire on every square inch near it. Ledlie's division rushed forward and occupied the crater. But there the whole maneuver stopped short; for everything hinged on Ledlie's movements; and Ledlie was hiding, well out of danger, instead of "carrying on." After a pause Confederate reinforcements came up and drove the leaderless division back. "The effort," said Grant, "was a stupendous failure"; and it cost him nearly four thousand men, mostly captured.

August was a sad month for the loyal North. It was then, as we have seen, that Lincoln had to warn Grant about the way in which his orders were being falsified in Washington. It was then that Sherman asked for reinforcements, so as to be up to strength before and after the taking of Atlanta. And it was then that Halleck warned Grant to be ready to send some of his best men north if there should be serious resistance to the draft. Nor was this all. Thurlow Weed, the great election agent, told Lincoln that the Government would be defeated; which meant, of course, that the compromised and compromising Peace Party would probably be at the helm in time to wreck the Union. With so many of the best men dead or at the front the whole tone of political society had been considerably lowered— to the corresponding advantage of all those meaner elements that fish in troubled waters when the dregs are well stirred up. There were sinister signs in the big cities, in the press, and in financial circles. The Union dollar once sank to thirty-nine cents. To make matters worse, there was a good deal of well-founded discontent among the self-sacrificing loyalists, both at the home and fighting fronts, because the Government apparently allowed disloyal and evasive citizens to live as parasites on the Union's body politic.

The blood tax and money tax alike fell far too heavily on the patriots; while many a parasite grew rich in unshamed safety.

Mobile was won in August. But the people's eyes were mostly fixed upon the land. So a much greater effect was produced by Sherman's laconic dispatch of the second of September announcing the fall of Atlanta. The Confederates, despairing of holding it to any good purpose, had blown up everything they could not move and then retreated. This thrilling news heartened the whole loyal North, and, as Lincoln at once sent word to Sherman, "entitled those who had participated to the applause and thanks of the nation." Grant fired a salute of shotted guns from every battery bearing on the enemy, who were correspondingly depressed. For every one could now see that if the Union put forth its full strength the shrunken forces of the South could not prevent the Northern vice from crushing them to death.

September also saw the turning of the tide on the still more conspicuous scene of action in Virginia. Grant had sent Sheridan to the Valley, and had just completed a tour of personal inspection there, when Sheridan, finding Early's Confederates divided, swooped down on the exposed main body at Opequan Creek and won a brilliant victory which raised the hopes of the loyal North a good deal higher still.

Exactly a month later, on the nineteenth of October, Early made a desperate attempt to turn the tables on the Federals in the Valley by attacking them suddenly, on their exposed left flank, while Sheridan was absent at Washington. (We must remember that Grant had to concert action personally with his sub-commanders, as his orders were so often "queered" when seen at Washington by autocratic Stanton and bureaucratic Halleck.) The troops attacked broke up and were driven in on their supports in wild confusion. Then the supports gave way; and a Confederate victory seemed to be assured.

But Sheridan was on his way. He had left the scene of his previous victory at Opequan Creek, near Winchester, and was now riding to the rescue of his army at Cedar Creek, twenty miles south. "Sheridan's Ride," so widely known in song and story, was enough to shake the nerves of any but a very fit commander. The flotsam and jetsam of defeat swirled round him as he rode. Yet, with unerring eye, he picked out the few that could influence the rest and set them at work to rally, reform, and return. Inspired by his example many a straggler who had run for miles presently "found himself" again and got back in time to redeem his reputation.

Arriving on the field Sheridan discovered those two splendid leaders, Custer and Getty, holding off the victorious Confederates from what otherwise seemed an easy prey. His presence encouraged the formed defense, restored confidence among the rest near by, and stiffened resistance so much that hasty entrenchments were successfully made and still more successfully held. The first rush having been stopped, Sheridan turned the lull that ensued into a triumphal progress by riding bareheaded along his whole line, so that all his men might feel themselves once more under his personal command. Cheer upon cheer greeted him as his gallant charger carried him past; and when the astonished enemy were themselves attacked they broke in irretrievable defeat.

This crowning victory of the long-drawn Valley campaigns, coming with cumulative force after those of Mobile, Atlanta, and Opequan Creek, did more to turn the critical election than all the speeches in the North. The fittest at the home front judged by deeds, not words, agreeing therein with Rutherford B. Hayes (a future President, now one of Sheridan's generals) who said: "Any officer fit for duty who at this crisis would abandon his post to electioneer for a seat in Congress, ought to be scalped."

The devastation of everything in the Valley that might be useful to Lee's army completed the Union victory in arms; while Lincoln's own triumph in November completed it in politics and raised his party to the highest plane of statesmanship in war.

From this time till the early spring the battle of the giants in Virginia calmed down to the minor moves and clashes that mark a period of winter quarters; while the scene of more stirring action shifts once more to Georgia and Tennessee.

CHAPTER XI
SHERMAN DESTROYS THE BASE: 1864

Sherman made Atlanta his field headquarters for September and October, changing it entirely from a Southern city to a Northern camp. The whole population was removed, every one being given the choice of going north or south. In his own words, Sherman "had seen Memphis, Vicksburg, Natchez, and New Orleans, all captured from the enemy, and each at once garrisoned by a full division, if not more; so that success was actually crippling our armies in the field by detachments to guard and protect the interests of a hostile population." In reporting to Washington he said: "If the people raise a howl against my barbarity and cruelty, I will answer that war is war, and not popularity seeking. If they want peace, they and their relatives must stop the war." He also excluded the swarms of demoralizing camp-followers that had clogged him elsewhere. One licensed sutler was allowed for each of his three armies, and no more. Atlanta thus became a perfect Union stronghold fixed in the flank of the South.

The balance of losses in action, from May to September, was heavily against the South: nearly nine to four. The actual numbers did not greatly differ: thirty-two thousand Federals to thirty-five thousand Confederates. (And in killed and wounded the Federals lost many more than the Confederates. It was the thirteen thousand captured Confederates that redressed the balance.) But, since Sherman had twice as many in his total as the Confederates had in theirs, the odds in relative loss were nine to four in his favor. The balance of loss from disease was also heavily against the Confederates, who as usual suffered from dearth of medical stores. The losses in present and prospective food supplies were even more in Sherman's favor; for his devastations had begun. Yet Jefferson Davis was bound that Hood should "fight"; and Hood was nothing loth.

Davis went about denouncing Johnston for his magnificent Fabian defense; and added insult to injury by coupling the name of this very able soldier and quite incorruptible man with that of Joseph E. Brown, Governor of Georgia, who, though a violent Secessionist, opposed all proper unification of effort, and exempted eight thousand State employees from conscription as civilian "indispensables." Then, when Sherman approached, Brown ran away with all the food and furniture he could stuff into his own special train; though he left behind him all arms, ammunition, and other warlike stores, besides the confidential documents belonging to the State.

Brown had also weakened Hood's army by withdrawing the State troops to gather in the harvest and store it where Sherman afterwards used what he wanted and destroyed the rest. Yet Hood kept operating in Sherman's rear, admirably seconded by Forrest's and Wheeler's raiding cavalry. Late in October Forrest performed the remarkable feat of taking a flotilla with cavalry. He suddenly swooped down on the Tennessee near Johnsonville and took the gunboat *Undine* with a couple of transports. Hood had meanwhile been busy on Sherman's line of communications, hoping at least to immobilize him round Atlanta, and at best to bring him back from Georgia for a Federal defeat in Tennessee.

On the fifth of October the last action near Atlanta was fought thirty miles northwest, when Hood made a desperate attempt on Allatoona with a greatly superior force. Twelve miles off, on Kenesaw Mountain, Sherman could see the smoke and hear the sounds of battle through the clear, still, autumn air. But as his signalers could get no answer from the fort he began to fear that Allatoona was already lost, when the signal officer's quick eye caught the faintest flutter at one of the fort windows. Presently the letters, C—R—S—E—H—E—R, were made out; which meant that General John M. Corse, one of the best volunteers produced by the war, was holding out. He had hurried over from Rome, on a call from Allatoona, and was withstanding more than four thousand men with less than two thousand. All morning long the Confederates persisted in their attacks, while Sherman's relief column was hurrying over from Kenesaw. Early in the afternoon the fire slackened and ceased before this column arrived. But Sherman's renewed fears were soon allayed. For Corse, after losing more than a third of his men, had repulsed the enemy alone, inflicting on them an even greater loss in proportion to their double strength.

Corse was still full of fight, reporting back to Kenesaw that though "short a cheek bone and an ear" he was "able to whip all hell yet." Sherman thanked the brave defenders in his general orders of the seventh for "the handsome defense made at Allatoona" and pointed the moral that "garrisons must hold their posts to the last minute, sure that the time gained is valuable and necessary to their comrades at the front."

The situation at the beginning of November was most peculiar. With the whole Gulf coast blockaded and the three great ports in Union hands, with the Mississippi a Union stream from source to sea, and with Sherman firmly set in the northwest flank of Georgia, Hood made the last grand sortie from the beleaguered South. It was a desperate adventure to go north against the Federal troops in Tennessee, with Kentucky and the line of the Ohio as his ultimate objective, when Lincoln had been returned to power, when Grant was surely wearing down Lee in Virginia, and when Sherman's preponderance of force was not only assured in Georgia but in Tennessee as well. Moreover, Thomas, the "Rock of Chickamauga," had been sent back to counter Hood from Grant's and Sherman's old headquarters at Nashville on the Cumberland. And Thomas was soon to have the usual double numbers; for all the Western depots sent him their trained recruits, till, by the end of November, his total was over seventy thousand. Hood's forty thousand could not be increased or even stopped from dwindling. Yet he pushed on, with the consent of Beauregard, who now held the general command of all the troops opposed to Sherman.

The next moves were even more peculiar than the first. For while Hood hoped to close the breach in Georgia by drawing Sherman back, and Sherman expected that when he went on to widen the breach he would draw Hood back, what really happened was that each advanced on his own new line in opposite directions, Hood north through Tennessee, Sherman southeast through Georgia. So firm was the grip of the Union on all the navigable waters that Hood could only cross the Tennessee somewhere along the shoals. He chose a place near Florence, Alabama, got safely over and encamped. There, for the moment, we shall leave him and follow Sherman to the sea.

The region of the Gulf and lower Mississippi being now under the assured predominance of Union forces, Grant, with equal wisdom and decision, entirely approved of Sherman's plan to cut loose from his western base, make a devastating march through the heart of fertile Georgia, and join the eastern forces of the North at Savannah, where Fort Pulaski was in Union hands and the Union navy was, as usual, overwhelmingly strong.

Sherman's March to the Sea at once acquired a popular renown which it has never lost. This, however, was chiefly because it happened to catch the public eye while nothing else was on the stage. For its many admirable features were those about which most people know little and care less: well-combined grand strategy, perfection in headquarter orders and the incidental staff work, excellent march discipline, wonderful coördination between the different arms of the Service and with all auxiliary branches — especially the commissariat and transport, and, to clinch everything, a thoroughness of execution which distinguished each unit concerned. As a feat of arms this famous march is hardly worth mentioning. There were no battles and no such masterly maneuvers as those of the much harder march to Atlanta. Nor was the operational problem to be mentioned in the same breath with that of the subsequent march through the Carolinas. Sherman himself says: "Were I to express my measure of the relative importance of the march to the sea, and of that from Savannah northward, I would place the former at one, and the latter at ten—or the maximum."

The Government was very doubtful and counseled reconsideration. But Grant and Sherman, knowing the factors so very much better, were sure the problem could easily be solved. Sherman left Atlanta on the fifteenth of November and laid siege to Savannah on the tenth of December. He utterly destroyed the military value of Atlanta and everything else on the way that could be used by the armies in the field. Of course, to do this he had to reduce civilian supplies to the point at which no surplus remained for transport to the front; and civilians naturally suffered. But his object was to destroy the Georgian base of supplies without inflicting more than incidental hardship on civilians. And this object he attained. He cut a swath of devastation sixty miles wide all the way to Savannah. Every rail was rooted up, made red-hot, and twisted into scrap. Every road and bridge was destroyed. Every kind of surplus supplies an army could possibly need was burnt or consumed. Civilians were left with enough to keep body and soul together, but nothing to send away, even if the means of transportation had been left.

Sherman's sixty thousand men were all as fit as his own tall sinewy form, which was the very embodiment of expert energy. Every weakling had been left behind. Consequently the whole veteran force simply romped through this Georgian raid. The main body mostly followed the rails, which gangs of soldiers would pile on bonfires of sleepers. The mounted men swept up everything about the flanks. But nothing escaped the "bummers," who foraged for their units every day, starting out empty-handed on foot and returning heavily laden on horses or mules or in some kind of vehicle. If Atlanta had been a volcano in eruption, and the molten lava had flowed to Savannah in a stream sixty miles wide and five times as long, the destruction could hardly have been worse, except, of course, that civilians were left enough to keep them alive, and that, with a few inevitable exceptions, they were not ill treated.

The fighting hardly disturbed the daily routine. Sherman was never in danger; though wiseacre Washington, supposing that he ought to be, used to pester Lincoln, who always replied: "Grant says the men are safe with Sherman, and that if they can't get out where they want to, they can crawl back by the hole they went in at." This seemed to allay anxiety; though the truth was that Sherman's real safety lay in going ahead to the Union sea, not in retracing his steps over the devastated line of his advance.

On approaching Savannah a mounted officer was blown up by a land torpedo, his horse killed, and himself badly lacerated. Sherman at once sent his prisoners ahead to dig up the other torpedoes or get blown up by those they failed to find. No more explosions took place. Savannah itself was strongly entrenched and further defended by Fort McAllister. Against this fort Sherman detached his own old Shiloh division of the Fifteenth Corps, now under the very capable command of General William B. Hazen. As the day wore on Sherman became very impatient, watching for Hazen's attack, when a black object went gliding up the Ogeechee River toward the fort. Presently a man-of-war appeared flying the Stars and Stripes and signaling, *Who are you?* On getting the answer, *General Sherman*, she asked, *Is Fort McAllister taken?* and immediately received the cheering assurance, *No; but it will be in a minute.* Then, just as the signal flags ceased waving, Hazen's straight blue lines broke cover, advanced, charged through the hail of shot, shell, and rifle bullets, rushed the defenses, and stood triumphant on the top.

Before midnight Sherman was writing his dispatches on board the U.S.S. *Dandelion* and examining those received from Grant. He learned now, from Grant's of the third (ten days before), that Thomas was facing Hood round Nashville and that the Government, and even Grant, were getting very impatient with Thomas for not striking hard and at once. A week later the Confederate general, Hardee, managed to evacuate Savannah before his one remaining line of retreat had been cut off. He was a thorough soldier. But men and means and time were lacking; and the civil population hoped to save all that was not considered warlike stores. Thus immense supplies fell into Sherman's hands. Savannah was of course placed under martial law. But as the wax was now nearing its inevitable end, and the citizens were thoroughly "subjugated," those who wished to remain were allowed to do so. Only two hundred left, going to Charleston under a flag of truce.

The following official announcement reached Lincoln on Christmas Eve.

Savannah, Georgia, December 22, 1864.

TO HIS EXCELLENCY PRESIDENT LINCOLN,
WASHINGTON, D. C.

I beg to present you as a Christmas gift the city of Savannah, with one hundred and fifty heavy guns and plenty of ammunition, also about twenty-five thousand bales of cotton.

W. T. SHERMAN, Major-General.

In the meantime Hood's desperate sortie had struck north as far as Franklin, Tennessee. Here, on the last of November, General John Schofield, commanding the advanced part of Thomas's army, gallantly withstood a furious attack. On this the closing day of a lingering Indian summer the massed Confederates charged with the piercing rebel yell, and charged again; re-formed under cover of the dense pall of stationary smoke; and returned to the charge again and again. Many a leader met his death right against the very breastworks. Another would instantly spring forward, only to fall in his turn. Thirteen times the gaunt gray lines rushed madly through the battle smoke and lost their front ranks against the withering fire before the autumn night closed in. Schofield then fell back on Brentwood, halfway on the twenty miles to Nashville. He had lost over two thousand men. But Hood had lost three times as many; and Hood's were irreplaceable except by a very few local recruits.

Hood now concentrated every available man for his final attack on Thomas, who had odds of twenty thousand in his favor. Hood marched his thirty-five thousand up to Nashville, where he actually invested the fifty-five thousand Federals. By this time even Grant was so annoyed at what seemed to him unreasoning delay that he sent Logan to take command at once and "fight." But on the fifteenth of December Thomas came out of his works and fought Hood with determined skill all day. Having gained a decisive advantage already he pressed it home to the very utmost on the morrow, breaking through Hood's shaken lines, enveloping whole units with converging fire, and taking prisoners in mass. After a last wild effort Hood's beaten army fled, having lost fifteen thousand men, five times as much as Thomas.

The battle of Nashville came nearer than any other to being a really annihilating victory. Out of the forty thousand men Hood had at first in Tennessee not half escaped; and of the remainder not nearly half were ever seen in arms again. As an organized force his army simply disappeared. The few thousands saved from the wreckage of the storm found their painful way east to join all that was left for the last stand against the overwhelming forces of the North.

CHAPTER XII
THE END: 1865

By '65 the Southern cause was lost. There was nothing to hope for from abroad. Neither was there anything to hope for at home, now that Lincoln and the Union Government had been returned to power. From the very first the disparity of resources was so great that the South had never had a chance alone except against a disunited North. Now that the North could bring its full strength to bear against the worn-out South the only question remaining to be settled in the field was simply one of time. Yet Davis, with his indomitable will, would never yield so long as any Confederates would remain in arms. And men like Lee would never willingly give up the fight so long as those they served required them. Therefore the war went on until the Southern armies failed through sheer exhaustion.

The North had nearly a million men by land and sea. The South had perhaps two hundred thousand. The North could count on a million recruits out of the whole reserve of twice as many. The South had no reserves at all. The total odds were therefore five to one without reserves and ten to one if these came in.

The scene of action, for all decisive purposes, had shrunk again, and now included nothing beyond Virginia and the Carolinas; and even there the Union forces had impregnable bases of attack. When Wilmington fell in January the only port still left in Southern hands was Charleston; and that was close-blockaded. Fighting Confederates still remained in the lower South. But victories like Olustee, Florida, barren in '64, could not avail them now, even if they had the troops to win them. The lower South was now as much isolated as the trans-Mississippi. Between its blockaded and garrisoned coast on one side and its sixty-mile swath of devastation through the heart of Georgia on the other it might as well have been a shipless island. The same was true of all Confederate places beyond Virginia and the Carolinas. The last shots were fired in Texas near the middle of May. But they were as futile against the course of events as was the final act of war committed by the Confederate raider *Shenandoah* at the end of June, when she sank the whaling fleet, far off in the lone Pacific.

For the last two months of the four-years' war Davis made Lee Commander-in-Chief. Lee at once restored Johnston to his rightful place. These two great soldiers then did what could be done to stave off Grant and Sherman. Lee's and Johnston's problem was of course insoluble. For each was facing an army which was alone a match for both. The only chance of prolonging anything more than a mere guerilla war was to join forces in southwest Virginia, where the only line of rails was safe from capture for the moment. But this meant eluding Grant and Sherman; and these two leaders would never let a plain chance slip. They took good care that all Confederate forces outside the central scene of action were kept busy with their own defense. They also closed in enough men from the west to prevent Lee and Johnston escaping by the mountains. Then, with the help of the navy, having cut off every means of escape—north, south, east, and west— they themselves closed in for the death-grip.

By the first of February Sherman was on his way north through the Carolinas with sixty thousand picked men, drawing in reinforcements as he advanced against Johnston's dwindling forty thousand, until the thousands that faced each other at the end in April were ninety and thirty respectively. On the ninth of February (the day Lee became Commander-in-Chief) Sherman was crossing the rails between Charleston and Augusta, of course destroying them. A week later he was doing the same at Columbia in the middle of South Carolina. By this time his old antagonist, Johnston, had assumed command; so that he had to reckon with the chances of a battle, as on his way against Atlanta, and not only with the troubles of devastating an undefended base, as on his march to the sea. The difficulties of hard marching through an enemy country full of natural and artificial obstacles were also much greater here than in Georgia. How well these difficulties could be surmounted by a veteran army may be realized from a recorded instance which, though it occurred elsewhere, was yet entirely typical. In forty days an infantry division of eight thousand men repaired a hundred miles of rail and built a hundred and eighty-two bridges.

Sherman took a month to advance from Columbia in the middle of South Carolina to Bentonville in the middle of North Carolina. Here Johnston stood his ground; and a battle was fought from the nineteenth to the twenty-first of March. Had Sherman known at the time that his own numbers were, as he afterwards reported, "vastly superior," he might have crushed Johnston then and there. But, as it was, he ably supported the exposed flank that Johnston so skillfully attacked, won the battle, inflicted losses a good deal larger than his own, and gained his ulterior objective as well as if there had not been a fight at all. This objective was the concentration of his whole army round Goldsboro by the twenty-fifth. At Goldsboro he held the strategic center of North Carolina, being at the junction whence the rails ran east to Newbern (which had long been in Union hands), west to meet the only rails by which Lee's army might for a time escape, and north (a hundred and fifty miles) to Grant's besieging host at Petersburg. Sherman's record is one of which his men might well be proud. In fifty days from Savannah he had made a winter march through four hundred and twenty-five miles of mud, had captured three cities, destroyed four railways, drained the Confederate resources, increased his own, and half closed on Lee and Johnston the vice which he and Grant could soon close altogether.

Nevertheless Grant records that "one of the most anxious periods was the last few weeks before Petersburg"; for he was haunted by the fear that Lee's army, now nearing the last extremity of famine, might risk all on railing off southwest to Danville, the one line left. Lee, consummate now as when victorious before, masked his movements wonderfully well till the early morning of the twenty-fifth of March, when he suddenly made a furious attack where the lines were very near together. For some hours he held a salient in the Federal position. But he was presently driven back with loss; and his intention to escape stood plainly revealed.

The same day Sherman railed down to Newbern over the line repaired by that indefatigable and most accomplished engineer, Colonel W. W. Wright, took ship for City Point, Virginia, and met Lincoln, Grant, and Admiral Porter there on the twenty-seventh and twenty-eighth. Grant explained to Lincoln that Sheridan was crossing the James just below them, to cut the rails running south from Petersburg and then, by forced marches, to cut those running southwest from Richmond, Lee's last possible line of escape. Grant added that the final crisis was very near and that his only anxiety was lest Lee might escape before Sheridan cut the Richmond line southwest to Danville. Lincoln said he hoped the war would end at once and with no more bloodshed. Grant and Sherman, however, could not guarantee that Davis might not force Lee and Johnston to one last desperate fight. Lincoln added that all he wanted after the surrender was to get the Confederates back to their civil life and make them good contented citizens. As for Davis: well, there once was a man who, having taken the pledge, was asked if he wouldn't let his host put just a drop of brandy in the lemonade. His answer was: "See here, if you do it unbeknownst, I won't object." From the way that Lincoln told this story Grant and Sherman both inferred that he would be glad to see Davis disembarrass the reunited States of his annoying presence.

This twenty-eighth of March saw the last farewells between the President and his naval and military lieutenants at the front. Admiral Porter immediately wrote down a full account of the conversations, from which, together with Grant's and Sherman's strong corroboration, we know that

Lincoln entirely approved of the terms which Grant gave Lee, and that he would have approved quite as heartily of those which Sherman gave to Johnston.

Next morning the final race, pursuit, defeat, and victory began. Grant marched all his spare, men west to cut Lee off completely. He left enough to hold his lines at Petersburg, in case Lee should remain; and he arranged with Sherman for a combined movement, to begin on the tenth of April, in case Johnston and Lee should try to join each other. But he felt fairly confident that he could run Lee down while Sherman tackled Johnston.

On the first of April Sheridan won a hard fight at Five Forks, southwest of Petersburg. On Sunday (the second) Lee left Petersburg for good, sending word to Richmond. That morning Davis rose from his place in church and the clergyman quietly told the congregation that there would be no evening service. On Monday morning Grant rode into Petersburg, and saw the Confederate rearguard clubbed together round the bridge. "I had not the heart," said Grant, "to turn the artillery upon such a mass of defeated and fleeing men, and I hoped to capture them soon." On Tuesday Grant closed his orders to Sherman with the words, "Rebel armies are now the only strategic points to strike at," and himself pressed on relentlessly.

Late next afternoon a horseman in full Confederate uniform suddenly broke cover from the enemy side of a dense wood and dashed straight at the headquarter staff. The escort made as if to seize him. But a staff officer called out, "How d'ye do, Campbell?" This famous scout then took a wad of tobacco out of his mouth, a roll of tinfoil out of the wad, and a piece of tissue paper out of the tinfoil. When Grant read Sheridan's report ending "I wish you were here" (that is, at Jetersville, halfway between Petersburg and Appomattox), he immediately got off his black pony, mounted Cincinnati, and rode the twenty miles at speed, to learn that Lee was heading due west for Farmville, less than thirty miles from Appomattox.

On Thursday the sixth, Lee, closely beset in flank and rear, lost seven thousand men at Sailor's Creek, mostly as prisoners. The heroes of this fight were six hundred Federals, who, having gone to blow up High Bridge on the Appomattox, found their retreat cut off by the whole Confederate advanced guard. Under Colonel Francis Washburn, Fourth Massachusetts Cavalry, and Colonel Theodore Read, of General Ord's staff, this dauntless six hundred charged again and again until, their leaders killed and most of the others dead or wounded, the rest surrendered. They had gained their object by holding up Lee's column long enough to let its wagon train be raided.

Grant, now feeling that his hold on Lee could not be shaken off, wrote him a letter on Friday afternoon, saying: "The results of the last week must convince you of the hopelessness of further resistance." That night Lee replied asking what terms Grant proposed to offer. Next morning Grant wrote again to propose a meeting, and Lee answered to say he was willing to treat for peace. Grant at once informed him that the only subject for discussion was the surrender of the army. That evening Federal cavalry under General George A. Custer raided Appomattox Station, five miles southwest of the Court House, and held up four trains. A few hours later, early on Sunday, the famous ninth of April, 1865, Lee's advanced guard was astounded to find its way disputed so far west. It attacked with desperation, hoping to break through what seemed to be a cavalry screen before the infantry came up; but when Lee's main body joined in, only to find a solid mass of Federal infantry straight across its one way out, Lee at once sent forward a white flag.

Grant, overwrought with anxiety, had been suffering from an excruciating headache all night long. But the moment he opened Lee's note, offering to discuss surrender, he felt as well as ever, and instantly wrote back to say he was ready. Pushing rapidly on he met Lee at McLean's private residence near Appomattox Court House. There was a remarkable contrast between the appearance of the two commanders. Grant, only forty-three, and without a tinge of gray in his brown hair, took an inch or two off his medium height by stooping keenly forward, and had nothing in his shabby private's uniform to show his rank except the three-starred shoulder-straps. When the main business was over, and he had time to notice details, he apologized to Lee, explaining that the extreme rapidity of his movements had carried him far ahead of his baggage. Lee's aide-de-camp, Colonel Charles Marshall, afterwards explained that when the Confederates had been obliged to reduce themselves simply to what they stood in, each officer had naturally put on his best. Hence Lee's magnificent appearance in a brand-new general's uniform with the jeweled sword of honor that Virginia had given him. Well over six feet tall, straight as an arrow in spite of his fifty-eight years and snow-white, war-grown beard, still extremely handsome, and full of equal dignity and charm, he looked, from head to foot, the perfect leader of devoted men.

Grant, holding out his hand in cordial greeting, began the conversation by saying: "I met you once before, General Lee, while we were serving in Mexico.... I have always remembered your appearance, and I think I should have recognized you anywhere." After some other personal talk Lee said: "I suppose, General Grant, that the object of our present meeting is fully understood. I asked to see you in order to ascertain on what terms you would receive the surrender of my army." Grant answered that officers and men were to be paroled and disqualified from serving again till properly exchanged, and that all warlike and other stores were to be treated as captured. Lee bowed assent, said that was what he had expected, and presently suggested that Grant should commit the terms to writing on the spot. When Grant got to the end of the terms already discussed his eye fell on Lee's splendid sword of honor, and he immediately added the sentence: "This will not embrace the side-arms of the officers, nor their private horses or baggage." When Lee read over the draft he flushed slightly on coming to this generous proviso and gratefully said: "This will have a very happy effect upon my army." Grant then asked him if he had any suggestions to make; whereupon he said that the mounted Confederates, unlike the Federals, owned their horses. Before he had time to ask a favor Grant said that as these horses would be invaluable for men returning to civil life they could all be taken home after full proof of ownership. Lee again flushed and gratefully replied: "This will have the best possible effect upon the men. It will be very gratifying and do much toward conciliating our people."

While the documents were being written out for signature Grant introduced the generals and staff officers to Lee. Then Lee once more led the conversation back to business by saying he wished to return his prisoners to Grant at the earliest possible moment because he had nothing more for them to eat. "I have, indeed, nothing for my own men," he added. They had been living on the scantiest supply of parched corn for several days; and this famine fare, combined with their utter lack of all other supplies—especially medicine and clothing—was wearing them away faster than any "war of attrition" in the open field. After heartily agreeing that the prisoners should immediately return Grant said: "I will take steps at once to have your army supplied with rations. Suppose I send over twenty-five thousand; do you think that will be a sufficient supply?" "I think it will be ample," said Lee, who, after a pause, added: "and it will be a great relief, I assure you."

Then Lee rose, shook Grant warmly by the hand, bowed to the others, and left the room. As he appeared on the porch all the Union officers in the grounds rose respectfully and saluted him. While the Confederate orderly was bridling the horses Lee stood alone, gazing in unutterable grief across the valley to where the remnant of his army lay. Then, as he mounted Traveler, every Union officer followed Grant's noble example by standing bareheaded till horse and rider had disappeared from view.

Grant next sent off the news to Washington and, true to his sterling worth, immediately stopped the salutes which some of his enthusiastic soldiers were already beginning to fire. "The war is over," he told his staff, "the rebels are our countrymen again, and the best sign of rejoicing after the victory will be to abstain from all demonstrations in the field."

In the meantime Lee had returned to his own lines, along which he now rode for the last time. The reserve with which he had steeled his heart during the surrender gave way completely when he came to bid his men farewell. After a few simple words, advising his devoted veterans to become good citizens of their reunited country, the tears could no longer be kept back. Then, as he rode slowly on, from the remnant of one old regiment to another, the men broke ranks, and, mostly silent with emotion, pressed round their loved commander, to take his hand, to touch his sword, or fondly stroke his splendid gray horse, Traveler, the same that had so often carried him victorious through the hard-fought day.

North and South had scarcely grasped the full significance of Lee's surrender, when, only five days later, Lincoln was assassinated. "It would be impossible for me," said Grant, "to describe the feeling that overcame me at the news. I knew his goodness of heart, and above all his desire to see all the people of the United States enter again upon the full privileges of citizenship with equality among all. I felt that reconstruction had been set back, no telling how far." "Of all the men I ever met," said Sherman, "he seemed to possess more of the elements of greatness, combined with goodness, than any other."

On the very day of the assassination Sherman had written to Johnston offering the same terms Grant had given Lee and Lincoln had most heartily approved. Three days later, on the seventeenth, just as Sherman was entering the train for his meeting with Johnston, the operator handed him a telegram announcing the assassination. Enjoining secrecy till he returned, Sherman took the telegram with him and showed it to Johnston, whom he watched intently. "The perspiration came out on his forehead," Sherman wrote, "and he did not attempt to conceal his distress. He denounced the act as a disgrace to the age and hoped I did not charge it to the Confederate Government. I told him I could not believe that he or General Lee or the officers of the Confederate army could possibly be privy to acts of assassination." When Sherman got back to Raleigh he published the news in general orders, and experienced the supreme satisfaction of finding that not one man in all that mournful army had to be restrained from a single act of revenge.

After much misunderstanding with Washington now in lesser hands, the surrender of Johnston's and the other Confederate armies was effected. Each body of troops laid down its arms and quietly dispersed. One day the bugles called, the camp fires burned, and comrades were together in the ranks. The next, like morning mists, they disappeared, thenceforth to be remembered and admired only as the heroes of a hopeless cause.

It was a very different scene through which their rivals marched into lasting fame with all the pride, pomp, and circumstance of war. On the twenty-third and twenty-fourth of May, in perfect weather, and in the stirring presence of a loyal, vast, enthusiastic throng, the Union armies were reviewed in Washington. For over six full hours each day the troops marched past—the very flower of those who had come back victorious. The route was flagged from end to end with Stars and Stripes, and banked with friends of each and every regiment there. Between these banks, and to the sound of thrilling martial music, the long blue column flowed—a living stream of men whose bayonets made its surface flash like burnished silver under the glorious sun.

Then, when the pageantry was finished, and the volunteers that formed the vast bulk of those magnificent Federal armies had again become American civilians in thought and word and deed, these steadfast men, whose arms had saved the Union in the field, were first in peace as they had been in war: first in the reconstruction of their country's interrupted life, first in recognizing all that was best in the splendid fighters with whom they had crossed swords, and first—incomparably first—in keeping one and indivisible the reunited home land of both North and South.

BIBLIOGRAPHICAL NOTE

Thousands of books have been written about the Civil War; and more about the armies than about the navies and the civil interests together. Yet, even about the armies, there are very few that give a just idea of how every part of the war was correlated with every other part and with the very complex whole; while fewer still give any idea of how closely the navies were correlated with the armies throughout the long amphibious campaigns.

The only works mentioned here are either those containing the original evidence or those written by experts directly from the original evidence. And of course there are a good many works belonging to both these classes for which no room can be found in a bibliography so very brief as the present one must be.

The War of the Rebellion: a Compilation of the Official Records of the Union and Confederate Armies, 128 vols. (1880-1901), and *Official Records of the Union and Confederate Navies in the War of the Rebellion*, 26 vols. (1894-), form two magnificent collections of original evidence published by the United States Government. But they have some gaps which nothing else can fill. *Battles and Leaders of the Civil War* (1887-89), written by competent witnesses on both sides, gives the gist of the story in four volumes (published afterwards in eight). *The Rebellion Record*, 12 vols. (1862-68), edited by Frank Moore, forms an interesting collection of non-official documents. *The Story of the Civil War*, 4 vols. (1895-1913), begun by J. C. Ropes, and continued by W. R. Livermore, is an historical work of real value. Larned's *Literature of American History* contains an excellent bibliography; but it needs supplementing by bibliographies of the present century. Inquiring readers should consult the bibliographies in volumes 20 and 21 (by J. K. Hosmer) in the *American Nation* series.

There are many works of a more special kind that deserve particular attention. General E. P. Alexander's *Military Memoirs of a Confederate* (1907), the *Transactions of the Military Historical Society of Massachusetts*, Major John Bigelow's *The Campaign of Chancellorsville* (1910), and J. D. Cox's *Military*

Reminiscences, 2 vols. (1900), are admirable specimens of this very extensive class.

The two greatest generals on the Northern side have written their own memoirs, and written them exceedingly well: *Personal Memoirs of U. S. Grant,* 2 vols. (1885-86), and *Memoirs of General W. T. Sherman,* 2 vols. (1886). But the two greatest on the Southern side wrote nothing themselves; and no one else has written a really great life of that very great commander, Robert Lee. Fitzhugh Lee's enthusiastic sketch of his uncle, *General Lee* (1894), is one of the several second-rate books on the subject. Colonel G. F. R. Henderson's *Stonewall Jackson and the American Civil War,* 2 vols. (1898), is, on the other hand, among the best of war biographies. Henderson's strategical study of the Valley Campaign is a masterpiece. Two good works of very different kinds are: *A History of the Civil War in the United States* (1905), by W. Birkbeck Wood and Major J. E. Edmonds, and *A History of the United States from the Compromise of 1850,* 8 vols. (1893-1919), by James Ford Rhodes. The first is military, the second political. Mr. Rhodes has also written a single volume *History of the Civil War* (1917). *American Campaigns* by Major M. F. Steele, issued under the supervision of the War Department (1909), deals chiefly with the military operations of the Civil War.

The naval side of this, as of all other wars, has been far too much neglected. But that great historian of sea-power, Admiral Mahan, has told the best of the story in his *Admiral Farragut* (1892).

An interesting contemporary account of the war will be found in the five volumes of Appleton's *American Annual Cyclopædia* for the years from 1861 to 1865. B. J. Lossing's *Pictorial History of the Civil War,* 3 vols. (1866-69), and Harper's *Pictorial History of the Rebellion,* 2 vols. (1868), give graphic pictures of military life as seen by contemporaries. Personal reminiscences of the war, of varying merit, have multiplied rapidly in recent years. These are appraised for the unwary reader in the bibliographies already mentioned. Frank Wilkeson's *Recollections of a Private Soldier in the Army of the Potomac* (1887), George C. Eggleston's *A Rebel's Recollections* (1905), and Mrs. Mary B. Chestnut's *Diary from Dixie* (1905) are among the best of these personal recollections.

The political and diplomatic history has been dealt with already in the two preceding *Chronicles. Abraham Lincoln: a History,* by John G. Nicolay and John Hay, in ten volumes (1890), and *The Complete Works of Abraham Lincoln,* in twelve volumes (1905), form the quarry from which all true accounts of his war statesmanship must be built up. Lord Charnwood's *Abraham*

Lincoln (1917) is an admirable summary. To these titles should be added Gideon Welles's *Diary*, 3 vols. (1911), and, on the Confederate side, Jefferson Davis's *The Rise and Fall of the Confederate Government*, 2 vols. (1881), and Alexander H. Stephens's *A Constitutional View of the Late War Between the States*, 2 vols. (1870). The best life of Jefferson Davis is that by William E. Dodd in the *American Crisis Biographies* (1907). W. H. Russell's *My Diary North and South* (1863) records the impressions of an intelligent foreign observer.

The present *Chronicle* is based entirely on the original evidence, with the convenient use only of such works as have themselves been written by qualified experts directly from the original evidence.

INDEX

Alabama, secedes, in 1864, threatened,

Alabama, Confederate raider, *Kearsarge* and, and *Hatteras*,

Albatross, ship,

Albemarle, Confederate ram, Cushing destroys,

Albemarle Sound, command lost,

Alexandria (Louisiana), State Seminary of Learning and Military Academy,

Allatoona (Georgia), Johnston evacuates, Corse's defense of,

"Anaconda policy,"

Anderson, Colonel Charles, quotes Lee,

Anderson, Major Robert, commands at Fort Moultrie, at Fort Sumter, surrender, leaves Fort Sumter, appointed to Kentucky command, superseded by Sherman,

Annapolis, Union troops at,

Antietam (Maryland), battle,

Apache Cañon, fight in,

Appomattox Court House (Virginia), Lee's surrender,

Appomattox Station, Custer raids,

Aquia, McClellan's troops at,

Archer, J. T., Confederate brigadier,

Arizona, "War in the West,"

Arkansas secedes,

Arkansas, Confederate ram,

Arkansas Post, capture of,

Arlington, home of General Lee,

Baylor, Captain J. R., proclaims himself Governor of New Mexico,

Beauregard. General P. G. T., sons at Louisiana Military Academy, and Fort Sumter, on the Potomac, at Bull Run, preparation for Shiloh, battle of Shiloh, Corinth, and Confederate plans, attacks Butler, telegram to Lee, command of troops opposed to Sherman,

Beauregard, Fort,

Beaver Dam Creek (Virginia), Porter's front at Mechanicsville,

Bee, General B. E., Bull Run, killed,

Bell, Commodore H. H.,

Belmont (Missouri), Grant attacks,

Benjamin, J. P., Confederate Secretary of War,

Benton, flagship,

Bentonville (North Carolina), battle,

Bering Sea, *Shenandoah* in,

Bermuda Hundred (Virginia), Butler seizes,

Beverly (West Virginia), Confederates retire to,

Big Black River (Mississippi), Grant's victory at,

Birge, H. W., and sharpshooters,

Bixby, Mrs., letter to,

Blackburn's Ford (Virginia), McDowell at,

Blair, General F. P., fight for Missouri, as a general,

Blockade, declared, effectiveness, blockade-runners, on Mississippi, attempts to break, double line necessary,

Bloody Angle, salient in Spotsylvania action,

Bonham, General M. L., Bull Run,

Boonville (Missouri), battle,

Boston Mountains, Confederates hold,

Bowling Green (Kentucky), Johnston at, Johnston abandons,

Brackett, Colonel A. G., quoted,

Bragg, General Braxton, at Baton Rouge, preparations for Shiloh, succeeds Beauregard, invasion of Kentucky, march on Nashville, sends out Morgan, Chickamauga, Chattanooga, Missionary Ridge,

Carolinas, danger from West Virginia, secede, effective for South (1864), menace to, Sherman's march through, scene of action (1865), *see also* North Carolina, South Carolina

Carondelet, Federal gunboat,

Castle Pinckney,

Catlett's Station (Virginia) Shields at, Banks near

Cayuga, Federal gunboat,

Cedar Creek (Virginia), Sheridan's ride to,

Cedar Run (Virginia), battle,

Cemetery Hill (Gettysburg), Early fails at,

Centreville (Virginia), in Bull Run campaign, Confederate base, McDowell's corps at,

Chambersburg (Pennsylvania), Federals at, Stuart's raid,

Champion's Hill (Mississippi), fight of,

Chancellorsville (Virginia), battle of, plans, Federal defeat,

Charleston (South Carolina), forts, beginning of hostilities, United States Arsenal seized, surrender of Fort Sumter, menaced, naval combats around, bombardment, defenses in Southern hands, Savannah citizens go to,

Charlestown (West Virginia), Patterson advances to,

Charlotte (North Carolina), Southern cannon made in,

Chase, S. P., Secretary of Treasury,

Chase, Colonel W. H.. demands surrender of Fort Pickens,

Chattahoochee River, Johnston crosses,

Chattanooga, Buell's objective, Bragg's base, Confederates retire on, Bragg at (1863), key to strategic area, battles on Missionary Ridge and Lookout Mountain, significance of victory, Grant moves headquarters from, Grant inspects, Federal headquarters, Sherman starts from,

Chestnut, James, Confederate officer at Fort Sumter,

Chickamauga (Georgia), battle, result of Federal defeat,

Chickasaw Bluffs (Mississippi), Sherman's assault,

Cincinnati, Grant's charger,

Cincinnati (Ohio), Confederate objective,

Macon (Georgia), Southern cannon made at,

Maffitt, Commander J. N., commands *Florida*,

Magruder, General J. B., and Butler, Yorktown, holds Richmond,

Mallory, S. R., Confederate Secretary of Navy,

Malvern Hill (Virginia), battle,

Manassas, Johnston at, Jackson at, location, Federal base, base destroyed, Battle of Second, *see also* Bull Run

Manassas, Federal ram,

Marshall, Colonel Charles, Lee's aide-de-camp,

Marshall, General H. M., with Johnston in Kentucky,

Martha Washington, story of Lincoln on board,

Martinsburg (West Virginia), Jackson marches on, Patterson occupies, Confederates reach, Jackson destroys Federal stores at,

Maryland, border slave State, Confederate hope for, Southern sympathy in, sea-power keeps for Union, Jackson's plan to enter, Confederate invasion, Federals massed in,

Mason, Fort, Lee from,

Matamoras, contraband imported into,

Matthews Hill, battle of Bull Run,

Meade, General G. G., quoted, as a general, succeeds Hooker in command, Gettysburg, Lincoln's dissatisfaction with, Army of Potomac under, headed for Richmond, Cold Harbor, Petersburg,

Mechanicsville (Virginia), battle,

Memphis, Confederate rams lost at, Confederate fleet at, Grant in command at, Sherman's army from, Grant returns to, Grant leaves, Grant considers retirement on,

Mercedita, Confederate gunboats attack,

Meredith, Solomon, "Iron Brigade" at Gettysburg,

Merrimac, only Confederate man-of-war, duel with *Monitor*, destroyed,

Mesilla (New Mexico), Baylor establishes capital at,

Roe, Commander of the *Sassacus*,

Rosecrans, General W. S., succeeds McClellan, Army of Mississippi under, holds Memphis-Corinth rails, replaces Buell, victory at Corinth, commands Army of Cumberland, Stone's River, maneuvers Bragg south, Thomas supersedes, Confederate plan to crush, Chattanooga,

Sabine Cross Roads (Louisiana), Banks's defeat at,

Sabine Pass (Texas), in Confederate hands,

Sable Island, Butler's troops at,

Sailor's Creek (Virginia), Lee's defeat at,

St. Louis, Haskins goes to, Lyon commands at, Lyon marches prisoners through, Harney makes peace, conference, Frémont's headquarters, Frémont fortifies, Halleck's headquarters,

St. Louis, Federal gunboat,

St. Philip, Fort,

Salem Church (Virginia), Jackson reaches,

San Antonio (Texas), surrender to State, Lee at, Sibley's retreat,

San Carlos, Fort,

Santa Rosa Island, Slemmer defends,

Sassacus, fight with *Albemarle*,

Savannah (Georgia), South holds, Sherman plans march to, Sherman reaches, Hardee evacuates,

Savannah (Tennessee), in Shiloh campaign,

Schofield, General John, Nashville campaign,

Scott, General Winfield, General-in-Chief, orders to Slemmer, and Lee, military adviser at Washington, civilian interference with, Grant's admiration for, prevision, "Anaconda policy,"

Seddon, J. A., Confederate Secretary of War,

Sedgwick, General John, Virginia campaign,

Selma (Alabama), Southern cannon made at,

Seminary Ridge, Lee's headquarters,

Semmes, Captain Raphael of *Alabama*,